LETTING GO WITH
LOVE AND CONFIDENCE

~

Kenneth Ginsburg, M.D., M.S.Ed.

and

Susan FitzGerald

LETTING GO
with
LOVE
and
CONFIDENCE

~

RAISING RESPONSIBLE, RESILIENT,

SELF-SUFFICIENT TEENS

IN THE 21ST CENTURY

AVERY

A MEMBER OF PENGUIN GROUP (USA) INC.

New York

Published by the Penguin Group
Penguin Group (USA) Inc., 375 Hudson Street, New York, New York 10014, USA •
Penguin Group (Canada), 90 Eglinton Avenue East, Suite 700, Toronto, Ontario M4P 2Y3,
Canada (a division of Pearson Penguin Canada Inc.) • Penguin Books Ltd, 80 Strand,
London WC2R 0RL, England • Penguin Ireland, 25 St Stephen's Green, Dublin 2, Ireland (a division of
Penguin Books Ltd) • Penguin Group (Australia), 250 Camberwell Road, Camberwell,
Victoria 3124, Australia (a division of Pearson Australia Group Pty Ltd) • Penguin Books India Pvt Ltd,
11 Community Centre, Panchsheel Park, New Delhi–110 017, India • Penguin Group (NZ),
67 Apollo Drive, Rosedale, North Shore 0632, New Zealand (a division of
Pearson New Zealand Ltd) • Penguin Books (South Africa) (Pty) Ltd, 24 Sturdee Avenue,
Rosebank, Johannesburg 2196, South Africa

Penguin Books Ltd, Registered Offices: 80 Strand, London WC2R 0RL, England

Most Avery books are available at special quantity discounts for bulk purchase for sales
promotions, premiums, fund-raising, and educational needs. Special books or book excerpts also
can be created to fit specific needs. For details, write Penguin Group (USA) Inc. Special Markets,
375 Hudson Street, New York, NY 10014.

Library of Congress Cataloging-in-Publication Data

Ginsburg, Kenneth R.
Letting go with love and confidence: raising responsible, resilient, self-sufficient teens in the 21st century /
Kenneth Ginsburg and Susan FitzGerald.
p.   cm.
ISBN 978-1-58333-429-4
1. Parent and teenager.   2. Teenagers.   3. Parenting.   4. Adolescent psychology.   I. FitzGerald, Susan.
II. Title.
HQ799.15.G563   2011   2011009539
155.5'1824—dc22

Printed in the United States of America
1   3   5   7   9   10   8   6   4   2

Book design by Katy Riegel

~

To my three girls

Ilana and Talia, you are becoming the young women I envisioned—kind,

generous, thoughtful, and committed to justice and repairing the world.

You'll always be my little girls, but the more you have grown—inside

and out—the more I have found there is for me to love.

Celia, you are the model the girls follow. Thank you

for being a true partner, not just in raising

our children, but in life.

K.G.

~

To my father, Hubert FitzGerald, whose love and support are a constant source

of strength and inspiration for me. And to the four other men who bring

tremendous love and joy to my life—my husband, David Cochran,

and our sons, Sean, Patrick, and Christopher.

S.F.

~

ACKNOWLEDGMENTS

~

This book took shape with the help of many people. We want to begin by thanking the most important people—the scores of parents who were interviewed for this book. They generously gave of their time and shared their parenting experiences. We decided to change the names of parents so they would feel free to talk openly about their children and their lives. We learned so much from them, and their wisdom permeates these pages even when they are not directly quoted.

Our agent, Joanne Wyckoff, was our rock as this project evolved over several years. She encouraged us, challenged us, and pushed us. Her fine eye for editing and storytelling served us well as we expanded our idea into a book proposal. Joanne is positive, pleasant, and smart—just what we needed in an agent.

Lucia Watson, our editor at Avery, also brought confidence and a can-do attitude to this project. She believed in the concept for the book and gave us the needed time to make it work. Assistant editor Miriam Rich tended to so many details. Her organizational skills kept us on track. Lucia and Miriam were committed to producing a book that would both guide parents as they raised their adolescents and reassure them that taking care of themselves in the process was a selfless act. We also want to thank a number of other people at Avery who got behind this book: president and publisher William Shinker; editorial director Megan Newman; publicist Adenike Olanrewaju; marketing coordinator Jessica Chun; Lisa Johnson, vice president/associate publisher; and Linda Rosenberg, copyediting chief. We appreciate all you did.

FROM KEN

I want to thank fate and good fortune for introducing me to Susan FitzGerald. In working with her I have found a true partner who shares a passion for the well-being of teens. Her wisdom and insight brought clarity to so many of our discussions, and this book never could have come to fruition without her unwavering commitment to produce a work that would really allow families to thrive through and beyond adolescence.

Much of this book is rooted in the philosophy of the youth development and resilience movements. I offer my deepest gratitude and respect to the leaders of these movements who have informed and inspired me. Rick Little and his team at The International Youth Foundation first clarified the importance of the essential ingredients needed for healthy youth development—Confidence, Competence, Character, Connection, and Contribution. I have added Coping and Control to their core ideas to create the Seven Cs model offered in this book. I have been fortunate enough to know Dr. Richard Lerner of Tufts University, who was part of that original team and is undoubtedly one of the premier developmental psychologists of our era. Dr. Lerner has proven that efforts aimed at promoting positive development make a real difference in the lives of youth. In the field of adolescent health and medicine, Robert Blum, M.D., and Michael Resnick, Ph.D., have led the field in shifting from a risk-based to a strength-based approach to youth; Karen Hein, M.D., has made the clarion call that youth are a resource to be nurtured. Similarly, Karen Pittman of the Forum for Youth Investment has tirelessly taught us that our goal must be to build youth because "problem free is not fully prepared." Peter Benson of the Search Institute has helped communities and parents understand that when we develop core assets in children they are positioned to thrive. The Communities That Care process developed by doctors David Hawkins and Richard Catalano has helped communities take active steps to promote positive development while simultaneously preventing problem behaviors in youth.

I thank my professional mentors, Donald Schwarz, M.D., and Gail Slap, M.D., who have nurtured me both professionally and personally. I pay tribute to the person who may have first inspired me to care so deeply about adolescents, the best teacher I ever had, Dr. Judith Lowenthal. I thank my colleagues at The Craig-Dalsimer Division of Adolescent Medicine at The Children's Hospital of Philadelphia for always serving as role models of compassionate and committed care. Much of what I know about the power of prevention, I have learned at the hospital's Center for Injury Research and Prevention, where I have spent the last several years studying teen driving. I am fortunate to have had colleagues as creative and effective as doctors Flaura Winston and Dennis Durbin to guide this important work. I am particularly grateful to State Farm Insurance Company for supporting our efforts to save teens' lives.

My family has had the greatest and most enduring influence on me. From my parents, Arnold and Marilyn Ginsburg; my grandmother, Belle Moore; and my brother Len, I have learned the power of unconditional love and the importance of *inter*dependence. I am blessed with a wife, Celia, who supports me and enriches me, and with two precious daughters, Ilana and Talia, who serve as constant reminders to me about what really matters.

Finally, I thank the young people and their families who have allowed me to be a part of their lives. I am honored to work on behalf of military families through the Military Child Education Coalition and the U.S. Army's Child, Adolescent, and Family Behavioral Health Office. I am overwhelmed by the resilience and strengths of military families and their communities. I am moved by the love I see when parents bring their children to me at The Children's Hospital of Philadelphia and am humbled by the opportunity to serve them. I find myself rejuvenated as I bear witness to the resilience of many of the patients I care for, but, in particular, the youth of Covenant House Pennsylvania consistently remind me of the strength of the human spirit.

FROM SUSAN

This book began as a nugget of an idea when I was a children's health reporter at *The Philadelphia Inquirer* and I wrote an article about "when" kids are old enough to do certain things. My then editor, Paul Nussbaum, told me the concept would make for a great book. The idea really took off several years later when I met with Ken at his office at Covenant House in Philadelphia. I told him about my "when" idea and before I knew it he had pen and paper in hand and was sketching out a plan for a much bigger and better book. From his years of working with teens and their families, he felt strongly that the promotion of resilience needs to be at the core of every decision parents make. That conversation marked the beginning of a terrific partnership, and Ken's expertise on teens and parenting became the voice of this book. Ken is the kind of coauthor that every writer hopes for. He is creative, always enthused and energetic, and has a great knack for thinking two or three steps ahead. His positive way of seeing the world is infectious.

It would be impossible to name the many friends and colleagues who provided me with advice, encouragement, and welcome diversions during the reporting and writing process, but I will acknowledge just a few. Jane Eisner kindly referred me to our agent, Joanne Wyckoff. Arlene Morgan and Dotty Brown have been in my life as both editors and mentors over the years. Another colleague and friend, Marian Uhlman, pushed me to pursue this project and helped me to get it launched. Friends Chris Bak, Huntly Collins, and Ellie Fitzpatrick were there for me, as always.

I am blessed to have the support of a large, loving family. My mother, Nancy McKee FitzGerald, instilled in me a love for journalism and writing. She would have been thrilled to see this book. My father, Hubert FitzGerald, inspires me and shows me by example that every day should be embraced and treasured. I also want to thank my three sisters, Mary Scaccia, Sally Mika, and Pat Aichele, and my brother, Roche FitzGerald, who helped me in so many different ways while I was reporting and writing this book. And added thanks to Pat and to Tina Gregor for organizing parent discussion groups around topics in this book.

Finally, I thank my husband, David Cochran, who continually shows our three sons what it means to be a loving and committed husband and devoted father. He read portions of this manuscript and offered comments, and kept our lives running when deadlines loomed. I couldn't possibly do what I do without his love and support. I thank our three sons, Sean, Patrick, and Christopher, for the privilege and joy of being their mom. My guys have taught me to like puppies, sports, and roller coasters (well, kind of), and for that and much, much more I am forever grateful!

CONTENTS

~

SECTION III
How to Talk . . . About the Really Tough Stuff

INTRODUCTION

~

LETTING GO

"HEY, DAD, can I take the car?"

Steve, the father of two teens, was feeling uneasy about his older son's plans. To celebrate his eighteenth birthday, Mike wanted to drive to an amusement park with some friends. The trip would take two and half hours and involve the interstate. The idea didn't sit well with Steve because even though his son had been driving for a while, he had never ventured outside their hometown.

"I'd really be thoughtful about this before letting him drive," I told Steve when he approached me for advice. I worried that the road trip was a disaster waiting to happen. Mike had no highway experience and the long drive to the park would be tiring. Also, even if Mike was a responsible teen, he might very well get distracted or show off for his friends by speeding.

I advised Steve, however, not to outright shoot down the plans. Instead, he should calmly talk with Mike to find out what his son really wanted. If Mike's ultimate goal was to spend a day at the amusement park with friends, there were other ways to make that happen.

A few weeks later Steve e-mailed me an update. Mike was furious at first at not being allowed to drive and accused his father of trying to ruin his birthday. But afterward, he hugged and thanked his dad and mom for figuring out a way for his friends and him to get to the park using a train, bus, and taxi. Mike's eighteenth birthday turned out to be memorable after all.

~ ADOLESCENCE: A TIME OF "WHEN" AND "HOW"

I thought of Steve as I began to write this book because his story illustrates what you as a parent face every day with your growing child. During infancy and early childhood, there are a lot of *What* questions that you can look up in a child care book. What are those red spots? What should I do for a fever? What about teething and toilet training?

But as adolescence approaches, you grapple with different sorts of questions—questions that revolve around *When* and *How*.

When is my daughter ready to walk to school by herself?

When is she mature enough to go to the mall with friends?

When is my son ready for a cell phone?

When and *How* do I talk to him about sex?

Unlike *What* to do for a rash or fever, the answers to *When* and *How* aren't easily reduced to alphabetized entries in a reference book. Dealing with the *When*s and *How*s can be confusing and even frightening for parents because we instinctively want to protect our children from anything that could hurt them or make them sad. From the time of birth, parents are repeatedly urged to draw their children close. But the *When*s and *How*s are aimed at a different parenting goal: learning to let go. I don't mean *Letting Go* in merely the physical sense—should Steve let his son go to the amusement park? I'm talking about the much bigger process of helping your adolescent toward self-sufficiency because it's best for him, and for you. It's about learning to *let go with love and confidence.*

∼ WHY I'M WRITING THIS BOOK

I'm a pediatrician who specializes in the care of adolescents, which means that by extension I care for families, too. In my work at The Children's Hospital of Philadelphia I treat all kinds of adolescents, from healthy, well-adjusted youth to marginalized, homeless teens. On almost a weekly basis I see how horrific problems such as serious illness and addiction can over-whelm families. But I also see how more often it's the everyday issues around adolescents wanting more independence that give most parents their biggest struggles. In more than two decades of caring for adolescents, I've come to understand that there is no such thing as problem-free teen years, but that teens and parents can embrace strategies that enable them to handle problems well. I've also witnessed that most kids turn out quite well even if they suffer a few bruises or setbacks along the way.

So what makes for a smoother adolescence? Getting to the heart of that question is important to me because I'm not only an adolescent medicine doctor but also the father of teens. My twin girls, Ilana and Talia, are fifteen, and the *When*s and *How*s of *Letting Go* have come at me fast. When should I begin to let them take public transportation by themselves? Are they up for the intensity of sleep-away soccer camp? Should they be allowed to choose where to go to high school? The questions tug at me and aren't easy to resolve, even for someone who's made a career out of taking care of kids.

I began to examine what makes for a successful journey through ado-lescence in three previous books, most recently in *Building Resilience in Children and Teens: Giving Kids Roots and Wings* (American Academy of Pediatrics, 2011).

Resilience means having the ability to bounce back from difficulties and handle stressful situations without becoming derailed. Resilience isn't a trait children come equipped with; it's an acquired ability that parents can help cultivate.

My research and work with adolescents and their families repeatedly remind me that when parents take a positive, proactive approach to parenting, they greatly increase the chances that their children will learn to capitalize on their strengths, manage stress, and embrace healthy choices instead of getting stuck in destructive behavior. *Letting Go with Love and Confidence* is designed to show you practical ways to use the many *When* opportunities of adolescence to promote, not undermine, your adolescent's resilience so she is poised to thrive throughout life.

I'm fortunate to meet hundreds of parents in my work each year and I'm repeatedly struck by how parents are eager to do their best. They don't want to be scolded or blamed for their children's struggles; they want to know what works, from both a research and real-world perspective. Whether it's considering if their seventh grader should have text messaging or their tenth grader is mature enough to date, parents want to make safe, sensible decisions. Unfortunately, in our hectic, mobile world, most of us don't have a wise aunt down the block or a childhood friend around the corner to turn to for advice. We're lucky if we get snippets of parental wisdom on the soccer sidelines or while waiting for back-to-school night to begin, but we lack that proverbial village to help us raise our children.

For that reason, I hope that *Letting Go with Love and Confidence* will feel like a comfortable chat among friends or family who don't consider any question or dilemma you face with your adolescent silly or too obvious. So many books approach the topic of adolescence from a cynical point of view or fixate on the frightening extremes of adolescent behavior. While this book will tackle some tough topics, I think you'll find it refreshing and reassuring. It reflects my firm beliefs that teens are wonderful people and that parents shouldn't dread the approach of adolescence. In fact, there are so many good things to look forward to. As I always tell my own children, I love watching them grow up because every day there's more of them to love.

The tendency nowadays is to portray the world as a random and dangerous place where bad guys scheme to nab children and teens face intense stresses unlike those experienced by previous generations. Just look at the public's fascination with news accounts of school shootings and catch-a-predator TV shows. At the same time, there's a sense that technology—PET (positron-emitting tomography) scans, functional MRIs (magnetic resonance imaging)—will soon unmask the secrets of the brain and reveal why we think and behave as we do. The notion of the "teenage brain"—short on reasoning and all lit up with firing neurons when temptation comes along—is intriguing but an oversimplification of still unfolding scientific knowledge. As appealing as it may sound, no MRI scan will ever be able to tell you *When* your teen is capable of taking the train to the city. You have to learn to think through the *When*s and *How*s of adolescence using *your* brainpower, taking into consideration not only what you know about your child but where you stand as a parent.

In fact, adolescence is a lot about you. Are you ready to loosen the reins? Are you ready to set a precedent or tackle a sensitive topic? Are you ready to accept that *Letting Go* is an act of love? Are you equipped with the knowledge to make the decisions around *Letting Go* with confidence?

∼ HOW THIS BOOK WILL HELP YOU

When and *How* are easy ways to think about what we're going to discuss in the chapters ahead, but those two categories are catchalls that embrace much more. I want you to start thinking of the *When*s and *How*s of adolescence not as distinct events to which you must react in the moment, but rather as a series of more deliberate steps that will allow you to gradually let go. If you're coming to this book as a parent of a child under ten years of age or a preteen, you'll get a leg up because the unfolding of adolescence begins well before physical changes are obvious. If you have a young or middle teen and already are feeling a bit challenged, I hope this book will allow you to make the most of this critical time in your child's development.

Letting Go with Love and Confidence will help you achieve five key goals:

- **Manage your emotions around *Letting Go*:** Many of the struggles of adolescence occur because you are conflicted about your child growing up. A desire to keep things the way they've always been or an unwillingness to accept a child's need for independence often gets in the way of wise parental decision making. You need to acknowledge the very real emotions you are experiencing around *Letting Go,* but then help make the transition easier by taking time for yourself and preparing to reenter an adult-centered life. There is nothing selfish about focusing on your own well-being—it will create a happy home and set a good example for your child.

• **Reduce conflict around the *Whens* by turning them into opportunities for growth:** It's everyday issues, even seemingly mundane ones, that trigger most parent-child struggles. Your child thinks she should be allowed a new privilege just because she's a certain age— "I'm almost thirteen!"—or because her friends are doing it—"Jessica's mom lets her go to the mall!"—but she might lack the skills needed to manage the situation. If you focus on preparing your adolescent for scenarios sure to arise, you will turn potential sources of conflict and rebellion into opportunities for your child to master new skills and demonstrate responsibility.

• **Minimize anxiety over the *Hows*:** Certain subjects cause parents great discomfort not only because the topics are tough to talk about with kids, but because the stakes in getting the conversation right seem so high. *How* in the world do you talk about sex or peer pressure? You will learn to approach sensitive subjects with honesty and clarity, upping the chances that your child will hear what you say. Your angst will be eased because you will begin to talk and listen in a way that earns your child's trust.

• **Become confident with your parenting ability:** So often parenting seems haphazard, but it shouldn't be. This book is not a "cookbook" for good parenting, but it does provide an approach for you to apply to each situation so that your child is prepared to thrive. You'll be more objective and less emotional in decision making because you'll have new insight into adolescent development and your child's individual strengths and weaknesses.

• **Understand that nurturing independence is an act of love:** The words *Letting Go* imply that you're giving up something valuable, but by the time you're done with this book, you'll understand that you are giving a lifelong gift when you allow your teen to learn to thrive on his own. The ultimate goal of parenting is not to make a happy sixteen-year-old, but to produce a happy, healthy, well-adjusted thirty-five-year-old. The gift of independence is a profound expression of parental love.

This book draws on the latest findings on adolescent behavior and parenting, including my own research on teens. I first met my coauthor, journalist Susan FitzGerald, nearly ten years ago when she was a *Philadelphia Inquirer* reporter covering children's health. She interviewed me about a study I had done on teens' beliefs about which ingredients they needed in order to succeed. I have my two daughters and Susan has three sons—which means we have five different parenting perspectives between us. But that wasn't nearly enough when it came to writing this book. *Letting Go with Love and Confidence* also contains the collective wisdom of scores of parents from around the country who themselves have wrestled with the *When*s and *How*s. They generously shared their ideas and experiences and helped us focus on eighteen *When* scenarios that come up all the time for parents and six *How* topics that merit special attention. These parents' stories will reassure you that you aren't the first or even the millionth parent to go through this process. You won't feel so alone after you meet Alex, who opened his phone bill to discover his son had three thousand texts. Or Debbie and Rich, who were torn over what to do when their teens started balking at going to church. You'll also feel encouraged by the perspectives offered by parents who are delighting in their young adult children after weathering some rocky teen years.

IT'S NOT ABOUT AGE

Let's go back now to Steve's dilemma over whether to allow his son to go on a road trip to the amusement park. Notice that I didn't offer Steve an age guide to decide whether his son was ready for the responsibility. That's because arriving at an appropriate answer to *When* or *How* isn't about numbers at all. It's not about what age your child is or what date appears on the calendar, but rather about understanding where your child is developmentally, emotionally, and socially. Whether Mike was ready to drive his friends to the park had little to do with his age, which was well past his state's licensing age of sixteen, but rather with his experience and track record. Steve was immensely proud of his son and wanted to let go, but not until he was confident that Mike was prepared for highway driving and the responsibility of taking a carload of friends.

It might be easier, I suppose, if confronting the *When*s and *How*s was as simple as checking your datebook. In fact, so many of life's most memorable events are age determined. Children raised in the Catholic faith usually make their First Communion in second grade. Jewish children have their bar or bat mitzvah at age thirteen. For girls of Latino heritage, the fifteenth birthday is the occasion for the *quinceañera* celebration. We can vote at eighteen and legally consume alcohol at twenty-one. But I won't say that your son is old enough to stay home alone at age eleven or that your daughter is capable of handling a job at fifteen, because I don't know your son or daughter or the circumstances of your lives. I also won't tell you that there's a perfect age to talk about sex or drugs. What you will find in the pages ahead is a thoughtful strategy that emphasizes preparation. The answer to *When,* you see, is about recognizing *when* there are enough pieces in place so the chances for a positive outcome are enhanced. A request by your fourteen-year-old to spend the afternoon at the mall won't have to hinge on answering on the spot "Is she old enough?" if you've taught her, in part through your example, about spending wisely and treating clerks and other shoppers with respect. The day your teen begins to drive won't be quite so nerve-racking if you've made a habit of modeling safe driving behavior and made it clear that you will monitor your teen's progress even after he gets his license.

I'll also give you fresh ways to think about the *How*s. In today's sound-bite world, we're conditioned to think that everything requires a quick, clever response. But I want you to think of the *How*s as ongoing conversations with your child. Just like there isn't an age chart for the *When*s, I won't give you a scripted formula for the *How*s. Instead, I'll show you ways to position conversations as your child moves toward and through adolescence. Sex is a perfect example. You won't have to fret over *How* to deliver The Big Sex Talk if you begin years before to talk in developmentally appropriate language about sexuality—meaning love, respect, and relationships. By setting the stage over time for issues that matter, you're more apt to have effective communication throughout the many permutations of *Letting Go* that lie ahead.

How This Book Is Organized

Letting Go with Love and Confidence is divided into three sections. The opening one will focus a lot on your role as parent as you launch your adolescent on the path toward adulthood.

There are entire books devoted to topics such as adolescent development, discipline, effective communication, and peer pressure, but what I've done here is synthesize the most pressing points so you have a clear framework of knowledge to build on as you face this time of growth. I hope you'll feel more confident going forward because you'll understand yourself better as a parent and know how to assess your child's changing needs.

This opening section will address these key topics:

- **The emotional side of *Letting Go*:** Your love for your child shouldn't hinder his progress toward independence. I'll help you make sense of your feelings of loss and encourage you to plan for your next stage of life.
- **The importance of cultivating resilience:** I'll introduce the "Seven Cs of Resilience"—the seven essential ingredients that go into raising a strong, capable teen.
- **The basics of decision making:** There's a litmus test to apply to every decision you make: Is it safe? Is it practical? Does it meet my standards for morality and decency?
- **The effect of parenting style:** I'll show you ways to promote positive behavior and improve communication. I'll teach a discipline strategy that will put an end to nagging and empty threats.
- **The role of temperament and development:** Your child's temperament and maturity level influence how he handles new challenges. By knowing your child's individual profile, you can play to his strengths.

- **The social dynamics of peers:** I'll teach you three survival skills your teen can use to resist peer pressure while still holding on to friends.

By the time you're done with this opening section, you'll have a rationale to draw on every time you consider granting a new *When* privilege or tackle a *How* discussion. If you're armed with the right information, adolescence will seem less like a mystery to be figured out and more like a well-mapped journey you can help your child navigate.

The next two sections of the book—one devoted to the eighteen *When*s and another focused on the six *How*s—are arranged by topic. Some of the *When* scenarios, like driving, are uniquely tied to the teen years, but others, such as walking to school or staying home alone, are about providing early opportunities that allow your child to begin to gain confidence that he can master his world. Likewise, certain *How* topics might feel like they should be saved for adolescence and they certainly should be discussed then— topics like drinking and drugs—but your child is more likely to listen to what you're saying if you start broaching these subjects much sooner.

You don't have to read the *When* and *How* chapters in order. You can start with an issue that you're dealing with at the moment—and turn, for instance, to the *When* chapter on cell phones if you're being badgered with "I'm the only kid in my class without a cell!" If your child is feeling defeated after doing poorly on a test, you might want to turn right away to the chapter on *How* to talk about success as well as its flip side, disappointment and failure. Each *When* and *How* chapter is informed by the topics in the opening section of the book, so, if you like, you can begin in the second or third section and work your way back to further explore certain concepts.

No matter what approach you choose for reading this book, I hope you pick it up often as you begin the exciting work of *Letting Go with Love and Confidence*. So *When* should you get started? *How* about now?

SECTION I

~

SETTING THE STAGE

CHAPTER ONE

~

Preparing to Let Go
It's a Lot About You

When my daughters were about to turn thirteen, I pulled out photographs and keepsakes to prepare myself psychologically for their birthday. As I looked through old pictures of parties, vacations, and family gatherings, I kept asking myself, "How can it be that they're teenagers when it feels like they just arrived?" In the program for our girls' baby-naming ceremony, my wife and I had included a poem from Kahlil Gibran's book *The Prophet* about the fleeting nature of childhood and the important but limited role of parents. I thought I knew so much then! Since that time I have written three books on parenting adolescents, produced parenting videos, and counseled hundreds of parents on *Letting Go*. I also have furthered my intellectual understanding of the many phases of adolescent development, including the painful period of in-your-face independence that often comes before a mature "interdependence," in which young adults come to realize that they can stand on their own *and* depend on their parents to be there for them. It all makes perfect sense to me. Then why do I—an "expert" on adolescent development—feel so conflicted, confused, and emotionally vulnerable (that's man talk for *teary*) when I think of my girls growing up?

The fact is—as I discover almost every day—that *Letting Go* is hard stuff. It's hard because there's a deep but often ignored emotional issue at play. Helping our children move toward a responsible, self-sufficient adulthood is every parent's goal, but in accomplishing it we are planning ourselves out of a job that gives us tremendous pride and joy. There's a real sense of loss as we begin to get glimpses of childhood's end. This may be especially true for our generation of highly involved parents, who make it our business to be there for as many games, recitals, and award banquets as possible. It can be difficult for parents to admit how we're feeling, perhaps because we focus so intently on the feelings of our kids. But as you start down the road of *Letting Go,* I want you to take stock of yourself:

- Is she "not ready" or am I not ready to see her grow up?
- Am I getting in the way of her growing up because I cherish her innocence and dependence?
- As I evaluate each situation, do I consider his current abilities, or do I still see him through a nostalgic lens that lets him stay a little boy in my eyes?
- What am I feeling as I see her becoming more independent? Excitement for her newfound skills and confidence? Loneliness? Jealousy?
- Am I unintentionally communicating that I feel left behind or that the way to please me is to always need me?
- As he broadens his capabilities to function without me, am I using the opportunity to reinvest in myself and my relationships?

There is no right or wrong answer to these questions, and your answers may depend on the given day. Melinda, Cara, and Jane are friends who each has a child who soon will be starting college, but they differ a lot in how they feel about the next chapter in their lives.

"It's sad for me thinking she won't be my child in the same way," said Melinda, as the three friends compared notes. She's already seen her oldest son graduate from high school and head off to college, so she thought it would be easier the second time around. But as she anticipates her daughter leaving home, she once again feels sad and even gets a bit weepy at the thought.

You might be feeling wistful like Melinda, but it's also possible that your emotions are more like Cara's—you have ambivalent feelings when you think ahead to what life will be like when your child no longer bounds through the door at the end of the day. Or you even might be feeling relieved that carpools, piles of laundry, and at least some of your worrying will be over.

"I'm almost afraid to admit I'm looking forward to my son going away to college," said Cara, who then backpedaled on her statement by declaring, "Don't get me wrong. I love my son, but he's *so* ready."

Maybe part of the reason adolescents present us with challenges is to get us ready for the reality that they're so very ready. You don't have to rationalize or apologize for whatever it is you're feeling. Acknowledging that your child is "ready" is part of successfully *Letting Go*. So, too, is recognizing and understanding your own feelings so they don't end up interfering in the work you have to do to successfully launch your child.

If you get stuck on the idea that your life is going to be empty without your child, you may create a conflict of interest. Your desire to keep the status quo in your family will get in the way of making decisions that allow your teen to become a well-adjusted adult. Let this point sink in for a moment. It's hard to imagine that the intensity of the love we have for our children could hurt their development, but if we feel empty without them, we have something to gain by preventing them from standing on their own. We may have a conflict of interest between what we intellectually know is best for our teens and what we emotionally feel might be best for us.

On the other hand, if you overreact to the signals your teen sends about being "ready" (perhaps he caustically reminds you that "I'm so outta here"), you might unwisely abandon your vital monitoring role or adopt a "teens will be teens" attitude. In other words, you loosen the reins too quickly, essentially giving up. Adolescents sometimes put up a fight with their parents over being "ready" for concerts or the mall or whatever because they're trying to convince themselves that they are.

Jane seems to have found just the right balance around *Letting Go*. She has four children ranging from grade school to college, so her wisdom comes in part from hard-earned experience.

"You can't help but be emotional about your kids because they're the best thing that ever happened in your world," she explained to her friends. "But every decision I make I try to focus on 'What makes for a capable person out in the world? What makes for a moral person out in the world?'"

Those forward-looking questions have allowed Jane to accept that her children's lives won't always revolve around her and that they need to arrive at their own set of goals and values for life.

While *Letting Go* isn't easy, it will be *easier* if you think ahead and put in place a plan that prepares your child for increasing freedoms as you move gradually into the background. It also will be easier if you simultaneously start planning for your coming life—one where your teen no longer lives in the bedroom next door.

Creating, or perhaps re-creating, a full life for yourself—one filled with satisfying pursuits and relationships—not only benefits you but sends a powerful message to your adolescent. By being good to yourself, you teach your child the importance of self-care; you reduce your stress, which helps in the trying moments, and you strengthen your relationship with your spouse, partner, or friends, which has a positive ripple effect on the entire family. Because you want to raise someone who thrives as a thirty-five- or even fifty-year-old, it is good for your teen to see you as an adult model of balance.

Parents often say that raising teens is more rewarding than the baby years, perhaps because you discover your own voice in these middle years. That's exactly what Rebecca is experiencing now that she has one child in college, one soon to go, and another in grade school. "Once my daughter left, I thought, 'I can be really sad about this or start to reinvent my life back to what it was like before I had kids,'" Rebecca explained. It wasn't that she was longing to be twenty-five again, but she recognized that amid the round-the-clock demands of work, marriage, and raising children, a long list of personal interests and people had gotten set aside. She now works out several times a week and is feeling so much more confident about herself that she competes in triathlons. She has also reconnected with girlfriends she hadn't seen much over the years.

"Now I feel like I'm either with my kids, working, or doing something else I really like to do," she said. I think it will be easier for Rebecca as her younger children leave home, and I'm certain they'll be emotionally healthier, too, because they see a mother who is happy both with them and on her own.

Some parents of teens try to cram a whole lot of family time into their schedules, anticipating that those days will soon be over. While you may often feel like you're shortchanging your kids, economics professors and researchers Garey Ramey and Valerie A. Ramey at the University of California, San Diego, found that today's parents actually spend more time in activities with their children than parents did in the 1990s. That added kid-focused time seems like a positive trend, but it could mean couples are spending less exclusive time with each other.

Of course it's good to spend as much time as you can with your adolescent, but not at the expense of tending to your own well-being. Researcher Ellen Galinsky, president and cofounder of the Families and Work Institute, conducted a large, much-quoted study in which she surveyed children and teens to find out their views on their families and their parents' work lives. When she asked them what their "one wish" would be if they could change something, many of them wished that their parents would be less stressed and less tired. (Parents, on the other hand, tended to assume that their children's "one wish" would be to spend more time with them.) That's a good thought to keep in mind if you're feeling selfish, focusing on yourself and your spouse. In the long run, you're helping to preserve a stable home that will meet your teens' needs.

In truth, many of the *When*s and *How*s are bound to put teens in some degree of conflict with parents. The essential question that must be answered by every adolescent is "Who am I?" Part of the answer has to be, "I am not my parents," which is why adolescents rebel to test their own limits and pretend they aren't listening to you, even when they are. In fact, when kids are growing up and rejecting their parents' values, it's a roundabout compliment because they know exactly what their parents' values are and where they stand on things, but they also know that they don't want to be there for now. While this push back may sometimes feel downright hurtful, you should take some comfort in remembering what your child did at other major developmental stages. When he was starting to walk and fell down, he wasn't content to sit in your arms while you soothed him. Instead, he wriggled free and took off again. When she was learning to talk and couldn't quite get a sentence out, she didn't sit quietly while you completed her thoughts. Instead, she babbled right over your words, saying "Me, me, me!"

Now your child faces yet another developmental stage—a big one. In fact, I liken the period of adolescence to having to cross a chasm that is a thousand feet deep with hungry crocodiles and sharp metal spikes at the bottom. (Think action adventure movie.) If you had to get across such a chasm, you wouldn't simply stand at the edge and jump because you'd never make it. You would back up, cover your eyes, and take a running leap. Parents might wish they could build a bridge across the chasm so that their adolescent wouldn't have to jump with eyes closed and arms and legs flailing, but the truth is that your teen has to accomplish much of the crossing from childhood to adulthood on his own. That means your teen might sometimes do ridiculous things that make you think he has regressed in maturity (the backing up to get a flying leap) and is wearing blinders (eyes closed) to pitfalls you clearly see. It can be scary for your teen to think of what's really ahead.

You can't prevent the emotional jolts that are a normal part of an adolescent's breaking away, but by preparing both your child and yourself for all that's involved in the crossing to independence, *Letting Go* won't seem so formidable or so final.

One more image comes to mind as we start to explore the process of *Letting Go.* Think back to when you used a baby monitor. When you first brought your newborn home, you kept the monitor close to your ear, carrying it around as if you were a security guard. Then came the day when you wandered from the monitor as you got familiar with your baby's rhythms and knew you'd hear his crying. Eventually you turned down the monitor but periodically tiptoed into your baby's room to make sure he was all right. Finally, you no longer felt compelled to have the monitor at your bedside.

Letting Go of your adolescent will be much like that, too. You'll gradually go from uneasiness to confidence, not in a straight line, but moving forward nonetheless. You'll worry, you'll hover, you'll let go and sometimes grab hold again. That's all part of the process.

CHAPTER TWO

~

BUILDING RESILIENCE
The Secret to Lifelong Success

SANDY HAS A favorite memory that she draws upon whenever her two sons are facing a new challenge. The three of them are kayaking on a gorgeous, sun-drenched day, and for the very first time, her sons are navigating the white water of a river near their home, Mom no longer seated with them.

"I can remember paddling behind them, each of them in their own little kayak. I was so scared for them, but I was so joyful they were taking on this risk with confidence. I wanted to cry, I was so happy," Sandy said. That day on the river offered a lasting lesson. "I think both of them believe they can do anything."

Sandy's story provides a nice way to conceptualize resilience. When adolescents are resilient, they aren't invulnerable, but they are equipped to handle change and rebound from adversity, rather than feeling victimized or hopeless. They can maneuver the white water because they have mastered the skills and therefore gained needed confidence. They have the mind-set that they can overcome the odds; if the kayak flips over they have the experience and know-how to right themselves. The rushing waters energize them because they represent a challenge to be met.

Now I know what you're probably thinking because I'm a parent, too. None of us likes to see our children go through turbulence or disappointment, in part because we know from our own experiences how awful that feels. When something bad comes along, we want to spring into a fix-it mode, just like we did when we tried to keep our babies from crying by rattling a toy. While it's an understandable desire to want the path to always be smooth for your child, it's neither possible nor wise, because sheltered children turn out to be unprepared adults. To flourish in the long run, adolescents must learn to manage trying situations so they don't become disillusioned and suffer lasting damage to their spirit. Resilient children will grow up to have the tools to adapt and thrive in a changing world.

Just like Sandy taught her sons to kayak the whitewater, you can use this period of adolescence to help your child cultivate resilience. Every *When* opportunity—*When* to allow your adolescent to walk to school alone? Manage his time and schedule?—can help foster resilience if your child is prepared to take on the challenge. Likewise, every *How* conversation you have—*How* to talk about success and failure, for instance—can be positioned so your teen develops confidence, not fear, and sees possibilities, not roadblocks.

WHAT WE KNOW about resilience comes from researchers from various disciplines, including sociology, anthropology, and psychology, who studied which factors allowed individuals, communities, and cultures to thrive and survive. When it comes to children and teens, researchers wanted to understand why some children from tough circumstances such as poverty or an unstable family life end up doing fine, while others can't beat the odds stacked against them. In medicine, we used to try to set kids on the right path by identifying what they were doing wrong—smoking, drinking, skipping school—and then attempted to convince them to give up their bad habits by offering targeted advice. But the research on resilience points to a different tactic—if we want to turn out happy, healthy kids prepared for life's challenges, we need to focus on what they are doing well. Play to strengths instead of magnifying shortcomings. I began to use that approach with my own patients and started to see a real difference in how they responded.

That bit of background on the resilience movement leads back to you because now I'm going to introduce a resilience-building strategy that you can implement with your child. I drew from the work of the great thinkers in the positive youth development movement and the extensive body of resilience research to develop a strategy I call the Seven Cs of Resilience. It consists of the seven key factors (all C words) that help in the formation of resilient children: Competence, Confidence, Connection, Character, Contribution, Coping, and Control. The Seven Cs are the focus of my book *Building Resilience in Children and Teens: Giving Kids Roots and Wings*, and I regularly teach the strategy to parents and professional organizations. All of the Seven Cs are intertwined, but we'll look at each component separately. Your child might already be strong in some areas, while other areas might require more attention and support. You'll hear about the Seven Cs throughout this book because the *When* decisions and *How* discussions of adolescence all should be aimed at putting these important pieces into place for your adolescent.

∼ COMPETENCE

Competence is about having the knowledge, skills, and experience to do something well. In a bigger sense, it's about your teen being able to handle himself without you. Competence is tied to confidence because you develop confidence when you get good at something. Likewise, confidence allows you to master something new.

Every *When* situation requires that specific skills be in place. Can your adolescent walk you through his plans? Does he have a contingency plan in case Plan A doesn't work out? Does he have any prior experiences that show he's capable of taking on this new challenge?

But competence involves much more than having a game plan. It's about being able to consider a problem, weigh the options, and come up with a solution. It's about being able to reconsider a decision when something doesn't seem quite right. Getting a sound education and acquiring good work skills are key to an adolescent becoming a competent adult, but so, too, are the many insights gleaned from everyday life.

We'll discuss in detail in the pages ahead about how you can use the *When*s and *How*s of adolescence to enhance competence in its many forms. Micromanaging your child's homework won't promote competence; it will keep your child from becoming a diligent student. Lecturing your adolescent might allow you to get things off your chest, but it's an ineffective teaching tool that sends a loud message: "I think you're incapable of figuring this out unless I tell you what I know."

Part of *Letting Go* is accepting that things won't always go smoothly despite how well you prepare your teen for what's next. Competence comes from practice, and often that entails figuring out how to regroup after mistakes so the next time can turn out better. If you step in as mop-up crew every time your adolescent slips up, you end up hindering his development of competence. Often the best way to help your child learn is to get out of the way. In some cases, you have to give the go-ahead even when you're fairly sure your child will fail because you know the experience will provide a valuable lesson.

The challenge is in knowing when to get out of the way, when to give gentle guidance, and when to allow your protective instincts to take over.

~ CONFIDENCE

Confidence flows from the realization that you're competent. A confident adolescent is able to take the steps necessary to make wise choices, stick to his principles, or think differently from his friends. Confidence isn't something you can give your teen, but you can help cultivate it, although not in the way you may be accustomed. So many parents shower their kids with compliments because they want to boost self-esteem. They fawn over art projects and tell their kids, "You're so smart."

You need to shift gears because confidence is not gained through inflated compliments. In fact, research shows that lavish praise can paralyze efforts and keep children from pushing on when they feel they've met their limit.

Carol Dweck, a Stanford University psychology professor and researcher and author of *Mindset: The New Psychology of Success* (Ballantine Books, 2007), measured how schoolchildren performed on puzzle tests after being praised for either their intelligence or their effort. Those students who were told they were smart after the first round of testing worried they would slip up next time, and ended up doing worse or took the easy way out on subsequent tests compared to those students who were instead complimented for working hard. Effort, unlike intelligence, is something children feel they can control, so they work at it.

Your teen likewise will develop more confidence if you are specific with your praise and criticism. Replace the "You're so smart!" with "Your studying really paid off." Instead of reacting to a bad grade by saying "You're becoming a slacker," try "What do you think went wrong? Is there something you could do differently for the next test?" You need to retrain yourself to notice effort. When our kids were small, we made a point to catch them being good as a way to reinforce positive behavior. Parents of adolescents tend to focus on the extremes—the successes and failures—but preparation and effort should be acknowledged whether the end result falls short or exceeds expectations.

~ CONNECTION

If I could share with you only one finding that's emerged from the research on resilience, it would be this: Young people will be resilient if the important adults in their lives believe in them, love them *unconditionally,* and hold them to high expectations.

Unconditional love is not blind acceptance of every behavior, but it is an unwavering stance that communicates, "I have your back and I'm not going anywhere." High expectations are not about demanding that your child gets straight As, but it is about expecting the very best of her nature. The daughter in front of you might be sporting purple hair and talking back, but she still has the same capacity for goodness as she did when she was five and let her jar of fireflies go free.

Despite what some cynics profess, parents are the most important people in teens' lives, and it is that safe, unconditional connection that gives a young person the confidence to take on challenges and overcome tough situations. Even though your teen is spending more time away from you, your home should still be the place where he feels most secure, loved, and respected, a place where he is able to voice what he's thinking without fearing condemnation or ridicule.

Connections with other stable, caring adults also matter a lot at this age—a grandparent, your teen's dance instructor or coach—and you should look for ways to encourage those interactions, though not insist on them. Don't take it too personally if your son seems happier going to the ball game with his friend's father than with you, or if your daughter starts quoting Mrs. So-and-So as the authority on everything from fashion to politics. Each of the circles your adolescent moves in—extended family, school, community, religious or cultural groups—provides him with critical reference points as he goes about developing his own slate of values, goals, and traditions. As you make decisions around whether your adolescent is ready to branch out into something new, consider whether the activity provides an opportunity for your child to strengthen a constructive relationship or make a meaningful new connection.

~ CHARACTER

I saw this definition of character, attributed to former Oklahoma congressman J. C. Watts, on a poster at a high school I toured with my daughters: "Character is doing what's right when no one is looking."

Each of us has our own list of character traits we admire most—honesty, empathy, reliability, compassion, loyalty, tolerance, a sense of fairness. The possibilities go on and on. There's no one way to define what it means to "have a good character" but I usually use this general rule: Adolescents who have a good sense of themselves, a respectful attitude toward others, and an awareness of what's going on in their bigger world are on their way to becoming caring, responsible adults.

Character can't be taught like a lesson in school; it's learned mostly by observing. We model kindness to our kids when we bring in the mail for a neighbor recuperating from surgery or make a casserole for a family with a new baby. We model patience when we listen attentively as our spouse talks about a hard day at work even though we've had a bad day, too. Our kids learn by listening to our reactions to a news story about a devastating earthquake or a rally to mark a pivotal moment in history. Through our daily actions, we teach our children the importance of consideration for others and what it means to be a committed member of a family and a community. We also, without realizing it, model character traits we don't wish for our kids—pettiness, close-mindedness, a quick temper.

You need to encourage connections between your teen and others who display the character traits you admire. Older cousins or college-age neighbors provide real proof that working hard in school and avoiding trouble pay off. On a school sports team, everyone is expected to keep their grades up and stay out of detention.

While having good role models is essential for a child's character development, you still need to be clear with your teen where you line up on character-related issues, whether it's lying, cheating on tests, spreading malicious text gossip, or judging people based on race, religion, or sexual identity. Ideally, parents should instill in their children not only a strong sense of right and wrong in terms of personal behavior, but also a desire to take a stand against what's wrong around them and try to change it. When you invite your teen to hand out campaign flyers with you, for instance, he sees that people care about voting issues.

You should approach all the *When*s and *How*s of adolescence with the goal of promoting character. Will this activity reinforce my child's sense of worth? Will it strengthen her belief that her actions matter? Will it introduce her to new ideas, offer a broader view of life, or open her eyes to people who are less fortunate than she is?

～ CONTRIBUTION

Teens who experience the rewards of service feel more positive about themselves. Teens are forever hearing, unfairly so, that their generation is self-absorbed and content to live in a virtual world. When teens are surrounded by thank-yous, rather than condemnation, from those who are grateful for their help, it reminds them that people value them and count on them to do good things.

Contribution can happen in many ways—it doesn't have to entail a service trip to a village on the other side of the world. Liz tells the story of how her son set off to fulfill his school's required service hours by cleaning up an elderly woman's yard, but ended up spending most of the afternoon talking over ginger ale and pretzels. Her son didn't physically do much; his contribution was listening.

Teens who get involved in service also experience another benefit— they get comfortable with asking for help for themselves. Because teens feel good when they help someone out, they come to realize that doing service is partly a selfish act. Later on when they need help, teens are less likely to feel ashamed because they know the other person isn't judging them or pitying them but genuinely wants to help. The ultimate act of resilience is being able to turn to another person and say, "I need a hand."

～ COPING

We all have ways of coping with stress. We work out at the gym, play around on the computer, or perhaps stretch out in front of the TV with a beer and a bag of chips. Our kids also have techniques for coping, not all healthy ones, either. The negative behaviors parents fear so much— smoking, drinking, cutting—aren't necessarily due to your teen's "weak character" or even peer influences, but may be your child's answer to dealing with stress.

Part of being resilient involves having healthy coping skills in place that you can turn to almost automatically when a stressful moment overtakes you or excessive worry threatens to settle in for the long haul. Teens with good coping skills are less likely to turn to dangerous quick fixes when they're overwhelmed; they are more likely to thrive in new and unexpected situations. I'll share in Chapter 26 the details of my Ten-Point Stress-Management Plan for teens, which includes breaking big problems into little ones and taking an "emotional vacation" from what's bothering you.

~ CONTROL

Adolescence should be a time when your child learns to follow his inner sense of control so that he makes decisions that prepare him to thrive in the future rather than to live only in the moment. You help your child achieve self-control when you use a discipline strategy that grants privileges in response to consistent responsible behavior and ties consequences directly to undesired behaviors. When your teen has inner control, he no longer thinks things "happen to me," but instead appreciates that his decisions and actions influence the outcome. In the next chapter on parenting style, we'll talk about how the right type of discipline can enhance your adolescence's sense of inner control amid a peer world that often feels unpredictable and sometimes even out of control.

ONE OF THE HARDEST parts of *Letting Go* is slowly leaving behind the fantasy that you can protect your child from the world. The truth is that it was never possible and, more important, overprotected children don't recover very well when times are tough. Our challenge is to prepare our teens to navigate the world—with all of its joys and knocks—on their own. Keep asking yourself this question: "In what ways does my reaction or decision develop or undermine resilience?"

CHAPTER THREE

~

Doing a Gut Check
Safety, Practicality, Morality

Every parent has a tool that needs to be used more often: It's called the gut instinct. Your adolescent tells you his plans for the evening, but something doesn't quite feel right. That's your gut talking and you need to pay attention. That's not to say that *no* is the only possible response, but your gut is waving a red flag to signal, "Slow down. Get some more information."

The gut check is at the core of the *three-prong litmus test* that you can apply to every *When* decision and every *How* discussion: *safety, practicality, and morality*. While those categories seem daunting, think in terms of three simple questions: Is the proposed scenario safe? Is it practical? Does it meet my standards for morality and decency? We live in a society where many parents make it their job to keep their kids happy, but you need to consider whether your teen's wishes square with basic safety measures and your family's values.

An honest consideration of those factors is important in decision making because sometimes you tend to exaggerate the possible downsides of a situation when you're afraid you won't be there to pick up your child if he fails. On the other hand, you might makes decisions too casually because your adolescent has a fierce need for independence or a rebellious nature that makes it easier to give in.

∼ SAFETY

To feel responsible *Letting Go* you have to start with safety, because anything that compromises safety can't be tolerated. If a situation genuinely puts safety at risk, the answer is "No!" Period.

Adolescents must understand that while we want to foster their increasing freedom, we will always give appropriate boundaries so they can progress toward independence safely. When your child was little, you didn't wring your hands over whether he could cross the street by himself. You simply said, "You can't cross the street without me." Likewise, parents of adolescents need to take an unwavering stand when safety is at stake. Anytime your gut reaction is that you're dealing with a safety issue, you have to trust that feeling and do what is necessary to protect your child. Anxiety serves a purpose. Sometimes we intuitively know that danger exists, even though we can't rationally explain it. This is a biological instinct that took root in our ancestors as a survival tool. Don't let your analytical self override your gut. If something "feels" dangerous to you, it likely is. (If you know yourself to be a worrier or particularly anxious, you should still trust your gut when it speaks to you strongly. But you might choose to run your thoughts by someone else who is safety minded and cautious, but less anxious, to check out your instincts.)

Part of the safety check involves being able to objectively assess the potential for danger. We live in a media-saturated world where unlikely risks such as kidnappings get magnified, while real and preventable dangers—reckless driving, binge drinking, date rape, drowning, gun injuries—aren't fully appreciated. The leading killers of teens are "unintentional injuries" (mostly car crashes), homicide, and suicide. Public health experts have moved away from using the word *accident* because it implies there was nothing that could have been done to prevent the unfortunate turn of events. It was bad luck, your number was up, you happened to be in the wrong place at the wrong time. For sure, horrible, inexplicable things do happen, but many accidents are preventable.

A parent can't—and shouldn't—control everything. And the ultimate responsibility for your child's behavior does lie with him. But parents really do matter and they can prevent many problems by establishing appropriate rules and boundaries around curfew, driving, and other issues and then effectively (much more on what it means to be effective later!) monitoring those rules. Once you accept that fact, you can shift from the comfortable denial that says, "I have no control anyway," or the fallback position of "Good parents let kids learn through their mistakes," into an active stance that says, "I can't control everything, but I will play the odds as best as I can . . . with my eyes wide open."

Although this absolute approach to safety is part of loving parenting, your teen will probably say you're treating her like a baby or that "You care too much." She may have seen other teens take the same chance many times with no consequences, and knowing they ended up okay may have extinguished her own worries.

Barbara's sixteen-year-old son lashed out when she said he couldn't have friends over while she and her husband were gone, a rule she considered very much a safety issue. "This is not a fun house. No one wants to come here because this is not a fun house," he protested before storming off. His words stung Barbara because she and her husband always welcomed her son's friends into their home and had gone to the expense of making the basement kid-friendly by adding an air hockey table. "But then I thought that if a 'fun house' means there are no parents home, no supervision, that it's like living in a college dorm, then that's okay," she recalled.

Barbara waited to calm down and then revisited the issue with her son. "You know, I thought about the comment you said about this not being a fun house," she told him. "It's not my job to provide you with a 'fun house.' But this is a loving home, it's a safe and accepting home, and your friends are welcome here. You have space, and you can have privacy with your friends."

Judith Smetana, a professor of psychology and researcher at the University of Rochester, has studied adolescent attitudes and behavior for decades and found that teens draw a distinction between what they think are legitimate issues for their parents to be involved with and those that are off-limits. Things having to do with safety or the teaching of socially acceptable behavior fall into the acceptable category. Most things related to friends are in the hands-off column. If you make it clear that your concern is about safety, not about how you feel about your teen's friends, your teen is more likely to accept that you're not trying to control or punish him. Your words should convey the sense "Yes, I do trust your judgment, and yes, you are showing me more every day how much you are growing up, but I care about you so much that I can't let you take this chance." The bottom line is that this is about safety, not control.

Barbara's experience with her son underscores the importance of the language and tone used in discussing safety concerns. If you seem hysterical—"You're going to die if you go out on a night like this!"—or suspicious—"I don't trust your friends to be in my house when I'm not here"—your teen will reject anything more neutral you have to say because he's already concluded you're exaggerating things or, worse yet, dissing his friends.

In an ideal world, you shouldn't be the only person watching out for your teen's safety. There should be multiple layers of protection that come from parents, relatives, school, community, and even peers. Think of the shield around your child as a block of Swiss cheese. Each slice has many holes in it, but the chances are good that something can't get the entire way through the unsliced block. Your holes or blind spots as a parent can be compensated for by the next layer. At the same time, you can't pass off your responsibility because sometimes when everybody is watching the kids, no one is really paying attention. Think of what needs to happen around a backyard pool. There might be multiple adults present, but one has to be the designated lifeguard; otherwise no one takes full responsibility.

~ THE BENEFITS OF GROUP RULES

Kids want to be normal, and sometimes they will take stupid chances to prove they are. If you are the only parent with proper rules and boundaries, your child will always be bucking the trend, and that can be uncomfortable for him and hard on you because you'll constantly hear that you're being unfair. I like the strategy of parents who take the added step of getting together with other parents to decide group rules for what's considered safe and acceptable. If every kid on the football team is expected to be home by ten, you'll have fewer arguments. If parties involving your kid's circle of friends always have adult monitors, teens won't see the parties as lame.

Rose and Ed made a point of figuring out who was in each of their teens' close circle—it was easy in their son's case because he spent a lot of time playing drums in a garage band—and then went out of their way to get to know the parents. They periodically invited the other parents and their teens over for a picnic or an evening of socializing to create an opportunity to discuss and agree upon curfew and other communal rules.

"We talked about parties and how many sleepovers we thought were acceptable," Rose said. "We talked about the parameters for going to houses when parents weren't there." Curfew and alcohol—none of the latter would be served at parties and kids weren't allowed to come and go—were also on the agenda. Because they already had made the effort to get to know the other parents, Rose and her husband found it easier to pick up the phone when a big event like the prom came along to check if the other parents were okay with the all-night activities. Of course, the group consensus didn't prevent every problem, but overall the strategy seemed to work. "Having group rules helped the kids feel secure because they knew there were boundaries. I think they felt less pressured to do things because there wasn't that, 'Well he can do it. Why can't I?'" Rose said. "This is what we decided as a group and they accepted it."

Having a network of support can also help you psychologically during the inevitable moments when parenting feels like a lonely and thankless job. Teens sometimes lead their parents to believe they are the only ones not allowed to do something, which, of course, is rarely if ever true. "I try to surround myself with friends who are on the same page as me," said Betty, who has three kids. It's not that she and her friends talk all the time about what their kids are up to, but just knowing there are other parents who think the way she does about setting standards for safety and behavior is affirming when her teens try to wear her down with comments like "Oh my God! You're *so* overprotective!"

Now I want to acknowledge here that it's possible you'll experience a defensive response when you reach out to other parents. We sadly live in a world where adults get criticized for even gently correcting other people's children, and many parents get touchy about any hint that they're not as diligent as they could be or that their child has stepped out of line. I promise not to talk too much in this book about the "good old days," but it's fair to say that it didn't take much for word to get back to our parents that we were blasting our music out the window or speeding through the neighborhood.

I don't think we should as a society give up on the expectation that adults collectively must hold youth to high standards of behavior. While it might feel uncomfortable to call or e-mail parents to check about plans involving your adolescent and his friends, it will become less awkward if you get in the habit of doing it. You might very well be met with "Thanks for calling. I'm really glad you reached out," and better yet, you could start a trend where parents begin to check in with each other.

No matter what, don't underestimate the safety you offer your child by being known as a parent who keeps an eye on things. Your child might want to do the right thing but can't admit it to her friends that something goes against her better judgment. Let her instead blame you. ("Are you kidding? My dad is the strictest guy around!") You'll learn more about "shifting the blame" strategies in Chapter 6.

∼ PRACTICALITY

Practicality follows closely behind safety. Being practical often falls by the wayside in this era of indulgent parenting, but it's perfectly reasonable to make decisions based on whether your child's request falls within your family's budget, schedule, and priorities. I urge you to think about the message you're sending if you're constantly handing over $20 bills, cutting short your own plans to serve as a shuttle driver, or putting your teen's social life ahead of already scant family time.

Don't get me wrong. Your child should be secure in knowing she is always at the forefront of your concern and your love is boundless. However, adolescents should respect that their parents have responsibilities with work, home, younger siblings, and extended family and that last-minute requests aren't always possible to fill. Life in the long haul is about being practical, at least most of the time, and adolescents should learn to plan ahead and make trade-offs. Some parents have e-mail addresses like "Mom24/7." While parenting is far from being a day job, you simply can't do everything. You need downtime to stay healthy and rested and preserve family relationships.

I like the tactic that Pamela, who has three children, has adopted for staving off what she calls the "piling-on effect"—that feeling that no matter what a kid is doing, it's never enough. "Take Halloween," Pamela says. "It starts out with trick-or-treating, then the kids want to go to someone's house afterward for a party, then they want to have a sleepover, and then, since there's no school the next day, they want to go to the mall." Instead of always playing defense when her kids and their friends mount a full-court press, Pamela has learned the power of stating at the onset what's doable— "You can have a friend over, but she can't spend the night because we have to get up early tomorrow." That practical strategy has cut down on wearying debates with her kids.

You also have to be practical about money—how to stick with a budget and save for the future. Some parents feel guilty that they can't afford to buy their kids the latest clothes, cell phone, or laptop. Children learn a lifelong lesson when you tell them you're saving for a family vacation or have to put off buying something because the roof needs replacing. Parents need to teach their children the difference between what you want and what you need, and that there's pleasure to be had in delaying gratification and saving up for something special. Before you know it, your teen will be on his own and paying his bills, and you want him to be ready for the economic realities of life.

∾ MORALITY

Every decision you make as a parent should be in keeping with your standards for what is right and wrong, whether it involves a core character value such as honesty or fairness, or one of your nonnegotiables, such as underage drinking. Parents will sometimes preach one thing and then condone the opposite. Let's take telling the truth as an example. You tell your child from an early age that lying is wrong and hurtful to relationships, but then you say it's okay for your adolescent to go to a party where the host's parents are out of town and have no idea of what's going on. You preach the importance of inclusion in society, but then let your child have a sleepover that includes all but a couple of classmates.

Even very young children absorb morality lessons all around them, so take advantage of everyday experiences to set high expectations for morality and common decency. Remember, your child is listening to what you say about your neighbor or sister or boss. If you start preaching morality during mid-adolescence—something many parents do because they hit the panic button on sex or some other issue—your teen will probably tune you out or reject what you have to say precisely because it's coming from you. (This is not because of anything you've done right or wrong; it's just the nature of mid-adolescence. More on this later.) During adolescence, you need to talk less, but behave consistently with the very standards you want your child to have. Adolescents are really good at spotting hypocrisy, and anything that flies in the face of the principles you espouse will be held against you with a vengeance.

Ask yourself when you're wrestling with a decision that makes you uncomfortable whether you're considering giving in because you want your teen or his group of friends to like you. It's a huge mistake to believe you can parent most effectively as your adolescent's "best friend." Kids need adults to be the proverbial lighthouse on the shoreline that provides a steady reference point on what is safe and right.

Rebecca, who grew up in an Irish Catholic family, says that now that she's a parent she sees the wisdom in her mom's loving but unmovable stand when it came to things that really mattered.

"When you tried to work on her to change her mind, she had a simple answer: 'Not while I'm God,'" Rebecca's mother liked to say, though always with a twinkle in her eye. Rebecca doesn't pull that line—at least not often—on her own three children, but she sometimes hears her mother's words as she reminds herself that she needs to stand firm and unapologetic in situations where her kids' safety or well-being is at risk.

"I never want to be my kids' best friend. I want to be the adult in their life that steers them in the right direction and gives them a heads-up when they're not going there," Rebecca said.

Every parent wants to make their kid happy, and it's pretty easy to create momentary happiness—just give them what they want. The bigger challenge is to make them prepared for a successful, balanced adulthood. This means they will have to learn to control impulses that offer momentary pleasure but risk safety. They will have to learn to be practical. We hope they will develop a deep moral sense that will drive them to make decisions that take into consideration how their actions are affecting others.

CHAPTER FOUR

~

LOOKING IN THE MIRROR
How Do You Parent?

THERE'S A TENDENCY nowadays to treat parenting as a profession, to approach it with the same outcome-oriented zeal with which we attack our paying jobs. We may not talk in terms of productivity or meeting objectives, but we measure our worth by what we "do" for our kids and what they "do" in turn. Piano lesson—check! Baseball practice—check! We've all heard parents complain—or is it *brag?*—"I've been in the car all day!"

But parenting, at the end of the day, is not about managing your child's life or keeping your car gassed and ready to go to the next activity. Parenting, at its essence, is about providing the right mix of *warmth, support,* and *monitoring* so your child learns to manage his own life and make his own good decisions. Most parents give some thought to parenting techniques when their children are babies and toddlers, but often don't think much as time goes on about the habits they've fallen into. Adolescence offers an ideal opportunity to reexamine your parenting style to see if what once felt comfortable is effective now that your child is beginning to push limits. In the chapter ahead we'll take a look at different parenting styles, as well as communication and discipline strategies. You may conclude that how you're doing things remains effective or decide to make adjustments to handle new circumstances. Either way, a bit of self-reflection prepares you to be flexible when you need to be!

∼ FOUR PARENTING STYLES

If you look around at the parents you know well—including your parents and yourself—you could probably put a label on them, ranging from lenient to strict. We all have somewhat of a strategy, whether we realize it or not, for how we raise our children, based on the type of family we grew up in, the temperament of our kids, and the culture and community in which we live. Psychologists who study parenting generally use four categories to describe parenting style, with each one varying in the degree of warmth, support, and monitoring that parents provide their children. Take a look at them:

- **Authoritarian parents** set a lot of rules and give their children a lot of directions, usually without much explanation. They operate from a position of power and can be harsh with punishment. They set high expectations for their children, but also foster a family dynamic in which conformity is expected, questioning authority is frowned upon, and discussion of concerns is discouraged. "Why? Because I said so" is a common theme, as is "As long as I'm paying the bills, you'll do what I tell you." Authoritarian parents certainly love their children, but may not demonstrate much warmth. They see the protection they offer their children as love. Children of authoritarian parents may miss the chance to learn how to problem-solve and seize ownership of their own decisions and behavior, and may end up rebelling against their parents' hard-line approach.
- **Permissive parents** are what most people would call indulgent. They usually spend a lot of time with their children and genuinely enjoy them. They are generous with affection, and are eager to meet

their children's wishes and needs. They tend to teach their children good values but fail to make many demands on them or establish the boundaries that help keep kids safe and behaving appropriately. They instead rely on an approach that says, "I adore you and I trust you to make good decisions." Permissive parents sometimes operate from a desire to be friends with their kids and go to great lengths to avoid conflict to assure that they are liked. One parent explained, "Our kids love us too much to do anything too crazy." Children of permissive parents end up having to mostly police themselves, which puts a lot of pressure on them. While they generally want to please their parents by doing the right thing, they are driven largely by a fear of being a disappointment. This can lead to a bit of neurosis and excessive worry about whether they are good or acceptable. In my office practice, parents with a permissive style will sometimes explain to me that their kids tell them everything because "we are like best friends." Unfortunately, I often learn in private sessions with their adolescents that they hide a lot of things from their parents because they don't want to hurt them.

Children who grow up in permissive households can get caught up in risky behaviors because their parents don't have needed rules and monitoring in place, and self-policing is not good enough for young people who are developmentally supposed to test their limits and don't yet have the experience to always know which actions can lead to danger.

- **Uninvolved parents** provide their children with not much at all in the way of rules, monitoring, *or* emotional support. They have difficulty empathizing with their children. In some cases, a parent's lack of involvement in their children's lives is due to personal struggles, such as mental illness or addiction, or overwhelming demands in other aspects of life. But most laissez-faire parents more deliberately adopt the attitude that "kids will be kids; they need to learn by their mistakes," perhaps as a reaction to their own upbringing or a sincere desire to have their children learn from life lessons. Uninvolved parents often go into overdrive, however, when a child gets into trouble, suddenly enforcing new rules and punishments. Because their parents only notice them when they get in trouble, children of uninvolved parents might do whatever it takes to get the attention they so desire and need. These children are at risk for a host of attention-getting problems, including drugs or truancy, and may have a difficult time with personal relationships as they get older.

- **Authoritative (as opposed to authoritarian) parents** offer a balance of warmth, support, and monitoring. They are nurturing, but not smothering. They promote their children's independence by encouraging new experiences, while at the same time setting reasonable boundaries, clear expectations, and consequences. They hold their children accountable in an age-appropriate way for their behavior, but usually avoid strong punishment. Authoritative parents are flexible and responsive to the circumstances at hand—sometimes providing their children more rules, other times loosening up—and they listen to their children's point of view and encourage them to make their own choices and solve their own problems. But for the issues that matter most—when safety is at stake, for instance—they take a firm "You'll do as I say" stand. There's a substantial body of research in support of the authoritative style of parenting. When adolescents are given clear boundaries and expect a reasonable amount of parental supervision, they are less likely to engage in worrisome behaviors, such as underage drinking and sexual activity, and more likely to do well in school. Later on, I'll tell you about some of my research that found that teens who describe their parents as authoritative are far less apt to get in car crashes.

~ ADJUSTING YOUR STYLE

The point of introducing you to the four styles of parenting wasn't to label you a good or bad parent or try to fit you into a box. Rather, I wanted to get you thinking about how you combine the various ingredients of parenting—warmth, support, and monitoring. Parents will often say they've got an easy kid or a tough kid, and there's certainly some truth to that, but in fact you can *choose* to parent in a way that promotes positive behaviors in your child. Let me really bring that point home. How your children turn out and whether your children participate in those behaviors you most fear is not simply a matter of luck and unforeseen circumstances. While you can't control everything, your approach to parenting can make a big difference.

We too easily fall back on the parenting "tapes" we have stored in our heads—those same reactions our parents had to us or the exact opposite because we're trying hard not to mimic what we experienced growing up. You can choose to turn off those tapes or add new ones to your mental library.

Connie, who has a daughter in high school and another in middle school, gives a lot of thought to her parenting style—in part because her own upbringing left much to be desired. The youngest of three siblings, she was raised in a suburban home by hands-off parents. Connie came and went as she pleased, with no curfew and few rules. "Other people thought it was cool that I didn't have those kinds of restrictions," she says, but she interpreted her parents' lack of involvement as meaning they didn't care about her. "I remember thinking, 'Don't you *want* to see my report card?'"

Connie and her husband, Greg, consciously strive to be authoritative (balanced) parents—they're clear and confident in their rules and decision making, but they're warm and responsive, too. They expect their girls to do well in school, participate in sports, and help around the house, but free time is for play and friends. Their older daughter, a high school sophomore, must provide details in advance on what she wants to do, but once Connie and Greg agree to her plans, they let her go and expect her to be where she says and return at the agreed-upon time. They don't pepper her with cell phone calls or texts when she's out with friends. "Once we decide something is okay, we have to trust her," Connie says.

If you decide to tweak or even significantly shift your parenting style, don't worry that it will be viewed as weakness or desperation. It will probably be welcomed by your adolescent—even though he may not verbalize what is different about your relationship—as a sign that you're listening to each other and learning a lot as you go.

∼ LISTENING AND TALKING WELL

So many parenting decisions are based on trusting that our children will tell us when they feel tested beyond their limits or need adult advice, support, or even protection, but the reality is that many children don't disclose. Parents often focus on finding out as much as they can about their teens' lives, but ultimately how much we know as parents comes down to how much our kids choose to tell us. You can increase the chances your child will reveal what's really on his mind by putting into place communication strategies that depend on *your* listening and talking skills. You probably think that you're already doing a lot of both as a parent, but you may not be listening or talking in a way that allows your child to feel secure in sharing much of what's going on in his life. Teens frequently tell me that their parents don't listen to them, a statement the parents would probably dispute by pointing out that they *always* respond to what their child tells them. That's the point precisely—parents react, but they don't really listen. They talk too much and listen too little.

Let's first take a look at what's entailed in good listening:

- **You don't interrupt.** You listen to your child with the intent of being a sounding board and you listen with genuine empathy and interest. When you listen well, you don't dismiss or make light of what your child is saying or jump in and tell him how you think he should feel.
- **You turn off your parent alarm.** So often parents react to something their kid is telling them by sounding their parent alarm. Your son tells you a teammate is having a postgame party on Friday night and your "parent alarm" goes off, propelling you into a lecture on the dangers of drinking and police busts. Your daughter tells you that she met a nice guy at summer camp and you interrupt with the pronouncement "You're too young to date." The parent alarm assumes imminent catastrophe even though the facts aren't yet clear, and it drowns out any chance for a meaningful discussion because it cuts your child's thoughts short. The parent alarm signals "I will tell you

what to do because I don't think you're capable." When you deactivate your parent alarm and avoid a rush to judgment, your teen is more likely to reveal what's on his mind. If your teen starts telling you about a cheating scandal at his school, for instance, don't warn, "Well, you better never cheat!" and then give a million reasons why. Instead, use responses that might get your teen talking about the pressure kids feel to get good grades. Questions such as "What do you think about that?" "Why do you think that happened?" and "How do you think things will turn out for the kids who were caught cheating?" will be more productive.

- **You listen more than you talk.** Eran Magen, a psychologist at the University of Pennsylvania, in collaboration with Paul Konasewich, a leadership consultant, developed a powerfully simple technique called "Supportive Listening" that teaches individuals and businesses how to improve their communication skills by doing a better job of listening to what others have to say. He recognizes that people are the best experts on themselves, so the goal in listening should be to get the other person to arrive at their own solutions. When you listen more than you talk, you put your adolescent in the position of being able to consider all sides of an issue, sort through his emotions, and reach his own wise conclusion. When kids arrive at an answer themselves, they own it and therefore have nothing and no one to rebel against.

Now let's talk about talking. Imagine what would get recorded if someone made a video of you talking to your teen. Would you like what you saw? It's not just the words you use. Your tone of voice, hand gestures, and body position convey messages, too. Are you dismissive or overly dramatic? Do you talk in a condescending or belittling manner? Do you take over the conversation?

When it comes to talking with your teen, you want to avoid lecturing. Here's why:

- **Adolescents usually don't comprehend lectures.** Parents assume their children are soaking in their wisdom as they shower them with rapid-fire warnings and advice, but such lectures are delivered in a style that adolescents' developing minds simply cannot process. Lectures don't work with teens because they are too abstract. Think about a typical parental lecture. In an attempt to get our points across quickly about things that terrify us, we careen in seconds from point A to point B to point C to point D and onward, stringing together a whole bunch of variables that come across like a complicated algebra problem: "If you drink (or do drugs) you'll get bad grades and not get into college. If you're not well educated, you'll end up in a low-paying job or unemployed. You could become homeless or even dead." The progression of points seems linear and logical to you (though admittedly a bit hysterical). But your teen will probably take in only "drink" and "dead" and not much in between. Your intended message comes across just like the *"Wah, wah, wah"* of the adults in Charlie Brown's world. Your teen gets that you're angry and that you thought she was foolish and incapable, but misses your point entirely. The next chapter, on adolescent development, will explain this in greater detail, but for now you need to know that early adolescents still see things very concretely. This means they understand what they can touch and smell, right here, right now. They don't think about future consequences—the very thing lectures tend to focus on. Older adolescents can think in abstract, nuanced ways, seeing possibilities and grasping future ramifications of decisions made now, but all people (adults and teens alike) revert to more concrete thinking when under stress or in a panic. This means that at the precise time when we tend to shift into lecture mode—times of stress—teens of all ages can't understand what we are saying. Let's use the example of the drinking and drug lecture again. Going from point A to point B makes sense: Drinking and drug use can lead to poor school performance. But you need to slow down and take it one step at a time. Once your teen has figured out point B, move along to C. One step at a time, like simple math, not algebra. Once they really grasp point C, you might want to calmly guide them to point D, but there is usually no need to cover everything at once.

- **Lectures backfire because they're one-sided.** The goal is to have your teen reach his own "aha" conclusion, but that can't happen when you're on a tear and talking *at* him at breakneck speed. Your teen will decide you need a chill pill, tune you out, and perhaps even choose to rebel to prove you wrong. Instead of delivering a lecture, you want to encourage two-sided discussion. That is more likely to happen if you use open-ended questions like "How do you think kids handle their schoolwork when they party every weekend?" Your teen's response could lead you to the next point you want to get across, or it could steer you in a direction you had not even considered.

- **Lectures tend to get too personal too fast.** Remember, teens think it's okay for their parents to talk about safety and how to behave in a socially acceptable way, but not about most issues having to do with their friends. When you respond to your parent alarm with a lecture, you're more likely to head into that forbidden territory and end up in a minefield because your teen has heard your message as saying: "And I don't trust your friends!"

- **Lectures tend to be badly timed.** So often lectures are delivered at a time of tremendous emotion. You're angry or scared or anxious about something coming up with your teen. It's not the time to opine on the perils of teen pregnancy when your daughter's prom date is at the door. Likewise, ticking off a list of don'ts—*don't drink, don't do drugs, don't have sex, don't be bad*—as you pull up to drop your son off at a party will merely fuel the anxiety he's already feeling and perhaps even make your worries a reality. Instead of delivering badly timed lectures, you want to seize on opportunities to draw your teen into impromptu discussions by using the external cues all around you—things you see on TV or pass by while driving. Questions such as "Have you ever seen your friends drink and drive?" won't go over well, but comments about a TV show might trigger a good discussion. In the *How* chapters, we'll give more examples of these kinds of conversations.

- **Not lecturing does not mean turning a blind eye.** You certainly should correct your child or express displeasure or concern when he's doing something wrong or worrisome. But that doesn't have to involve a lecture. Yelling isn't at all productive, either. For parents who grew up in homes where loud, emotional conversations were common, this habit can be hard to break, but you'll be surprised how your child starts responding to a gentler mode of communication. Liz said she decided to drop the dramatics and listen more after she noticed that not only were her kids' eyes glazing over when she went into lecture mode, but so were her husband's. A few months later, she received a gratifying text from her son following a discussion about class work. Previously, things would have heated up and ended in an unpleasant exchange of words, but not this time. "Thanks for understanding me," he texted. "It means a lot u were supportive and we didn't argue."

Listening and talking well are key to discipline because when you create an environment where your child is able to think things through, he's more likely to make smart choices and own up if something goes wrong.

~ DISCIPLINE

Effective discipline is not just about responding to a problem, it is about putting into place a strategy that will make it so your kid usually does the right thing. So often discipline fails to bring about the desired change in behavior because it comes too late in the game. Parents equate discipline with punishment—they react after the fact to what their child did wrong. The word *discipline* means to teach or guide. You'll be a more effective teacher if you embrace a discipline strategy that teaches adolescents that they can earn a new privilege by showing they're competent and responsible, and that they will lose that same privilege when they fail to act responsibly. You also need to provide a reasonable and predictable amount of monitoring that your child knows to expect.

Let's look further at those points:

Make sure your expectations are clear. That seems like stating the obvious, but often parents are ambiguous about what they expect. It helps if you get into a routine early on that involves stating clearly what you want your child to do and what will happen if he doesn't follow through. The more you establish a pattern in your household that desired behavior leads to the granting of a related privilege and misbehavior leads to the loss of the privilege, the less likely your child will disobey. Even in the case of simple requests, be clear about your needs. "I need you to help me weed the garden this morning or I won't be done in time to drive you to the skate park after lunch" is a simple, nonthreatening statement. The expectation is clear (help weed) and so is the consequence (don't help, no ride).

Always take into consideration your child's competence. You can't honestly expect your teen to do well at something new if he hasn't been prepared to handle it. Does he have the needed competencies for taking on a new privilege? For the many issues that will come along in adolescence, the underlying message of discipline should be, "I'm excited to see you grow up and I want you to become independent, but for me to give the go-ahead for more privileges you need to show me that you're ready to handle them." Think back to Steve at the beginning of the book. He wasn't comfortable allowing his son to drive to the amusement park because his son didn't have experience with highway driving. Steve said no, but then vowed to take the time to expose his son to more varied driving conditions.

As we begin to explore the various *When*s, we'll talk about what specific skills need to be in place for different scenarios, but the overall idea is that not only do you need to lay out what you expect your child to do—"You need to be home from the concert at eleven"—but you need to consider whether your teen is equipped to think through any number of scenarios that could come up. The eleven o'clock curfew makes sense, but meeting it could become complicated if a friend who doesn't have the same curfew is driving, the event is on the other side of town on a Saturday night, or your teen and his friends get separated in the crowd. When you set expectations, be sure that your teen has a plan for handling the "what ifs" and agrees to keep you in the loop on any changes.

Tie consequences directly to the behavior at hand. Consequences should be spelled out not as a threat, but rather with a tone that suggests, "If you don't demonstrate responsibility, we'll need to make sure you're only allowed to do what you've proven you can handle." Parents often punish their teens by taking away something that means a lot to them—the cell phone or car are favorite targets—when the unwanted behavior has nothing to do with that. For discipline to further the goal of helping your child become capable, tie the consequence to the specific behavior and make sure your child knows the possible repercussions. If you allow a later curfew because you think your child is ready to handle the expanded freedom, then failing to meet the curfew without a good reason should result in a temporary rollback until your child demonstrates more responsibility. Return to the level where she proved reliable; that will cement the lesson that she is given as many privileges as she can handle, not more. When children learn to equate discipline with appropriate consequences related to their actions and likewise know that they can earn more freedoms by acting responsibility, they're more likely to do the right thing. They can control the outcome. On the other hand, when children equate discipline with severe punishment, ridicule, or humiliation, they feel powerless, as if their fate is in another person's hands. In other words, they experience a loss of control, undermining their ability to develop resilience.

Catch your teen "being good." Discipline should also involve showing an appreciation for your teen's wise choices. A simple comment like "You do a great job at getting home by eleven" lets her know that you recognize the effort she makes to follow your family's rules. Emphasizing the positive was a good discipline strategy when your child was three; it will work with your teen, too.

Hold family meetings to hash things out. One strategy that can help you set both expectations and consequences in advance is to have sit-down meetings with your child starting as early as age nine or ten. Family meetings allow parents to come together and present a united front to their child. (Avoid taking a good cop/bad cop approach to these meetings because that will undermine each parent's standing and teaches kids to play people off each other to get what they want.)

You know what approach would work best for your family, but one strategy is to use these meetings to set up a "contract" of sorts to promote positive behaviors:

- Let your child ask for privileges he thinks he can handle.
- If you think the requests are developmentally or age appropriate, then tell him exactly why you think he has proven himself ready for the privilege (reinforce the positive).
- Tell him what you will need him to demonstrate to show he is responsible enough to keep the privilege. Then jot down your needs and expectations next to his request.

This approach to granting privileges makes discipline easier because it ensures that the consequences of both good and mistaken behaviors are understood in advance. For example, if your fourteen-year-old asks for a curfew of a certain hour, you might talk about such topics as the importance of homework completion, knowing where he is, and being home on time. If he fails to complete homework, the consequence is he needs to return home at the time when he was able to consistently complete his homework. On the other hand, if he is able to complete his work with a later curfew, you might consider his request favorably when he requests an even later curfew a few months later. This matter-of-fact agreement allows him to earn new privileges when he demonstrates responsible behavior and allows you to withdraw them without entering a cycle of threats. To keep the process always evolving, you might consider having regularly planned meetings with your child to allow you to give the go-ahead for a new privilege in response to a pattern of responsible behavior.

Don't underestimate the power of monitoring. There's such an emphasis these days on "tracking" kids—with GPS devices built into cars and cell

phones and all sorts of computer and cell phone monitoring technology—
that monitoring has unfortunately become synonymous with spying on
your kid. I think of monitoring not as a threat or intrusion, but as a positive, caring response. You want your child to know that you expect the best
of him but will always set reasonable boundaries to protect his safety and
will keep an eye out to make sure he's managing things as agreed. Good
parental supervision—whether it's requiring adults at parties, a check-in
call after arriving at a destination, insisting that computers be used in a
common space, or having an agreement where your child has to ask for the
car keys—gives kids the opportunity to demonstrate to their parents that
they are accountable for their actions and are ready for even more independence. Adolescents feel secure knowing a parent is looking out for them,
and it can give them a needed excuse in a peer-charged situation, something we'll talk about in Chapter 6.

Effective discipline is never a static force—you can loosen or tighten
the limits you set and increase or decrease your level of supervision depending on the circumstances and where your child is developmentally and
experience wise. An older child might complain that you let her little sister
or brother "get away with everything" (obviously not true), but different
siblings do respond to varying levels of rules and monitoring.

You want your teen to see there's a give-and-take—he acts responsibly
and is trustworthy and you back off a bit. Because you have thought through
limits and consequences in advance, you should find yourself less often in a
panic where you feel compelled to slap on unreasonable rules.

You want to be responsive to reasonable suggestions and requests. If
your teen makes a reasonable case for a new privilege or an exception to a
rule (curfew, for example), it is a good strategy to honor the request. When
you do this, point out exactly why his responsible behavior has made you feel
comfortable with your decision. This will keep him engaged and he will
learn that communication with you—as well as good behavior—pays off.

∼ AN END TO NAGGING AND UNREASONABLE PUNISHMENT

In case you were curious, I do live on this planet and my kids are not robots. I know these strategies do not always go smoothly. But I want to caution you against entering the all-too-familiar cycle of discipline using nagging and threats that makes our families dysfunctional when things get bumpy. Because kids don't always go along with our plans and because we love them so much, we give lots of second, third, and seventh chances. We make a request, they decline to follow, and we repeat ourselves—many times. The problem is that these constant debates, fueled by your child's whining, lead to a situation where nagging is the norm and calm communication the rarity. When your teen drags you to your breaking point, you may go beyond reminders and escalate into threats. If that happens, your precious time together gets wasted because hostility takes over. If your teen still does not comply after your threats, your punishment may be worse than his crime because it was forged in fear or anger. When the punishment is worse than the crime, the teen feels like a victim and learns little. Little learning means discipline hasn't really happened.

How do we get into these cycles? The answer is pretty easy. Kids recognize our patterns—requesting, nagging, yelling, threatening—and begin to see it as a normal way to engage us. They conduct themselves in precisely the manner that draws us in because they are craving our emotional energy.

You help break these dysfunctional cycles by giving your child all the love, attention, and communication they need without them doing anything wrong (the catch-them-being-good tactic). You also break the cycle when you and your teen think through the consequences beforehand and he knows what to expect. Good discipline minimizes parent-child conflict because nothing comes as a surprise.

It's understandable why parents caught up in the heat of the moment often lay down extreme punishments, and certainly serious infractions such as vandalism and driving under the influence of alcohol or drugs require equally serious parental reactions. But if you've been pacing the floor because your child isn't home on time and you haven't heard from him, the adrenaline coursing through your body is driving your response. "You're grounded for three months!" can seem like a fair punishment when you've been picturing your child in a ditch, and it meets your needs because you won't have to worry if your teen is padlocked to his desk. But grounding for months at a time ultimately will serve no teaching purpose—especially for a teen who considers it long-term planning to look ahead a few days— and can have the effect of breeding resentment and rebellion. You can usually avoid this by having agreed-to consequences in place and by having them be tightly tied to demonstrated responsibility. Then, no matter how angry you are, you can take a step back, wait until you are calm, and follow through on your plan.

Because life cannot always be scripted, and because you're human, you'll find yourself in situations where you're too stressed to be rational. Part of being a good disciplinarian—a good teacher—is recognizing when it's okay to pull back on an unreasonable punishment doled out on in anger or fear. Parents are constantly being told that consistency is key to parenting, but I think flexibility is even more important. That doesn't mean that you should back down on agreed-upon consequences. But it's healthy for our teens to see that when we overreact, we are willing to acknowledge that there's a more sensible response. The same goes for unfortunate statements said in anger or frustration. We all say things we regret, sometimes reserving them for the very people we care the most about. When you step up and apologize for a disparaging remark or unfair accusation, your teen will appreciate your vulnerability and honesty even if he only acknowledges the apology with a nod.

Once discipline starts working the way it should, your home will no longer be a place of nagging, threats, and anger, but one where you and your child respect the fact that you each honor your end of the agreement.

❋

WE'VE COVERED a lot in this chapter—parenting style, communication strategies, discipline—so let's come full circle and remind ourselves why we put so much energy into parenting, even on days when we feel like we're far from winning the Parent-of-the-Year Award. We parent (in the active sense of the verb) because we love our kids—that's the bottom line. Sometimes you have to make a conscious effort to fall back *in love* with your teen—not because you don't truly love him but because the day-to-day demands of parenting can muddy that deep, instinctual feeling that overcame you almost from the moment of birth. Remember how you soaked in the sight of your sleeping baby, amazed that such a perfect little person had come into your life? You need to create moments that allow you to bask in your adolescent's presence, too. Go for a walk with your daughter. Drive your son to practice and turn off the radio. Make it a priority to splurge on an occasional dinner out—no getting up to let out the dog or rushing off to a game. You'll come away from these uninterrupted moments reminded that your teen is just as you knew him to be—loving, insightful, and probably rather charming, too. Every now and then give yourself a parenting gift—make time to fall back in love with your kid all over again!

CHAPTER FIVE

~

SEEING YOUR CHILD
What's He or She Really Like?

TERRY, a mother of six, keeps a list taped inside one of her kitchen cupboards. It keeps track of the ages at which her children were allowed to do certain things, such as get their ears pierced, go on a date, begin to drive.

"No one can complain that someone was allowed to do something sooner," says Terry, who finds that the list of minimum-required ages spares a lot of fighting. If her master list says something is so, then it is and there is little room for her other children to argue that a date should be moved forward for them (though there is a family "appeals process").

I understand where Terry is coming from—everything happens sooner and faster these days and parents want to slow things down. I also applaud her desire to minimize sibling rivalry and to offer proof that privileges are earned over time, so be patient. But her master list, if it were taken strictly on face value, misses a couple of points. Chronological age, as we discussed earlier, should not be the driving factor in the *When*s because simply reaching a certain age does not make a child ready for anything. Also, a one-size-fits-all approach doesn't work for all families because siblings can vary dramatically in personality and rate of maturity. One kid might be ready to date at fifteen—and another not until eighteen. Even if your children scream "unfair" sometimes—or often—they will ultimately appreciate your recognition that each is an individual.

Instead of age, I want you to focus on this: What's your kid really like? "He's funny," "She's a good athlete," "He's creative," "She's bright" are among the answers I'd expect to hear. We all have mental snapshots of our kids—the way we describe them in a casual conversation with a coworker.

Now let me ask the question again: What's your child *really* like? With the emphasis on *really,* I suspect your answer will take on detail and nuance. In this chapter, I will challenge you to look beyond easy descriptors by viewing your child using multiple lenses. To get a well-rounded view, you need to consider your child's temperament, those innate traits that we carry through life that influence how we respond to people and our environment in general. By understanding your child's temperament, you can better predict how he'll handle the many new experiences of adolescence. We'll also take a look at the various stages of adolescent development. Knowing where your child falls on the spectrum of physical, cognitive, moral, emotional, and social growth will allow you to be more confident as you approach decisions around the *When*s and help you to tailor developmentally appropriate conversations around the *How*s.

~ TEMPERAMENT

Think about how you described your newborn to friends. "He's such an easy baby." "He's as predictable as clockwork." Or perhaps you used words like "fussy" or "difficult." Whether you realized it or not, you were talking about temperament—certain traits that we're mostly born with that have a bearing on how we act and react. We may be naturally calm or excitable, bold or hesitant, loaded with energy or content to plod along. Temperament tends to be fairly steady throughout life, though the way a person expresses traits can be altered somewhat by life experiences and the influences of other people.

I'm not suggesting that you put a label on your child or explain away troubling behavior by blaming it on temperament. Temperament doesn't make your child do or not do his chores, and temperament is distinct from your child's intellectual capacity and other abilities. But being sensitive to your child's temperament is useful because it helps elucidate why she approaches life as she does, whether it's dealing with peers or school or reacting to something you've said. Temperament has a lot to do with how your child manages transition—something that adolescence is filled with as preteens and teens try out new friends, start high school, and expand their social life. Having insight into your child's temperament will help you implement strategies that play to his inherent strengths, but also ones that encourage him to push beyond his easy comfort zone. Also, just as you can shift your parenting style to be more balanced, you can consciously adjust your way of interacting with your child to better accommodate her temperament.

Experts who study temperament have slightly differing ways of classifying the components that make up a person's overall style. My colleague Dr. William B. Carey at The Children's Hospital of Philadelphia—who has written a book called *Understanding Your Child's Temperament* (Xlibris Corp., 2005)—is among those in the field who focus on nine identified traits that occur in everyone to varying degrees. Let's use that list here.

While your child can't be defined by one temperament trait alone, there are probably several that stand out:

- **Level of physical activity.** Some people are naturally more physical than others. Watch your child as she loads her backpack, walks to the bus stop, and sits at the kitchen table doing homework. Does she move quickly or methodically? Does she squirm? Does she tap her pencil? Now think about what she does when you drop her off at practice. Does she wait on the sidelines until her coach arrives or does she run around and begin drills. Kids high in physical energy may have trouble being still in a structured environment such as a classroom. Kids who aren't the physical type may be happier with fine-motor activities, such as drawing or building.

- **Regularity.** Parents are elated if their baby is predictable—sleeping, eating, and perhaps even crying at set intervals—and often distraught if their newborn's schedule is a free-for-all. Physical regularity, or lack of it, may not be so apparent in adolescence, but you'll notice certain behavior rhythms if you pay attention. Does your child have an after-school routine—eat a snack, watch some TV, and then start homework, or is every day different? Does she get her gear together the night before a game or rush about at the last minute? Does she keep her room organized?

- **Initial reaction.** When facing something new—whether a person, place, food, or task—some people jump right in, others are cautious and hang back, and a lot of people are somewhere in between. To gauge where your child is on the spectrum, think about specific instances—such as how he reacts when he gets dropped off at day camp not knowing anyone, or goes to an ethnic restaurant that doesn't have the usual steaks and burgers on the menu.

- **Adaptability.** This trait has to do with the ability to adapt to situations. Does your child demonstrate flexibility and find ways to adjust to new or unexpected circumstances? Or does she stay out of sorts or refuse to go with the flow? Most people are somewhere between flexible and rigid. Recognizing your child's tendencies for both initial reaction and adaptability will help you figure out how best to approach spur-of-the-moment opportunities and life-changing events.

- **Intensity.** Everyone tends to have a certain degree of energy that they put into both positive and negative responses. We all know people who laugh hysterically and cry unabashedly, who get really excited when something good happens and really, really mad when provoked. Others barely react. During adolescence, your child's intensity will affect how he responds to the fickleness of friendships, accomplishments and setbacks at school, and the praise and criticism that come from you. No matter how intense your child is or isn't, you need to pay attention to what he's saying and not be persuaded by the volume.

- **Mood.** We all experience a range of emotions throughout the day. But at the same time, we have a fairly consistent disposition or outlook on life. Some people are naturally cheerful or the eternal pessimist. Mood is different from internal feelings at any given time—a sunny teen could actually be covering up sad feelings. Your child's mood might be very different from yours, which could cause a clash in style, particularly as the emotions of adolescence heat up. A child with a more negative mood might also have difficulty with peers. A significant change in your child's regular mood could help tip you off to trouble spots during adolescence, something we'll talk more about in the *How* section.

- **Persistence and attention span.** Parents often focus on this trait because it has to do with whether your child buckles down and does his work. Persistence and attention span can improve with age, but we tend generally to be either a stick-to-it kind of person or one who loses attention when things get tough or something more interesting presents itself. Parents often misinterpret this trait for laziness or accuse their kid of tuning them out. Being aware of your child's tendencies will help you establish realistic expectations around homework, after-school jobs, and extracurricular activities and might alert you to your child's need for some informal or formal learning support.

- **Distractibility.** This trait is related to persistence and attention span but isn't quite the same thing. A child can be easily distracted, for instance, but ultimately persistent. It's important to know whether your adolescent is easily sidetracked or it's just that our kids live in a multitasking world where doing three things at once has become the norm. Teens might think they can solve calculus problems while texting and watching TV, but that doesn't work for most kids.

- **Sensitivity.** The senses are at work with this trait. How much is your child bothered by things around her, whether a bright light, loud sound, scratchy sweater, or a strong odor or flavor? Some kids are wired to be more attuned to sudden changes in their environment. Understanding your adolescent's level of sensitivity will come in handy—yelling at a kid who is jarred by loud noises doesn't do any good, and some kids' taste buds simply can't handle certain foods, no matter how many battles you wage at the dinner table.

No child ever has a "perfect temperament," and no parent's temperament is ever perfectly in line with their child's. But parents can learn to accommodate their children's traits so there's less friction and disruption. For instance, if your child is slow to adapt to change, it makes sense to invest more energy in getting him ready for a move to a new school or neighborhood. You can also set expectations for your adolescent that will push him to move beyond what he's more comfortable with or to hold his natural tendencies in check. A shy adolescent should be expected to talk with relatives at family gatherings and to look people in the eye, and an intense child should be expected to learn to temper his emotions in the classroom and in certain social settings.

Now that we've talked about temperament, characteristics that stay fairly stable throughout life, let's move on to development—those changes that are beginning to happen in your adolescent even if you're not quite aware of them yet.

∼ A BIRD'S-EYE VIEW OF DEVELOPMENT

Before we parse the components of development, we first have to look at the whole picture. As a child transforms into an adult there is a developmental imperative: They must quickly answer the question "Who am I?" At least they believe they must.

We know, after we ourselves have struggled with this question for decades, that the answer to that question remains a lifelong quest—a source of both anxiety and driving force for much of what is exciting in life—but our kids don't know that yet.

To get an idea of the challenging developmental work your teen is facing, imagine a table covered with ten thousand pieces of a jigsaw puzzle.

The puzzle is titled "Who am I?" Not realizing he has a lifetime to complete the puzzle, your teen tackles it with ferocity because he believes he needs to get done by the time he graduates from high school or even by the time he writes his college essay. How does he do it? He begins with the corners and then creates the borders. Next, he looks at the picture on the lid to imagine how the pieces might fit together. Soon the puzzle gets tougher and your adolescent relies on trial and error—picking up pieces and turning them this way and that. You try to help, but your child waves you off. The puzzle work is—depending on the moment—intellectually challenging, frustrating, overwhelming, paralyzing, exciting, and tremendously rewarding.

Even though you have been shooed away, you are critical to the puzzle's completion. Boundaries and monitoring create those trustworthy borders that teens can push against as they try to manipulate the harder inner pieces on their own. Next, you are the picture on the cover against whom he compares himself. When teens have role models of what healthy adults look like, it becomes easier for them to formulate a picture of what they have to do to complete their own puzzle.

Now as if the "Who am I?" puzzle isn't enough to absorb your adolescent's energy, he has yet another nagging question to deal with: "Am I normal?" The latter question explains much of the angst associated with physical development and the ever-changing strategies utilized by preteens and teens in their quest to fit in. Get used to these two defining questions of adolescence—"Who am I?" "Am I normal?"—because we will return to them throughout this book.

If you're starting to wonder how in the world you're going to make sense of all these concepts, remember that you're not coming to this critical phase of your child's development without any knowledge. You went through it yourself, and the experiences you had provide a valuable starting point. Recall what specifically caused you to struggle as a teen—what overwhelmed you and in what instances you got stuck. Who or what helped you get through? Perhaps it was a coach who didn't let you slack off, a church youth group that provided friends outside of school, or a neighborhood band that offered an escape from a chaotic home. On the other hand, what kind of "support" did you reject with a vengeance? Going through this exercise will, at least, reinforce what I told you in the beginning of this book—even with all the fits and starts of adolescence, most of us turned out okay. Knowing your tender spots, which can still be surprisingly achy after all those years, is important because we often are hypersensitive when our kids experience the same discomfort and pain we did. If you were the quiet, awkward kid who didn't get invited places, you may overreact when your daughter comes home in tears because "everyone else but her" is going to a birthday party. If you were the short, clumsy kid who didn't hit your growth spurt until eleventh grade, you may take it personally when your late-bloomer rides the bench. Acknowledging in what ways you felt fragile and hurt might help you catch yourself when you get so swept up in your adolescent's developmental struggles that you can no longer be an objective sounding board.

∼ YOUR TEEN'S BRAIN

I get uneasy when I hear experts talk about the Teen Brain, using capital letters and exclamation points as if some odd entity has just been discovered. New scanning technology is enabling researchers to produce maps of various sections of the brain to highlight when emotions are firing and rational thought prevailing, but I worry that such findings can lead to the unfortunate conclusion that a teen's brain is completely impulsive, irrational, and out of control—downright crazy, some experts want you to believe. I also worry that the notion of a deficient Teen Brain prompts parents and educators to have low expectations of youth.

Teens are not broken and in need of being fixed, but it is our job as adults to help them meet their potential and safeguard their well-being. We must honor the creativity and intelligence that adolescents possess, enable them to develop a repertoire of strategies during calm moments that they can turn to when their emotions run high and interfere with reason, and protect them from the peer influences that can stir their emotions and lead to impulsive actions. I want you to think of *your* adolescent's brain in a positive light—it's an exciting work in progress that needs to be stimulated with new information and experiences but also shielded from harmful substances and situations, such as alcohol, cigarettes, and speeding cars.

So what basics do you need to know about adolescent brain development? A key point to understand is that different parts of the brain mature at different rates. In particular, the amygdala, an area deep inside the brain that is involved in emotional responses, aggression, and instinctual reactions to stimuli, develops sooner than the prefrontal cortex, a section behind the forehead that is a center for complex thinking and helps in the regulation of mood, attention, and impulsivity. The prefrontal cortex, which is sometimes described as the brain's CEO, continues to develop well into a person's twenties. This unevenness in brain development may explain why adolescents think sharply some of the time, but react with impulsivity or volatility to an unexpected trigger. We also know emotionality or impulsivity can be accentuated by the presence of peers.

Now let's talk about the various components of development. To make a complicated discussion lean, we'll take the approach used by many child development experts and divide adolescence into three parts: early adolescence, roughly ages eleven to thirteen; mid-adolescence, ages fourteen to sixteen; and late adolescence, from ages seventeen to twenty-one. At each stage, a child is undergoing physical, intellectual, moral, emotional, and social changes, but he doesn't necessarily progress through each of those categories at the same pace or in the same ways another child progresses. As much as your child wants to do what everyone else is doing, you need to factor into your decision your child's temperament and level of maturity.

Because development can be uneven, your child might be mature physically, while immature socially or emotionally. A fifteen-year-old boy with a man's body may still think more like a twelve-year-old. A fifteen-year-old girl may be articulate and insightful when it comes to schoolwork, but be ill at ease with her classmates. You probably have admired your teen's maturity one moment only to be struck the next by the thought that there's a tantrum-prone toddler living with you.

While the various types of development are interrelated—they drive each other—we'll examine each separately so you know what to expect at different phases of adolescence.

～ PHYSICAL DEVELOPMENT

Any discussion of physical development has to include the word *puberty,* even though I know it makes kids cringe. Puberty refers to the period in which the body begins to undergo sexual maturation and physically changes from child to adult. The range of normal puberty is wide—it can happen as early as age eight or nine for girls and not until age fourteen for some boys. In general, girls enter puberty sooner than boys, and there's evidence that today's kids are reaching puberty at an earlier age than in previous genera-tions. Why that's so isn't clear, although researchers suspect that better nutrition, exposure to environmental hormones, and the surge in childhood obesity may be pushing the trend. Most children are done with most of their growing by mid-adolescence. They're at or near their full height and have some meat on their bones. They've also developed sexually—boys can get girls pregnant and girls are physically capable of having babies.

Now set those generalities aside and let's take a look at a ninth-grade gym class. The variation in physical development is huge. Boys with side-burns and hairy legs sit next to boys with baby-smooth skin. Girls with breasts and hips stand in line with girls who could pass for sixth graders. Little wonder that body image looms so large: I'm too fat, too flat, too tall, too short. No one is "normal." Your child is not going to tell you that he feels insecure because he doesn't have underarm hair or that she feels like a freak because she's the only girl in her class who has gotten her period. But you need to be aware that adolescents, especially in the early teens, are especially sensitive about their looks and how they stack up against peers. You should provide your adolescent with factual, objective material—a good reference book, reliable Web sites—so they can read and see for them-selves how normal they really are. Our kids get so many distorted views of body image in the media they consume—just look at the sculpted abs that populate their favorite TV shows. Your child's doctor can also offer reas-surance that every body progresses on its own schedule—a good reason not to skip an annual checkup just because your kid is healthy.

Unfortunately, because we all sometimes judge books by their covers, you need to be sensitive to how your child might be typed by peers based on physical development. Adolescents who mature early are often expected to be leaders, and being a leader in peer culture is not always good. They might get too much sexual attention and may even feel pressure to take risks before anyone else does. Early maturers might get used to being the most popular or toughest kids around, only to be taken for a fall when other kids catch up and surpass them. Late-maturing kids, on the other hand, often assume the role of being "cute" or everybody's buddy. They might become the class clown or "the man" just to prove they can't be made fun of or pushed around.

Parents draw conclusions about their child's abilities and maturity based on physical appearance, too. They assume that their tall son should be good at sports, or that they don't need to worry about their daughter being sexually pressured because she is not yet curvy. Physical development usually occurs before maturity in other arenas, but not always. That's why you need to look beyond the cover and see what your child is like inside.

~ COGNITIVE DEVELOPMENT

Cognitive development refers to your child's growing ability to think and reason. It involves not just an expansion of knowledge but also an increasing capability to analyze complex scenarios, form thoughtful opinions, draw on past experiences as a reference point, and think through the implications of certain actions either ahead of time or as they're unfolding. Intelligence is a factor in cognitive development, and recognizing your child's intellectual strengths and weaknesses—he may lag in the classroom but can fix your computer or car in a flash—will allow you to better prepare for what challenges and opportunities lie ahead. But "thinking" in the sense we'll be talking about here isn't the same as smartness.

So many of the *When*s and *How*s of adolescence come down to whether your child's brain is developmentally ready to handle a multistep process that may unexpectedly change, or sort through complicated ideas. Taking a bus involves knowing how to read schedules and signs so that you can get from one place to another, but you also have to problem-solve if the bus doesn't come or changes routes because of a detour.

During adolescence, the ability to think and reason grows tremendously. An adolescent transforms from being that concrete thinker we talked about in the last chapter into a person capable of thinking abstractly. What do I mean by *concrete*? Concrete is a simple substance; it is exactly as it appears. Children view things simply, too. Something is pleasant or terrible, right or wrong. People are good or bad. Children live in the moment and have no concept of delayed gratification or planning ahead. By adulthood, abstract thinking usually has evolved. Think of an abstract picture—there's more to it than the strokes of paint that appear on the surface of the canvas. Adults usually can analyze a problem from various viewpoints, identify the pros and cons of a given action, and come up with a well-reasoned solution, or at least one that seems reasonable to them. They can set goals and know what is needed to get there. They may like someone, but still recognize that the person has flaws. The black and white of childhood takes on many shades of gray.

As you start to face your child's growing demands for expanded privileges and independence, it's important to remember that early adolescents are still very much in the concrete-thinking portion of this cognitive journey. Young adolescents think far more like children than adults, which means they often don't weigh the possibilities, project ahead to what could result from their actions, or recognize the subtleties of a situation. If a boy showers a girl with compliments and tells her he loves her, she'll probably believe it and maybe even agree to be sexual to seal the relationship. If a text goes out "rents out cum ova," chances are good the invite to a parent-free house will be accepted. As we discussed earlier, when something goes wrong, parents swoop in with one of those winding, abstract lectures that teens find incomprehensible. Often at this stage parents feel like their kids are blind to consequences and kids in turn feel as though their parents "just don't get" what they're feeling.

By mid-adolescence, cognitive growth is becoming more evident. Your teen will have opinions on politics, religion, history, and just about everything else, and he will embrace views that aren't necessarily just meant to counter yours—they could be based on something he heard in class, from friends, or on TV. He begins to manage his time and think longer term, gauging, for instance, what part of his math packet he needs to do on Tuesday to prepare for a test on Thursday. Life experiences are multiplying fast. At this point, it's more important than ever to notice your child "being good" and to link specific actions to consequences. Remember, your mid-adolescent still is making the transition from concrete thinker to abstract, so all the more reason that the punishment should fit the crime. In order to better help him grasp the connection between his action and a consequence, they should be tied together logically. For example, "Your staying out later than we agreed on means you were not able to handle the curfew. We will have to go back to the time you did manage well" will be more effective than "Since you were late, now you can't play video games for a week."

By late adolescence, most teens have a pretty good ability to think through more complex problems, detect nuances, and plan ahead, perhaps even to plan what career they hope to pursue. This transition to abstract thinking occurs not just because of brain development, but because the experiences of life are proving to be an excellent teacher. The same boy who used to e-mail his homework answers to other kids in hopes of being accepted by the cool crowd now questions the wisdom of teaming up in physics lab with a popular student who doesn't want to do any of the work. The same girl who once fell for "You're beautiful, I adore you, let's have sex," now thinks more critically about motives and consequences and brings to the equation the experience of having been burned by the boy who proclaimed she was the center of his universe.

Though they have this new capacity, older teens don't always draw on their abstract-thinking skills effectively—they are still learning. They sometimes act erratically and can still get caught up in risky situations without much thought to what could go wrong. That's why it's so important to help your adolescent cultivate an easily accessible set of coping skills and thought-out rationales for appropriate and safe action *before* crises hit. That way they do the right thing reflexively when their panicked mind can't sort through complexity. Remember that all people—even adults—lose their ability to think abstractly when stressed. Because your older teen is still prone to emotional moments, it remains important to continue to set some boundaries even as he demonstrates more signs of sound reasoning.

While it may have seemed easier when your child accepted everything as simple truths, enjoy this time when your teen begins to notice things that perhaps you don't, becomes passionate about ideas that are different from yours, and starts to wonder about why some questions have no answers. My unanswerable was "I get that the universe goes on and on infinitely, but how is that possible? Everything must end. But if it does end, then what is there, and when does that end?" I still haven't figured that one out.

∼ MORAL DEVELOPMENT

Moral development is hard to separate from cognitive development because as your child's thinking abilities become increasingly sophisticated, so, too, does his moral fabric. Your adolescent gradually transitions from a child who operates from the viewpoint "I don't want to get caught" to that person of character who decides to do the right thing even when no one is looking.

A young child's view of right and wrong, or good and bad, is largely me-centered and focused on external consequences: If I got a time-out or TV time taken away last time, I better avoid the behavior or at least do it when Mom or Dad can't nab me. Likewise, I'll be "good" because I'll get a reward.

By adolescence, moral thinking becomes more nuanced and outward directed. Teens still don't want to get caught (drinking, speeding, skipping school) by their parents or the law, but they begin to see their actions as part of a bigger picture that involves peers and consequences and the feelings of others. On to the downside, they can rationalize that it's okay to drink beer or smoke pot "because everyone does it" (which isn't true). Or, the upside, they can decide to avoid a behavior because they know it won't go over big with their friends or their parents or even the college admissions director.

By mid-adolescence, teens' views of right and wrong, good and evil also begin to expand beyond their own experiences. Middle and late teens often get involved in social justice or political causes—they want to stop war or put an end to sweatshops that pay their workers pennies to make expensive basketball shoes. They genuinely want to make a better world, but their generosity and empathy don't necessarily show up at home or in all their personal dealings. Your teen might urge you to "buy green" to preserve the planet, but balk when asked to take a shorter shower to save water. Adolescents take in so many new ideas at this age, and you can take advantage of the headlines or your teen's current events assignment to talk about pressing moral issues. It's okay to be opinionated, but don't preach— part of your teen's moral development involves arriving at his own set of spiritual, social, sexual, and monetary values—not simply accepting yours.

It usually isn't until late adolescence, or even adulthood, that a person begins to truly experience what it means to follow your own conscience— making personal decisions not just because laws or social norms or parents say it's right but because of an internal barometer. Some people never quite arrive at that point, instead continuing to rely on outside cues to tell them what is the right thing to do.

～ EMOTIONAL DEVELOPMENT

Let's go back to the "Who am I?" puzzle that your adolescent is busily piecing together. The answer to that question, as we discussed earlier, has to be at least in part "I am not my parents," which is why adolescents begin to separate from their parents as they begin to seek their own identity and autonomy. Your adolescent has to figure out the bulk of that puzzle on his own and that requires some space. You should still make it easier for him to piece together the puzzle by providing appropriate boundaries—the borders of the puzzle—and good role modeling—those identifiable colors and patterns shown on the box. But he has to do most of the hard work himself—turning the pieces in different directions and sometimes shoving them together, only to realize they're not a fit after all.

This process of self-discovery, this move from dependence to independence, unfolds during a time of strong and sometimes unsettling emotions for your adolescent. Part of emotional development is recognizing and dealing with not only your own feelings but those of others, and the two don't always square. Adolescence is often a time of quickly shifting emotions, but it's also a time when kids must learn how to modulate their emotions—dial down the anger, set their disappointment aside for another day—and channel overwhelming feelings into manageable ones.

Keeping your emotions in check when your child is in a state of heightened emotions is something you should strive for. Back off if necessary. Vickie said she discovered when her son was little that time-outs worked well when his emotions heated up—but she was the one who did the time-out behind her bedroom door until he calmed down. She continued the strategy throughout her son's teen years, heading off blowups that were brewing.

Keep in mind that kids usually reserve their meltdowns for their parents because they feel secure doing so. It's also good to remember when you reach rough patches with your teen that most kids really, really like their parents and come through adolescence with their family ties intact.

By early adolescence, children are beginning to do things to start the transition from dependence to independence. They may balk at family activities and be embarrassed to be seen with you in public. You may have to get good at transforming into the Present-But-Invisible Parent because that's how your teen prefers it when friends are over. Spending time with friends outside of a parent's view becomes your kid's goal. You may react by trying to keep things the way they were, scheduling outings and acting hurt (which you honestly are) when your teen announces he has another offer. But remember that *Letting Go* is what you ultimately have to do, so better to do it slowly. Remember, as soon as he gains confidence in his ability to stand alone, he'll come back to you.

Part of self-discovery is also spending time alone, and early adolescents often seek out the privacy of their bedrooms, to the alarm of parents who assume something bad must be going on. As hard as it is to go by that closed door, you need to honor your adolescent's privacy unless you fear for his safety or feel that he never comes out of the room. As part of the breaking away, your young teen may start being rude, less affectionate, critical of you and siblings, and dismissive of your ideas, and he may even try things simply to test parental limits. Mood swings can add to this new tension in your home. The same kid who lashes out at you with breathtaking words minutes later comes to snuggle with you in front of the TV. Because so much of their focus is inward, adolescents at this age often magnify whatever is going on in their lives, feeling self-conscious as though they're onstage with everyone watching them—an imaginary theater where they're the reluctant star. This is another reason why having you too front and center in the picture is uncomfortable—it's hard enough for a teen to manage himself onstage, let alone his parents!

By mid-adolescence, parent-child conflicts may intensify as teens spend less and less time at home and sometimes assume an air of caring little about what their parents think. It's important to note here that the emotional piece of development can look very different on girls than boys, but before I get in trouble for generalizing too much, I should say that there's more variation among the same gender than there is space between the genders. Your daughter will tend to engage when her emotions get heightened—she'll use her words to attack, latch on to something you say, and go after it, not letting anything go. Your son, on the other hand, will become deaf and tired, hearing just the first words of what you have to say and then staging a retreat. I wish I had a dollar for every parent of a teen boy who asks me to test his hearing because he's so nonresponsive, or check his blood for anemia because he seems forever tired.

Peers loom large in mid-adolescence and it will seem as though your teen can't get enough of her friends or look enough like them. With peer influences strongly in play, emotions heightened, and the ability to dampen down impulses and foresee consequences still uneven, mid-teens may be prone to risk-taking behaviors, including drinking, drug use, and unplanned and unprotected sex. In some cases, this troubling behavior falls into the category of experimentation, but if your teen is feeling stressed or depressed, the risk-taking may be more about finding an easy fix. People often say that teens think they're invulnerable, but that has been disproven by research. In fact, teens feel very vulnerable. Sometimes they behave as if nothing could hurt them, but that's usually to impress their peers. In the next chapter, you'll learn how to teach your child some skills that will help him get out of emotionally charged situations or, better yet, avoid them altogether.

Having said all that, I don't want you to be fearful of the emotional piece of mid-adolescence. It's exciting to watch a child shape his identity and channel his emotions and intellectual curiosity. There's so much possibility! Part of the development process involves your child moving from being "It's all about how I feel" to being aware and sensitive of the feeling of others, including parents. Using "I" statements instead of "you" ones will make your teen more receptive to what you're feeling. "You don't do anything around here. You act like I'm your maid" is one way to express frustration, but you will be met with defensiveness. There's almost no way to respond to a "you" statement except to say "no, I didn't" or "well, you started it when . . ." Now turn it around to an "I" statement and see the reaction you get. "I feel unappreciated when I cook a nice meal and you get up and leave your dishes on the table. I find it helpful when you clear things off because I can clean up faster." "I" statements make the listener want to help out or to fix the problem.

Hold on through mid-adolescence because development is on your side. Late adolescence into young adulthood is when the majority of the pieces come together for most kids. They're largely self-reliant and good at functioning independently from their parents, even if they're still financially dependent. Unlike in the earlier teen years, they don't feel the need to create friction with their parents and instead often show increased affection and respect. Older adolescents have a pretty good sense of who they are—likes, dislikes, talents, weaknesses—and even where they want to "go" in life. For parents who feel as though they were riding an emotional roller coaster with their teen, the years from high school graduation and on through college or a first job can be a very special time (though certainly not without setbacks). What you'll eventually discover is that out of the emotional push toward independence emerges an "interdependence"— a satisfying child-parent relationship that involves reciprocal support and sharing.

∽ SOCIAL DEVELOPMENT

Social development really goes right along with the emotional piece. Your adolescent is exploring "Who am I?" and worrying "Am I normal?" not in isolation but in the context of friends and the even larger peer culture. As she moves away from spending so much time with you and the family, she's turning to friends for support and validation. What better way to prove you're normal than to be just like your friends?

In early adolescence, kids tend to have intense, one-on-one friendships with a member of the same sex or a small group of same-sex friends, although interest in the opposite sex is increasing. Having a best friend or two is common. Along with that intensity, however, there is another force at play—the dynamics of peer culture are starting to percolate. In middle school, alliances can shift on a whim, and someone who's up one day may be down the next. The designation of being someone's "boyfriend" or "girlfriend" can also change with the wind. It's an environment where kids who still look and act very much like kids compete with peers who are physically mature and perhaps even trying out their sexuality. "Mean girl" behavior—exclusive lunch tables; spreading rumors via group texts— becomes more common in early adolescence, and there's bullying among both boys and girls as put-downs become a means to rise in the pecking order. Sadly, one of the best ways to feel normal is to define someone else as a loser or freak. It can be painful to see your adolescent sometimes struggle socially, but it's a mistake for you to get swept up in the day-to-day drama of your child's friendships. You want to be a supportive listener, but if you get emotional, you could end up magnifying whatever it is your child is feeling. You could also make the mistake of chiming in with a negative comment about someone who's back to being your child's BFF (best friend forever) the very next day.

Still, you can help prepare your child for the social dynamics of adolescence by introducing ideas at a young age about friendship, loyalty, avoiding gossip, and being inclusive. Adolescents need only a couple of really close friends, but it helps a lot if they draw their friendships from more than one pool. At any given time, your adolescent may not feel particularly connected to kids at school but enjoy being with friends at youth group or Boy Scouts. Having a couple of circles of friends also helps if one group starts migrating into activities or behaviors he doesn't want to be part of. One friend can never fill every need. Your preteen may even seem to be at different stages of development depending on who she is hanging out with. She might still like to play on the backyard swings with neighborhood friends, whereas she and her school friends try on clothes when they get together. You can help your adolescent have several circles of friends by encouraging participation in different activities.

Starting around early adolescence, you may not know all of your child's friends the way you used to. You can't arrange playdates for them anymore and you shouldn't. Barring your adolescent from a friend you don't like can only serve to make the attraction stronger, but you can make it easier for your child to hang out with certain friends by letting her invite someone along for a day trip or an afternoon of shopping. You can also make your home an attractive destination by stocking up on snacks and creating a space where your adolescent and his friends can watch TV or play video games outside of your constant view.

By middle adolescence, peer groups are fully in play and your child is working hard to fit into one of the many crowds that populate high school. Conformity with the group is big, and your teen might adopt the style of dress, music, and mannerisms of the crowd he identifies with—sending another signal that he's becoming a person apart from you . . . but just like his friends. Social development at this stage also means developing a sexual identity. Interest in the opposite sex is increasing, but contact is usually in a group setting. Teens may venture for the first time into one-on-one relationships and may experiment with sexual activity. By late adolescence, your teen and soon-to-be young adult will feel less need to be defined by a given group. Friendships become deeper now because your child is a lot more willing to share his ideas and values and even anxiety about what's coming next. Romantic interests can also have a powerful hold at this age, even if going on dates as we once knew it is less common.

~

MOST OF US have moments when we wish we could push a button and stop development just to keep our children small forever. But adolescent development—even with all its ups and downs—is an exciting process to watch. Your children will do well if you remain the constant in their lives, offering unconditional love, unwavering support, and guidance when necessary.

CHAPTER SIX

~

Social Skills Your Child Needs to Survive Peer Culture

Now that you've taken stock of your child's temperament and become familiar with the various stages of adolescent development, you need to step back and consider the peer environment. As you make decisions around granting new privileges, it helps to understand where your child fits into the landscape. You also will feel more confident if you teach your adolescent the three survival skills that empower teens to make good choices without fear of losing friends.

~ SO WHERE DOES YOUR CHILD FIT?

So much disturbing stuff is written about today's peer culture, it's often portrayed as an alien nation that sucks kids in and morphs them into unrecognizable creatures. But if you walked into your adolescent's cafeteria, it would probably feel familiar because there are the same sorts of cliques that were there in your day. The labels may be different, but the breakdown is fairly unchanged—jocks, popular kids, brainiacs, slackers, artsy kids. And then there are kids who have adopted an in-your-face style—black clothes, purple hair, multiple body piercings—that is meant to set them apart and challenge adult conventions. The truth is that those adolescents, like everyone else around them, are eager to belong, but do so by joining a group that at least on the surface seems not to care about being different.

Although you never want to make blanket assumptions about your teen by the group with which he affiliates, it really can give you a lot of information. At the least, you'll know something about the pressures to conform he is likely to receive. The habits and values held by a group can set the tone for things such as whether spending time with family, participating in school activities, or getting good grades is a priority. Negative behavior such as drinking may be more common in certain groups, though making assumptions based on what group your child falls into (for instance, assuming that Honor Society kids don't party) can be a mistake. You can't pick your child's group—just as you can't pick his friends—but you can increase the chances for healthy peer influences by encouraging your teen to be part of extracurricular activities that involve different circles of peers.

Many kids change the group they identify with as their interests take shape. Although this can be a positive thing, be on the lookout for when your adolescent appears to be switching groups because it might also signal a troubling change in behavior or an abandonment of previously held goals. In some cases, joining a new crowd means having to deal with a whole new set of expectations, and your adolescent may need to take some chances to fit in or prove himself.

Another important factor to think about as you consider how your child fits into the peer world is whether she tends to be a leader or a follower. Don't assume leaders are superior children (the team captain, the drum major) bound for great things and followers are wimpy kids who are easily manipulated and unlikely to be successful in life. Your child's temperament, which is innate, has a lot to do with where he positions himself, and being a leader in a peer group is not always desirable. It's one thing if your adolescent is setting the agenda for student council, but peer leaders can also feel the need to engage in risky behavior, such as supplying the liquor or fooling around with an upperclassman, to maintain their most-popular status. Followers, on the other hand, might be convinced to do things they wouldn't think of on their own, but they might also be highly observant, preferring to stay in the background to take everything in. Followers can turn out to be respected opinion leaders in peer groups, in part because they think things through and don't act brashly. The idea isn't to wish your child to be one or the other—a leader or a follower—but to recognize his tendency so that you can help him be prepared for the sort of pressure that he is most likely to encounter.

∼ IT'S NOT EASY BEING A KID

The swirling dynamics of peer culture can be tough and unforgiving no matter what group or groups your teen subscribes to and regardless of whether she tends to lead or to hang back. Because the "Am I normal?" question is so key, adolescents really want to be embraced by a crowd. In truth, most kids worry they don't quite belong. This is why it is such a big deal to adolescents what their friends or enemies or frenemies think of them, and why pressure is so deeply felt. Much of the drama and even pain of adolescence is caused by kids needing to prove they belong. Sometimes they shore up their position on the social ladder by pushing others down a few rungs. Be assured that teens do get far more forgiving of each other as they progress through high school.

Parents often think of peer pressure as a one-sided, confrontational force in which the tough kid thrusts a cup of beer in an innocent kid's face and says, "Drink this if you want to be one of us." Peer pressure is typically much more subtle. Adolescents can get caught up in doing things—smoking, driving fast—in response to the internal pressure they feel to fit in. Then, once they have joined the new desired club, they have an awful lot invested in not losing membership.

⤳ PEER PRESSURE ISN'T ALL BAD

The downsides of peer pressure get so much attention that the upside is easily overlooked. Peer pressure often is a positive force. Your son may work hard to boost his grades because he wants to stay with his friends in honors classes, or put in extra hours at his job because he and his buddies are going on a ski trip the next weekend and he wants to have extra spending money. Or maybe your daughter steers clear of a party because her field hockey team has a zero-tolerance alcohol rule and she doesn't want to jeopardize her starting position. Your child might even choose more positive behaviors because she knows that other teens follow her lead.

The social milieu of teens, with all its volatility and hurtful drama, also can be a very supportive place, where kids are protective of each other and forgiving of missteps that adults are loath to forget. It provides an excellent training ground for the interpersonal dynamics found in the adult world. Adolescents learn to follow rules and socially acceptable behavior, maintain relationships in an often hypercharged atmosphere, and negotiate with persuasive personalities and competing factions. Your adolescent can try on different personas and lifestyles—clothing, hair, music, manners of speech—at a time when a lot of other people are experimenting, too. They learn how to shift from group to group depending on the circumstances and even how to completely reinvent themselves—a vital skill for the workplace, where flexibility and adaptability are required. Another plus is that your adolescent can develop socials skills while still under the protective umbrella of family, school, and community. We will discuss more about the peer world in Chapter 27.

⤳ THE ESSENTIAL THREE SURVIVAL SKILLS

As you can surely tell by now, adolescents face conflicting forces. They want to fit in, but they also want to do the right thing. They want to be like everyone else, but at the same time they need to figure out who they are. You're conflicted, too. You want your child to be happy and have fun with his friends, but you also worry every time he steps out the door. For parents to trust that their child is ready for increased freedoms, they need to know their child can hold firm to his principles and decisions. But the truth is, when an adolescent is forced between a safe choice and saving face with friends, safety is often abandoned. No matter how many times your adolescent says he knows how to do the right thing or how hard you work to instill in him the importance of making wise choices, your adolescent will have trouble sticking to his position when caught in a stressful situation. We may fantasize that our kids will say, "I'm sorry, I reject this because it goes against my values and beliefs," but that's not reality.

I can't promise you that you'll ever stop worrying about your teen or even adult child—parents are wired that way for life—but you definitely can take steps that will lower anxiety around your teen's acculturation into a life that is more and more apart from yours. There are *three survival skills* you can teach your adolescent that will help her make good choices even in a peer-charged atmosphere. You're going to feel more secure knowing she can handle herself on her own and have a strategy to contact you when she needs you.

∿ SAYING NO AND KEEPING YOUR FRIENDS IN THE PROCESS

One of the best pieces of parenting advice I ever received was to raise my children using as few *nos* as possible. The tip sounds counterintuitive: We want to keep our kids safe and healthy, so we tell them, "No, you can't cross the street," or "No, you can't have cookies right before dinner." But saying *no* less often doesn't make you a pushover. By being selective, you're going to increase the chances that your *no* gets listened to and your child learns that the word is very powerful and protective.

Unfortunately, the effective use of *no* is something many teens haven't had the chance to learn because they've grown up amid confusing signals. Parents get in a pattern of saying *no* (when they really are thinking *maybe*) because they're tired or distracted or too angry to focus. And then comes the waffling, which leads to an about-face: "No, maybe, well, okay, why not?" A child soon comes to expect that a *no* holds plenty of possibility, and in fact might quickly turn into a *yes* if he turns on the whining or charm.

Your child needs to learn the power of the word *no!*—with the emphasis on the exclamation point. Girls especially must be emphatic because a halfhearted *no* can be misinterpreted as "Push me just a little more and you'll get a yes." You can model for your child how to use *no* for when it really matters. Say *no* in clear-cut terms for your nonnegotiables and make it clear why you did. Parents often hedge and apologize: "I'm sorry, I really know how much this means to you, but I think I really have to say no on this." There's no need to be sorry about taking a stand. "*No,* you can't have the car tonight because it's rainy and foggy. I'll be glad to drive you." Your *no* is clear and your reason specific (tonight, rain, fog). If you haven't made up your mind on something, say, "Let me think about it for a couple of days" or "I need more details from you before I can make a decision." It's okay not to have an on-the-spot answer.

Life-skills classes at school often teach kids to "reverse the pressure" as a technique to stave off peer pressure. The strategy is supposed to work like this: Someone offers your son a cigarette, saying, "Everyone smokes," and he then reverses the pressure by replying, "Well, I'm not everybody. I think for myself." Or a boy tells your daughter, "I love you; I want to show you how much I love you," and she's supposed to come back with, "If you love me, you'll wait."

The above technique may sound good when practiced in a classroom, but in the real peer world it may not work because what your teen wants more than anything is to keep his friends. Kids want to be liked and they want to be with their friends in the thick of things. While we hope young people can articulate where they stand and defy peer pressure, they won't do so unless they are equipped with an ability to also maintain their friendships. Teens need to be able to confidently say, "No, I don't want to go to the party tonight, but call me tomorrow to do something." Teach the following three-step technique: (a) Recognize when someone is giving you a line or you're feeling pressure. (b) State your position clearly and politely, but with no room for change. (c) Come up with something else to do, either now or in the future.

You can teach your adolescent (the younger the better) how to say *no* clearly and specifically, while not being off-putting. I'm not suggesting that you announce, "Let's role-play before I drive you to the party," but you can find opportunities while watching TV with your adolescent or discussing plans for an upcoming event to say things like, "Did you see how he fooled her with that line?" or "Do you think her *no* was convincing? What else could she have said?" Or "How do you think you would handle it if someone offers you a drink?" Commercials and pop-up ads provide fodder for talking about come-ons and manipulation. In the *How* chapters, we'll talk more about the subtle and not-so-subtle manipulation that can be part of peer dynamics.

By the way, children also need to learn to say *yes* with conviction. That way their peers will know they really mean what they say, yes or no. They remain in control.

∼ SHIFTING THE BLAME

Adolescents are more likely to get through a sticky situation if they can "shift the blame" for making a good decision to Mom or Dad or some factor that seems out of their hands. It's much easier for them to do the right thing if they can tell their friends that their annoying parents are to blame for their unpopular choice. "My mom checks the car like you wouldn't believe. Don't even think about smoking." Shifting the blame allows teens to save face, an all-important goal when you're moving in a world where no one wants to stand out. Shifting the blame is a technique you can practice with your child, even helping him come up with specific wording, such as "I can't go to the party because I have to get up early to work." One mom said she told her son he could use any colorful adjectives he wanted to describe her to his friends as long as it gave him an excuse for why he better behave.

Having in place a nightly "check-in rule" at your house will help your adolescent be able to shift the blame to you. Check-in works like this: Your teen must always come and say good night to you when he comes in, even if he has to come into your bedroom and wake you. The check-in rule allows you to know your child is home safe, but just as important, it allows your teen to have a face-saving reason to avoid drinking or blowing curfew. ("Are you joking? My dad smells my breath. If he catches me, I won't be going to the concert.")

The check-in rule shouldn't feel like an extreme measure, but rather as the next logical progression in the bedtime routines you established with your child over the years. You're no longer giving your child a bath or reading a book to him, but you should still close out the day with a reassuring "good night." The secret to making the check-in rule work to your child's advantage, and yours, is to use it every time, no exceptions. Your adolescent should check in whether he's coming home from a friend's house or a school activity, whether he comes in by himself or with a friend.

The check-in rule is an important piece of the supportive monitoring we talked about in Chapter 4. Parental monitoring ends up boosting a child's level of self-control. Your teen really is more apt to do the right thing when she knows you care and are paying attention.

~ USING A CODE WORD

The third protective social skill that all adolescents need involves the use of a code word to signal to their parents that they're caught up in a bad situation. Consider these two scenarios. Your teen goes to a friend's house, the friend sends out a group text, and soon the place is swarming with kids who arrived with a couple of cases of beer. Your teen calls you and says, "There's drinking going on, I'm feeling uneasy, and I'm afraid the police are going to bust the party. Can you pick me up?" Not quite. Your teen might say something like that if she's hiding in a closet and whispering into her cell phone so no one can hear, but remember, saving face is everything. With a dozen sets of ears around, she's probably more likely to take her chances and stay put. Now let's run through the scenario again, but this time you and your teen have agreed to a code word that she can use to call you in an uncomfortable situation or emergency, no questions asked. You get a call or text from her and she says, "I forgot to take out the dog." You know that "take out the dog" really means "Come and get me, now!" Or in a similarly prearranged agreement, "I forgot to take out the dog" might be your signal to start yelling into the phone that your daughter better get home and get her work done or she won't be going anywhere for a long, long time. Using the code word allows your daughter to put on a display to her friends that makes it look like you're the one spoiling the fun: "My mom's making me come home right now!" If she can't get home on her own, let her signal you by fighting a bit (normal teen behavior), and then you demand she meet you outside. Your teen gets home safely but she also saves face with her friends. The code word works best when it comes with an agreement that your teen will not be punished for reaching out for your help, even if she was involved in something you don't approve of.

It can even protect your child in nonpeer situations. Mariel's daughter had a code in place when she went to babysit in case the couple came home seemingly intoxicated. "Mom, you can come get me" was her way of saying, "They're drunk and not fit to drive."

Of everything I've written about parenting, I get the most feedback on the code word—parents have told me that the strategy saved their child's life. The code word is an easy strategy to put in place with a potentially huge payoff.

SECTION II

~

WHEN IS MY CHILD READY TO . . . ?

INTRODUCTION

~

WHY WHEN?

I HOPE the opening section gave you a good glimpse of what to expect during adolescence so you'll be less upset when your teen is no longer acting quite like the child you knew. I also hope it helped you realize that even though your child is changing, your love remains the constant force that will help your teen make it through all right.

I hope your confidence is building and that you're ready to get to work on the next step—the *When*s. Because adolescence is about figuring out what you can handle and who you are going to become, it is naturally filled with *When*s. Each topic in this section poses opportunities for trial and error and ultimately success. Your challenge is to make sure your adolescent learns from day-to-day mistakes rather than viewing them as catastrophes. At the same time you need to be vigilant in helping your teen avoid altogether those errors that could cause irreparable harm. Above all else, you want to ensure that your child doesn't miss out on the many possibilities for growth that are coming along.

A list of the *When*s of adolescence could be endless, but with the help of parents we narrowed it down to eighteen scenarios that families are likely to face and which present lessons that can be applied to other situations. There won't be a formula to how the *When*s are presented because they are so very different. But in all cases, you'll be given food for thought on the types of concerns or issues you should address. Each chapter will include an explanation of why this new experience presents an opportunity for growth, as well as the potential downsides. We'll also explore the competencies that need to be in place so your child has the confidence to take on the challenge, because you want each new experience to build resilience, not undermine it. In a number of the *When*s, I'll offer a step-by-step approach to implement as your child demonstrates that he's ready to assume more responsibility. Your new insight into adolescent development will come in handy with that. This stepwise strategy will help both your child and you gain confidence and will allow you to give a little bit of rope at a time and tighten up again as needed. Sometimes we will discuss steps you can take long before adolescence to prepare.

In some *When*s, I'll urge you to start by doing some observing. Think back to when you baby-proofed your home. If you just walked around your house and guessed what needed safeguarding, you might have missed some real opportunities to protect your baby. The first step to baby-proofing should be to get down on your knees and walk around, because then you see the surroundings at the same level as your toddler does. An adult sees a pan of boiling water on the stove and knows to be careful because it's hot, but a curious toddler looking up sees only the handle sticking out. It looks like a lever to be swatted or pulled down. Once you've been on your knees you know to turn that handle inward. That same sort of observing—getting a "kid's-eye view" of the mall or the route to school—will heighten your senses about the challenges your teen is likely to encounter. You'll see and think about things that haven't crossed your mind in decades. You might remember how routine things like taking public transportation felt at first. After you've done your observing, you'll be better positioned to think of how best to phase in a new privilege and what kinds of support and monitoring need to be in place to help things go smoothly.

Each *When* chapter has benefited from input from parents. They've gone through the very experiences you're facing and you'll learn from their observations, insights, and strategies. In some cases, you'll see names attached to stories, but in most cases know that our point of view was strongly flavored by the wisdom (often earned only through hindsight), and sometimes the mistakes, of the scores of parents Susan FitzGerald talked to.

By the time you're done with each chapter, you're likely to feel more comfortable recognizing *When* the time is right to introduce that specific new privilege or responsibility to your child. If a *When* you're thinking about isn't on our list, it's probably related to a topic that is, so feel free to mix and match the scenarios and strategies to suit what's going on in your life. Now let's get down to business—tackling all those *When* questions that can drive parents crazy but don't have to!

CHAPTER SEVEN

~

Walk Alone to School, a Friend's House, the Corner Store?

The first time Luanne let her daughter, then about nine, walk to school without her, she stood on the front step and watched until she disappeared from sight. Logically, Luanne knew there was not much to worry about— they lived in a low-crime suburban neighborhood with sidewalks, well-marked intersections, and crossing guards, and their home was just down the street from the school. But she wasn't able to calm her nerves until her daughter came back through the door at the end of the day.

"You're not comfortable with this, are you?" Luanne immediately asked her daughter, who did not dispute her mother's characterization of how she was feeling. The next day, Luanne went back to escorting her to school.

"There are a lot of strange people in the world," Luanne later explained of her decision to reverse course and keep on walking with her children until they were into middle school. "They're my children—everything I do in life is about my children. I would never put them in a situation where they'd be harmed." Waving them off to school in the morning wasn't good enough. "I need to see them go into the school."

While I don't doubt Luanne's sincerity in wanting to keep her children safe, I'm afraid that her fears might have caused her to miss a perfect opportunity to help her daughter begin to learn to safely move about her world. Walking (or biking) to school or the corner store is an important developmental milestone for children because it gives them a taste of being able to handle a tiny piece of their universe. It's a self-reliance skill that can build competence, boost confidence, and provide a sense of control—all key ingredients of resilience.

Still, parents often feel mixed emotions in letting their child head off without them, perhaps because walking alone is a metaphor for what will happen throughout adolescence. It's about a child flying the nest or taking the first steps to independence. Luanne focused on safety concerns, but maybe the bigger issue was that she wasn't ready to face that her daughter was growing up. Anxiety stems from a feeling of losing control, and parents often react by trying to regain control by putting very restrictive boundaries in place. The point of this book is not for you to be anxious or your child to be overly regimented. The point is to give you both confidence.

We purposely started the *When* section with walking alone because it's an easy one to take your pulse on. *What is my anxiety level around Letting Go? Am I transmitting my uneasiness to my child? How can I find ways to minimize worries and replace unrealistic fears with reliable information and commonsense strategies?*

Luanne's intense love for her kids certainly influenced every decision she made. But what if she instead had found a way to begin to build confidence, not reinforce her own uncertainties and fear?

~ SIZING UP SAFETY

I don't want to minimize the role parents play in keeping their children safe, and certainly young children should always be supervised. Moreover, only you can truly decide whether your particular community is a safe place for your child to be on his own, given factors such as traffic and the layout of intersections and streets. In some neighborhoods, gangs, drug trafficking, and gun violence are troubling realities, and parents in those circumstances need to be extra vigilant.

That said, I want you to put safety issues in proper perspective so that you don't allow unreasonable fear to interfere with your adolescent's need to branch out. Luanne's worry that her children could be harmed by strangers is understandable considering all the media attention on child abductions and the abundance of TV shows portraying children as victims. But in actuality, only a very small fraction of child abductions involve a stranger. According to the National Center for Missing and Exploited Children, the typical abductor is a family member or someone whom the child knows or is at least familiar with, not some unknown person cruising the neighborhood or hiding in the bushes. (Only about 115 cases a year in the United States conform to the standard notion of child snatchings.)

NCMEC and other child safety experts are working to educate parents about the shortsightedness of preaching to children too much about "stranger danger." It can have the unintended effect of making children unsure of themselves and overly fearful of their surroundings, while not savvy enough about likely hazards. When parents obsess about rare possibilities, they miss the chance to teach the everyday skills that should be in place when a child begins walking by himself: Always following crosswalk signals, never jaywalking, and sticking to a predetermined route are habits children absolutely must have.

IN HIS BOOK *Protecting the Gift: Keeping Children and Teenagers Safe (and Parents Sane)* (Dell, 2000) Gavin de Becker, an expert on predicting violent crime, outlines the pitfalls of the "Never Talk to Strangers" rule. He makes the case that when parents incessantly warn about strangers, they unintentionally imply that familiar people can be trusted not to hurt you. That certainly isn't true when it comes to most cases of child abductions or child abuse. Children instead need to know how to talk to strangers with the right balance of politeness and detachment because they undoubtedly will have to speak to people they don't know to buy a bus ticket or ask for directions. They also could have to ask a stranger to help them in an emergency—whether they're lost or have a flat tire. Children need to know how to seek out a "safe stranger," not just the obligatory police officer parents tell their child to look for (unfortunately, police don't magically appear when we need them) and how to elicit help without coming across as timid.

"Children raised to assume all strangers might be dangerous do not develop their own inherent skills of evaluating behavior," de Becker writes. He suggests that parents advise their children to seek out a woman (or maybe even better, a woman with children) if they get lost or feel in danger because women are unlikely to be sexual predators and are more apt than men to get involved in helping a child, instead of passing him off to a security guard.

~ WHY WALK?

With that general safety philosophy in place, let's circle back and focus on why it's a good thing for children to learn to walk places on their own.

At its most practical level, walking is good for kids' health. All you have to do is stand outside a school when classes let out and you'll see that health officials aren't exaggerating about an obesity epidemic. According to the federal government's National Health and Nutrition Examination Survey for 2007–2008, 19.6 percent of children aged six to eleven and 18.1 percent of those aged twelve to nineteen are obese. The reasons for the obesity epidemic are hotly debated—Too much fast food? Too much time in front of TV and video games?—but the long-term implications are potentially profound. Overweight kids are more likely to have weight problems as adults and they're at risk for high blood pressure, high cholesterol, and type 2 diabetes even before they reach adulthood.

Walking affords social benefits, too. It gives adolescents a chance to interact with their peers in an unscripted setting and often it provides them with a broader social base because they may walk to school with different kids than those they go to class with. Friendships for life, sometimes between older and younger children, can be made on the way to school.

On a deeper level, walking on their own presents a chance for kids to forge ahead by gaining confidence when they recognize their own increasing competence. Walking might seem like a mundane thing, but it's a big accomplishment because it signals to them, "Hey, I can handle this, I can figure out things on my own!"

∼ FIRST LITTLE STEPS

This is a *When* that is ideally suited to a stepwise approach. While young children are not ready to walk on their own because they developmentally lack the necessary thinking skills, it's never too soon for you to start pointing out traffic patterns, crosswalk signals, and the importance of sticking to a predetermined route. Crossing a street safely is not as simple as looking both to the right and left. You need to be able to judge distances and speeds and to anticipate that a driver is about to pull out of a parking space or switch lanes, something young children simply can't do. Young kids also react before they think, which is why they will dash after a ball that goes into a busy street and dart across the street to catch up with a friend.

Even though you walk the same streets every day with your child, I urge you to put on your "observer cap" and set out on your own to get a fresh sense of what lies along the way. We get so used to our everyday routes that we don't see the distractions or potential hazards. Pretend you just landed in your community. You might not normally pay attention to the stores that sell snacks because you don't frequent them, but many kids fall into the habit of buying something to eat on the way to or from school. The crossing signal that seemed well timed to you might seem like an eternity to a child who spots a buddy on the other side of the intersection.

You should help your child select a route that is least stressful and avoids potential trouble spots—unleashed dogs, gangs of kids, a neighborhood bully, a confusing intersection. The shortest route is not necessarily the best choice. Better to walk around a bothersome block or two than be anxious every day. Your child needs to know to stick to well-traveled roads, avoiding backyards, alleys, parking lots, and vacant lots, and to walk on the half of the sidewalk closer to the curb. Staying clear of cars is smart, but in the unlikely event that someone tries to pull your child in, teach her to wave her arms and scream, "I don't know this man" or "This man is not my dad" to attract attention.

Make sure your child can identify the markings for a pedestrian crosswalk and knows where crossing signals and school crossing guards are posted. He should also know the location of public buildings such as fire and police stations, libraries, and recreation centers. Introduce him to people you know who live along the route in case he needs to find an adult. Walk with him through test runs and ask him to point things out. If you're thinking about giving your child a cell phone in case something unexpected happens, that might be a fine idea, but read Chapter 12 first.

There are any number of ways to phase in this *When.* Cathy, the mother of three, took an approach that included talking her kids through the drill as they walked, pointing out street names and counting blocks. Your directions might sound something like this: "We're walking down Warner Street. . . . We're turning right on Maple. . . . We go three blocks and make a left on Walnut." Cathy also did what she calls "creative dramatics" with her children to role-play different scenarios that might unfold, whether being picked on by a bully or being approached by someone in a car.

"I always wanted my children to know the world is a wonderful place and people are wonderful, but that if they happen to meet someone who wasn't wonderful, they had verbal and physical skills they could use," Cathy said.

At one point, when work schedules made it impossible for Cathy or her husband to walk along to school, she paid an older child to accompany her daughter—a strategy that works nicely on an informal, unpaid basis, too. Your child gets a confidence boost from walking without you but still feels the security of a protective gaze. Later on, she can be the big kid who escorts a younger neighbor. Another variation on that theme is for neighborhood parents to take turns walking younger children to school as a group—creating what some safety experts call a "walking bus." It allows your child to be on her own on your off-duty days, even though she technically isn't.

Even with all those basic safety rules in place, you can't forget to factor in your child's social skills and temperament. Intellectually, your child might be quite capable of getting around, but might not be quite there with street smarts. When you're out in public, you need to be self-assured but not cocky, and polite while still minding your own business. Can your child avoid pressure from friends to show off? Does he dawdle so much that he might not get to school on time? Does he get picked on?

Carla had to take an honest look at her son, Tyrone, when he announced at age ten that he no longer wanted to be driven to school. She could understand why a boy his age didn't want to be seen with his mom outside school, but she worried that Tyrone wasn't yet socially mature enough to be on his own. He often got teased because he was overweight and he was easily distracted, sometimes to the point of being oblivious to what was going on around him. Getting to school would require both walking and taking a bus in a neighborhood where there were blocks with boarded-up homes and older kids hanging out on corners. Things weren't predictable.

Carla worked hard not to baby Tyrone, but her instincts in this case were telling her, "Hold on a minute." Carla listened with an open mind as Tyrone made his case, but ended up telling him he had to wait a while before he could set out on his own. Then she made a deliberate effort to teach him more about what to be on the lookout for in the neighborhood and how to conduct himself when walking down the street. "Walk with confidence when you see someone, like you know what you're doing," she told him. "Pay attention to your surroundings, but don't stare at people." By the start of the next school year, Tyrone was on his own and doing okay.

Bottom Line: Walking alone is a great metaphor for the journey everyone takes as they march toward adulthood. Your child has the ingrained capability to do this, but needs a bit of advanced planning to get started. Like the rest of life, this journey will start one step at a time.

CHAPTER EIGHT

~

STAY HOME ALONE?

THIS QUESTION TENDS to break down along two lines: whether your child is ready to routinely come home to an empty house after school and whether she's prepared to stay home alone while you go out. You might feel there's no choice on the after-school question because there may be no one around to watch your child if you're a working parent. Schools often discontinue extended-day programs in middle school, making latchkey kids a reality in many families. On the nighttime question, you may have reached the point where the babysitter is not much older than your child, so why shell out the money? Babysitters aren't cheap and can be hard to find.

Luckily, this is one of the easier *When*s because it can be phased in, starting with leaving your young adolescent at home while you run an errand. While being home alone at night might seem more challenging than allowing your child to be on his own after school, I think it's the easier of the two to reach a decision on because it can be made on a case-by-case basis. The after-school question needs added consideration because you have to be sure that your child can settle into a good routine every day until you come home.

∽ WHY HOME ALONE?

There's a lot to be said for staying home alone. Kids get good at fending for themselves, mastering such skills as putting together a simple meal or getting their homework or chores done without being nudged. They experience the relaxation that comes from being alone and get a break from always being dragged along with the adults. Just as with walking to school, children gain a sense of control when they can manage a well-defined piece of their day. This is a *When* that gives parents insight into how your child will respond to expanded freedoms—and hopefully the realization that she's doing okay will make the next *Letting Go* not so hard. There's another payoff for you, too. You're more likely to go to the gym or out to dinner with your spouse if you don't have to worry about finding a babysitter, and that gives you a nice preview of when you'll have a lot more time for yourself.

∽ DON'T INADVERTENTLY CREATE ANXIETY

You want this to be a positive experience that builds confidence rather than triggers anxiety, so you have to consider carefully whether your child's temperament and ability to solve problems are suited to being home alone. Parents sometimes make the assumption that their child is ready because she's reached a certain milestone, such as turning twelve or entering middle school. Your child being "too big" shouldn't be the driving reason to stop using babysitters or discontinue accepting help from a relative or neighbor, because sometimes slightly older children need *more* supervision, not *less*.

This might seem like stating the obvious, but a good starting point is to gauge whether your child is comfortable with the possibility of staying home alone. Some kids are spooked by the thought of being in a house or apartment by themselves, but may not readily admit it. Cell phones lend some peace of mind because you can check in and be reached in an emergency, but they can't eliminate all the anxiety. If your child falls into the jumpy category, you need to be even more deliberate in phasing in this responsibility a bit at a time. A quick trip to pick up another child provides the opportunity to say, "I need to go out for thirty minutes. Would you like to come along or stay here?" When you make the transition from daytime to nighttime, it might help your child's initial uneasiness to have a "buddy system"—your child invites a friend over while you go out for a couple of hours. If you have multiple kids, we'll talk in Chapter 16 about whether your child is ready to babysit younger siblings.

No matter what list of instructions you leave, your child still has to be able to think through problems for himself, and that requires a certain level of maturity. The instruction "Don't leave the house while I'm out" makes sense on a certain level, but some emergencies would call for a child to do exactly the opposite. Think of the unexpected that can happen over the course of a week—a thunderstorm knocks out the electricity; someone rings the doorbell to ask you to sign a petition; the fire alarm goes off in your building. You can begin to prepare your child for staying home alone by presenting him with scenarios, ideally using real-life examples that crop up. Instead of "Don't open the door for anyone," try something like, "What would you do if the doorbell rings?"

Fred and his wife went over the instructions before leaving their son for the evening, but when they got home fire trucks were lined up. Their son had built a fire in their fireplace and didn't open the damper, so smoke was everywhere. It hadn't occurred to the couple to say "Don't use the fireplace." It's a "Kids do the darnedest things" sort of story, but it's also a good reminder of the importance of looking at your home with fresh eyes as you ready your adolescent to be unsupervised. Make certain that locks on doors and windows are secure, the smoke and carbon monoxide detectors are working, and that your family has an agreed-upon fire escape plan. If you have an alarm system, your child should know how to turn it on and off.

Prescription pills need to be out of sight, and if you own a gun, be sure to lock it away. You need to have clearly defined expectations around answering the phone (do you want it answered, and if so, what should your child say?), and using the stove, oven, and microwave. If your child likes to cook and has shown he knows how to operate appliances, you might feel comfortable with him fixing a meal.

Emergency plans need to be in place, too. While cell phones make us feel safer, they have in some ways diverted attention away from some basic safety measures. A child needs to know his address and home phone number (he also needs to know how to use the landline) and how to identify what his house looks like if there's something unique about it. ("There's a white fence along the drive; it's the condo around back.") He should know your work number and where you work—something many kids don't know because all their numbers are programmed into their cell phones. Family phone numbers and emergency rescue numbers should be posted on the refrigerator or other prominent spot, along with the numbers of two or three trusted adults whom you have identified as people your child can call if she's feeling scared or unsure about something. Your child should be familiar with a couple of your friends in the neighborhood who have agreed to be people she could go to in an emergency, for example, if she is followed home from school or if she loses her key or gets locked out.

Many parents instruct their adolescents to stay inside so they won't get hurt or run into trouble. If you decide you'd like your child to get some fresh air and exercise after sitting all day, have a predetermined agreement on where he can go and how he will alert you of his comings and goings.

Time management also is an issue. It's easy to say, "Watch TV for half an hour, then do your homework," but most kids aren't that organized. Still, don't shower your child with phone calls because that says, "I'm anxious and you should be, too." Having your child call when she gets home is a sensible expectation and your placing a call when you're winding down at work serves as a subtle reminder to your child to get moving. Posting a specific but reasonable list of expectations can help with time management: Feed the cat, bring in the mail, set the table.

~ TOO OLD FOR A BABYSITTER?

In many ways, middle and older adolescents present more challenges than young adolescents. If you leave a twelve-year-old home alone, friends are unlikely to come by, but not so for a fifteen- or sixteen-year-old whose friends (or boyfriend or girlfriend) can drive. In the evening, a house without an adult at home can rapidly transform into a party spot because texting allows word to instantly spread that parents are out. Your teen might not have any intention of throwing a party, but if a carload of friends pulls up, it may be tough to turn them away.

You have to think about the implications of setting precedents for after school too soon, because you might want to have more supervision, not less, for your older teen. Research indicates that adolescents who are unsupervised after school are more likely to use alcohol, tobacco, or drugs, get mixed up in gang activity, and be sexually active. I'm not saying being home alone will lead *your* adolescent to have sex or take up smoking, but being involved in school and community activities can help kids stay out of trouble.

So often this issue gets cast as working moms versus stay-at-home moms, but our collective goal as a community of parents should be to keep all of our kids as safe and productive as possible. I appreciate the bind families find themselves in on the after-school question, but I urge you to think creatively about ways to vary your child's routine so at least he isn't home alone every day. Perhaps once or twice a week your child goes to see a grandparent, volunteers, or takes a class at your neighborhood rec center: Anything that breaks up the routine of coming home to an empty house will make it less likely that your teen falls into a pattern of unwanted behavior.

Families sometimes share sitters when their kids are small, but such cooperative arrangements can still work with older kids. An older child in the group can serve as a helper to the younger children, assisting with homework or practicing basketball, and perhaps get paid a few dollars for his time. Another strategy is to think of your babysitter needs in a different way. As Liz's children moved into adolescence, she hired a local college student for after school and made the point to refer to her as the driver.

The designation went down better with her kids, who thought they were too old for a sitter. By pairing your younger adolescent with a high school or college student, you could end up with a good role model or even someone who can explain geometry.

Some parents choose to have a "No One Allowed Over" rule, which, like the "Don't Go Out" rule, makes a lot of sense because no one wants their home to become known as the local hangout. But all-out restrictions can end up squashing some positive activity. Rose and Ed's son played drums in a neighborhood garage band, headquartered at their house, and the boys wanted to practice after school. The couple set rules on which specific boys their son could have over and what part of the house they could be in. Once in a while they would arrive home from work early and unannounced to see if things were running smoothly. It's the sort of monitoring that works well during adolescence. Another good strategy is to tell a neighbor that your adolescent is there by himself and to let you know if anything unusual comes up. Be sure to tell your teen, in turn, that a neighbor is keeping an eye out. You let your child know you trust him to do the right thing, but that you care so much for his safety and well-being that you'll do some monitoring to see if the arrangements need to be tweaked.

Bottom Line: Staying home alone offers an opportunity to build confidence in adolescents as they conquer fears and learn to manage some of their own responsibilities and needs.

CHAPTER NINE

~

TAKE PART IN SLEEPOVERS?

ALL-NIGHT TALK SESSIONS, nonstop video games, loads of junk food—what's not to like?

Back when we were kids, sleepovers often revolved around special occasions—a birthday party or end-of-summer campout in a backyard tent—but now they seem to happen all the time. Sleepover mania has taken hold in many communities, even with children still in kindergarten. For some adolescents, a weekend isn't complete without a night of sleeping on someone's floor or couch.

Parents often complain about the frequency or inconvenience of sleepovers—tired kids can be miserable kids!—but tend to go along with them because they seem pretty harmless. But no matter how routine sleepovers have become, you should be thoughtful about preparing your child for the possible downsides. A number of safety checks and social skills need to be in place so you can sleep comfortably while your child gets very little rest.

∼ THE GOOD STUFF

There is some real positive social growth that can come from sleepovers. A lot of bonding happens late at night and sometimes a rather intense intimacy can be reached when friends have a chance to trade deep thoughts and let down their guard. Kids can assume roles they don't normally take during daytime hours. The quiet girl in the group might be an awesome karaoke singer; the "B team" player might be a Ping-Pong whiz. There's also something inherently exciting about a freewheeling night without a bedtime, topped off by a breakfast that includes a rehash of all the funny things that went on.

For parents, sleepovers provide a chance to get to know their child's friends, something that's harder to do when many of your adolescent's interactions take place via computer or cell phone. If you keep some of the food in the kitchen, you create a perfect opportunity to talk to the guests without seeming nosey. Establishing your house as a gathering spot sets a precedent for later on when you'll be glad to have your seventeen-year-old and her friends in your basement instead of at an undisclosed location.

But there are also some potentially concerning issues. Safety is a key concern with sleepovers, in part because you're sending your child into a home that you might know very little about. Among the points to consider: Do you know the family and have you been in their home? Will parents be home the entire time? (If the parents are going to be out in the evening, they should say so.) Who else will be in the house, including older siblings, relatives, members of the opposite sex? Is there a swimming pool out back, and if, so, will the kids be using it? (This is a vital point if your child isn't a good swimmer.) Call the other parents before you make a decision. You can frame the conversation in a friendly, nonjudgmental way that acknowledges that while you're happy that your child has been extended the invitation, you want to run a few things by the parent. "Eliza told me Kaley invited her to sleep over Friday night. I always check in with parents to make sure the plans are okay." By stressing that "I always check in with parents," you're not suggesting that you question this particular parent's values or parenting skills. Volunteering to send along a snack for everybody will be welcomed and give you a reason to go to the door and chat with the host parent when you drop your child off. Don't skip a call just because you know the family or because the sleepover is part of a large birthday party. The same considerations should apply because safety isn't guaranteed in numbers—in fact, unwelcome peer dynamics often take over at sleepovers.

There are also practical issues, starting with whether your child is comfortable sleeping away from home. Sleeping at a friend's house can be tough for a child with a bedtime routine, such as sleeping with a night-light or a special blanket. A sleepover might seem like fun at nine P.M. but become a challenge as the night wears on. If your child isn't comfortable staying without you at a grandparent or cousin's house, that's an indication that a sleepover, even with a close friend, could be taxing. (All of the issues in this chapter apply to sleep-away camp as well.)

Sleepovers can be very disruptive to your child's routine, and yours, even if the event isn't held at your house. Your child loses sleep and your family experiences the fallout when she's struggling to finish her science project on Sunday night. Are you willing to deal with it? This is a *When* where your child's temperament has to be high up on the list of considerations. Some kids can recover quickly after losing sleep; others disintegrate. Some kids are good at getting their homework out of the way; others save everything for the last minute. Sleepovers present an opportunity for you to teach your child to plan ahead. "Sure, you can sleep over if you have your homework done and your gear packed for Monday morning." Then vow not to get caught up in any drama that might ensue the next day because your child is exhausted. Even with best-laid plans in place, sleepovers simply aren't a good match for some kids' temperaments. A mom whose son has attention deficit/hyperactivity disorder (ADHD) said that sleepovers were so wearing on her son—and the entire family—that she eventually instituted a ban. Her son could go to a friend's house, but she picked him up late in the evening. Don't ignore your own practical issues. If you have a big workweek coming up, losing sleep because of six shrieking girls in your living room is not what you need. Say *no* with conviction—and suggest another time.

The parents in Pamela's neighborhood became so worn down by their kids' constant sleepover requests that they jumped when one of the moms suggested an alternative called the "sleep-under." "A sleep-under has everything a sleepover has except you go home at eleven o'clock or midnight," explained Pamela. Pizza, popcorn, sodas, movies, and even PJs are part of the experience, but everyone goes to sleep in their own beds.

"My kids always start out by asking for a sleepover and I'll say, 'No, because we have too much going on tomorrow,' or whatever the reason, and invariably the next question is, 'How about a sleep-under?'" Pamela said. "I don't care how late kids stay. I'll drive them home as long as someone is up at the other end."

The sleep-under is a nice example of parents getting together around a shared concern and coming up with a creative response.

While sleepovers on the surface seem like uncomplicated affairs, a lot of tricky social stuff goes on. Sleepovers can be highly unpredictable, emotionally charged events, and you need to be realistic about how your child's temperament influences his ability to handle situations where the social dynamics can shift on a whim and boundaries of what's acceptable behavior might fade. Some kids secretly hate sleepovers, though they won't admit it to their friends, and are happy to have an excuse not to go. Some adolescents still are more comfortable with one-on-one relationships and aren't yet adept at handling the fickleness of group dynamics. Girls can start out being nice to each other and end up nasty as the night wears on. Cell calls and texting stir the pot even more by drawing in girls who aren't there. (One mom says she tries to ban cell phones when her daughter has friends over— but that's easier said than done since adolescents view phones as a safety line to home.) Adolescents of both sexes might think it's funny to send inappropriate texts, IMs, or cell photos, and porn sites and inappropriate movies could be part of the night's entertainment. In my day, making prank calls made for the perfect sleepover.

An upcoming sleepover presents an opportunity to reinforce with your adolescent the value of being inclusive—if there are only ten girls in the class, it's not okay to leave out just one or two of them—and the downsides of gossip, whether in person or in cyberspace. Secrets shared and photos taken at midnight can go viral almost instantly, becoming juicy postings on someone else's social networking page. Remind your child of the twenty-four-hour rule—don't ever respond in haste to a text or IM because you're angry or want to impress the person at the other end.

Sleepovers can present more challenges, the older kids get. Teens might get their first taste of alcohol at a sleepover if someone sneaks in a water bottle filled with vodka or the basement refrigerator is stocked with the parents' beer. Roaming or cruising around in the middle of the night or a midnight visit by members of the opposite sex who are sleeping at a nearby house could happen.

A number of parents said they felt uneasier about sleepovers involving older adolescents because what can go wrong is more consequential. Rose said she and the other parents in her son's group reached a communal agreement to tighten up on sleepovers once their boys reached high school, allowing them only on rare occasions and only if they were planned and approved ahead of time. A last-minute call from your teen to stay at a friend's house could be a completely innocent request—but it could also mean he doesn't want to have to face your check-in rule because he's high. If your teen calls at ten-thirty to ask to sleep out, you might be less likely to call the family to make sure that's okay because you don't want to wake someone up. Right there, you've broken an important link in your safety chain. No matter how late it is, follow through with a call to the other family, or insist your child calls you when he gets there and then have him put the parent on the phone. In the same way, if one of your adolescent's friends shows up last minute at your house, insist the friend call his parents and get on the phone to say that it's all right if the friend stays over.

Sleepovers usually turn out okay, but you still need to make sure your adolescent knows how to use the three survival skills we talked about in Chapter 6: (a) being able to say *no* firmly while preserving a friendship; (b) shifting the blame to you ("My parents are picking me up at eight in the morning, so I can't be hung over"); and (c) code word, which allows for an exit ("I forgot to feed the dog" really means "You need to insist I come home right now!").

A sleepover chapter would not be complete without a discussion of coed sleepovers, which have become popular in some communities after special events such as prom and graduation. All the same caveats and more apply, because these after-parties can career into emotionally volatile, alcohol-fueled gatherings that take on a life of their own, especially if they're hyped as one last hoorah before everyone goes their separate ways. You need to have both your comfort level and your teen's be your guide here. It's okay for you to be against coed sleepovers and it's okay for your teen to be uncomfortable with the idea of spending the night.

Isabelle said coed sleepovers were not in keeping with her standards for decency, so she made it clear to her teens early on, "This family does not do boy-girl sleepovers"—with her emphasis on *not*. With three kids through high school, Isabelle has stuck to her guns.

Coed all-nighters are usually billed as "just hanging out," but even if the guest list consists of a group of friends who aren't paired up, mere opportunity and close quarters might dial up sexual feelings. This generation approaches dating differently than we did—"group dating" is more common—but they also have different views of sexual activity. Getting picked up for a one-night stand at a bar or nightclub—the unsafe, promiscuous sex that defined some young people in the '60s and '70s—is less likely, but in some communities today the practice of "hooking up"—having sex with a friend with the understanding there are no strings attached—is acceptable. Your teen must have the confidence to handle unwelcome sexual banter or physical advances that could unfold during a long night. This is a situation where you should expect nothing less than precise details from the host family: By what time must the teens arrive at the house? Will they be forbidden from coming and going? Will the host parents collect car keys to prevent middle-of-the-night driving? Will the parents be there the entire time and chaperone throughout the night? Will the girls and boys sleep in separate areas? Is this an alcohol-free event?

Boy-girl sleepovers are a good example of when it can help for your teen to be able to accuse *you* of being the loser. If your teen says she's not allowed to stay over because she has to work the next day, she's got an out for why she's leaving at midnight. Be the parent who's willing to do late-night pickups—your teen will appreciate it and his friends will be glad you spared them the hassle of asking their own parents for a ride home.

Bottom Line: Sleepovers offer a great opportunity to build relationships outside of school, but they have to meet the test of practicality. This is a When where you may have to be more cautious with your older teen than early adolescent.

CHAPTER TEN

~

DECIDE ABOUT CLOTHES, HAIR, ADORNING THE BODY?

TAKE OUT YOUR high school yearbook and remind yourself what you looked like back in the day. It's a good bet that your parents weren't thrilled with your length (or height) of hair! You might remember times when you headed out the door in a parent-approved outfit, only to switch or shed clothes on the way to meet friends. You also probably spouted the "It's a free country" speech when your parents demanded you remove your eye shadow or sideburns.

The point is that kids and parents have been battling over clothes for eons and, in the process, sacrificing a lot of goodwill on something that has little bearing on whether someone grows up to be decent. I think parents are wise to save their energy for more significant issues and allow their children latitude on dressing as long as their choices fall within the bounds of commonly accepted decency. Body piercings and tattoos are a different matter—you have every right to veto an adolescent's request to make a permanent, and perhaps regrettable, statement.

~ WHAT STYLE SAYS

If you consider that key developmental question "Who am I?" it will make perfect sense why adolescents try out personas, using clothing and hairstyles that often are the opposite of what parents would pick. At the same time, the second developmental question—"Am I normal?"—propels many teens to copy what everyone else in their crowd is wearing. As much as you might have to bite your tongue when your daughter comes home with pink streaks in her hair, I urge you to look at the positives of your child's style. Creativity gets a chance to shine through dress—an eye for color, design, teaming up unlikely pieces that somehow make for a great look. Remember how you clapped when your toddler put mismatched clothes together, but accomplished getting dressed on his own? Your adolescent is exhibiting a similar ability to think for himself, so take a deep breath and celebrate it.

For some teens, clothes become a vehicle to express newly discovered interests and passions. They can make a statement about their concern for the environment or social justice by buying "recycled" clothes at thrift shops or shunning certain labels. The faded flannel shirt your son takes off only to get washed every so often may speak to his views on "conspicuous consumption."

On the downside, how your child dresses can send an unintended message (or sometimes all too intended). College students prepping for interviews are taught that it takes only a few seconds for prospective employers to form an impression, and snap judgments are tough to change. Adolescents are likewise sized up quickly. A teen dressed all in black with black makeup and nails or in sagging jeans with holes in the bottom makes a different first impression than a kid wearing a team T-shirt. And it's not just adults making assumptions—adolescents are judging each other, too.

While I'm all in favor of expression through dress, some boundaries need to be in place. Parents shouldn't tolerate clothing that makes an offensive or threatening statement—whether it's gang colors or symbols, or offensive slogans that are profane, racist, or sexist. Some T-shirts are emblazoned with alcohol, drug, or gun references, and those also need to be vetoed. Girls are so used to seeing exposed breasts and bellies on TV that dressing in a sexually suggestive manner (whether it's meant to come across that way or not) has become routine. Parents have the right to draw the line on clothing that is overly revealing. Another caveat: You should pay attention if your child suddenly adopts a drastic new look, because it could signal a shift in who he's hanging out with.

Otherwise, try to stifle your critique. Your teen might very well abandon the hat you despise once you stop harping on it. Some parents fixate on their child's appearance to the point that they apologize for their kid's clothes or hair to relatives or other parents. Kids have every right to feel humiliated when their parents call them out in public; you wouldn't want the same to happen to you.

~ MINIMIZE THE CONFLICTS

The conflicts over clothing will be reduced if you allow your child early on to pick out what she wants to wear. Some parents continue to lay out their kids' clothing even into middle school—a level of management that can only serve to make an adolescent want to rebel by wearing things she knows will irritate her parents. A good starting point is to reach some agreement with your adolescent on what is acceptable for school. Most kids get the fact that what they wear to class or Grandma's house has to be neater and more modest than what they choose for other times. Being able to make your own clothes selections should come with related responsibilities— placing clothes in baskets to be laundered and folding them and putting them away afterward. Your adolescent also needs to understand the money side of clothing—how to be a savvy shopper and stick to a budget, skills we'll talk more about in Chapters 13 and 14. Part of making smart choices involves reading labels—DRY CLEAN ONLY comes with a recurring cost.

Clothing is one of those areas where drawing your adolescent into casual conversation will go a lot further than preaching on the horrors of spaghetti straps and exposed boxer shorts. You won't have to spend much time in front of the TV before you can slip in a comment like, "How do you think that girl comes across to her friends?" or "What do you think he's trying to say with those clothes?" A wait in the dentist's office as you both flip through magazines could lead to a discussion on why designer labels are seen as status. You can use a trip to the beach, where all sorts of body adornments (some on wrinkled, saggy skin) are on display, to ask your son why people like to plaster themselves with tattoos.

School uniform requirements take away much of the debate over clothes and are thought to reduce bullying and the impact of economic inequities, though it's amazing how kids still find plenty of ways to express themselves while wearing the obligatory khakis and polo shirt. Dress codes help, too, though adolescents are clever at stretching the rules. Instead of going nuts playing fashion police every morning, let your adolescent pay the consequences if she gets flagged at school for wearing a skimpy top.

∼ PERMANENT STATEMENTS

Giving some ground on the clothing front will put you in a better position to say *no* to permanent modes of expression. You need to make clear where you stand on multiple piercings and tattoos, though it could backfire if you turn it into a control issue. Some teens like tattoos and piercings precisely for their shock value, and who better to shock than your uptight parents? Remember, teens think it's all right for their parents to focus on safety, so rather than rail against tattoos and tongue rings on aesthetic grounds, focus on health concerns, such as hygiene and the possibility of infection related to unsterile conditions. Your child is likely to point out he'd never be so dumb as to go to a nonprofessional place, so remember there's another valid argument in your arsenal: It's okay to care about how your child fits into society, and tattoos and body piercings are viewed negatively by many people.

The message to convey, in your own words, is "I don't care what you wear. I don't care if you pierce your ears. But I do worry about people judging you because of piercings or tattoos. When you're older and you're on your own, you can make that decision. But for now, I don't want you to do that."

Piercings at least grow back in when your teen gets tired of the look. But even though lasers can lighten tattoos (and maybe make them disappear), for all practical purposes tattoos must be seen as a statement for life. What's cute or funny or a declaration of love at eighteen (JACOB LOVES MINDY) probably won't be welcome at forty, especially if Jacob is married to Sarah. A colleague of mine helps teens come to their own decisions. She asks them what they would have chosen to tattoo on themselves when they were eight. They usually respond with characters like Tweety Bird, Eeyore, or Superman. She then asks how they'd like a Tweety now? Tastes change; tattoos remain. If your child really feels compelled to make a statement, henna tattoos fade away.

The tattoo and piercing discussion is worth revisiting with your older teen. Most kids will adhere to their parents' wishes while in high school, but some college freshmen consider it part of their rite of passage to arrive home for semester break with an eyebrow ring or tattoo—though the tattoo might be discreetly placed—and part of the shock value comes with not warning you.

Francine thought she had gotten off easy with her high schooler, but then her daughter returned from a summer program in South America with multiple ear piercings and a nose ring. She told her daughter she wasn't happy about what she had done to her body, but she then took the attitude that what was done was done. As it turned out, the nose piercing soon became infected and her daughter had to remove the ring.

I want to end this chapter on one final thought. Some parents, especially mothers, try to relate to their adolescents by dressing like them—though they might not consciously have thought it through that way. There is a danger in look-alike dressing because it inadvertently sends the message, "Hey, we're friends." You're a parent, not a friend. Let your adolescent celebrate who she is through dress, then you do the same. If you dress just like your child, she'll have to figure out another way to prove how different she is from you.

Bottom Line: Appearance is a pretty safe way for teens to assert their style. As long as your teen's style meets your standards of decency and doesn't leave any permanent marks, this probably shouldn't be one of your battles.

CHAPTER ELEVEN

~

Go Online?

Depending on who you talk to, the Internet is either a dangerous place for kids or a world of opportunity. It's either squelching kids' creativity or opening their eyes to a universe of new ideas. It's either ruining their ability to cultivate relationships or allowing them to be more connected than ever.

While all of those seemingly opposing views have merit to varying degrees, let's move beyond the usual good-versus-evil Internet debate and think practically. In just a few years we've gone from being glued to our desktop computers to reading e-mail on our cell phones in the checkout line. Who can say where technology will take us next? Too often parents either easily concede defeat on the Internet question—taking the attitude, "It's a different world we live in. I have enough things to worry about"—or go into such high-alert mode that they treat technology as the enemy without recognizing its benefits.

The safety issues can't be ignored—we've all heard the frightening stories about child molesters who hook their targets online and arrange a rendezvous, or cyber stalkers and harassers who take advantage of the easy access the Internet affords. You certainly do want to take advantage of whatever software you can to minimize the risk that your child will encounter such dangers. (See National Center for Missing and Exploited Children's Web site, www.missingkids.com.)

But at the same time, you need to think about safety more broadly to make sure the Internet and other technology is a constructive part of your child's life. A survey published in 2010 by the Kaiser Family Foundation found that kids between the ages of eight to eighteen spend on average a total of seven hours and thirty-eight minutes a day on the Internet, watching TV, playing video games, and hooked up to iPods—and that doesn't even count the other hour and a half spent fielding texts. These numbers are breathtaking considering that a child's day also includes going to school and sleeping.

~ WHAT'S NEEDED TO SUCCEED IN THE INTERNET AGE, OR NOT

This chapter and the next, on cell phones, are closely related, so I'm going to outline some common issues here. We know what it takes to raise strong, capable children—it's those Seven Cs of Resilience we talked about in Chapter 2. Children and teens need meaningful Connections to other people. They need to feel Competent and Confident. They need good Character and to believe that their Contributions to their family, school, and community matter. They need to feel they can Control the outcomes of their actions and decisions and can Cope with stress. None of that has changed even though the Web and cell phones have so changed our kids' world. Let's use the Seven Cs (in a different order than we earlier did) to consider your child's involvement in the online world.

Connection. You want your child to interact comfortably with peers. You want him to be able to talk respectfully and with confidence with adults, and be able to approach people for information and advice. You want to know that your own connection to your child is strong so that she'll tell you if she's bullied or comes across troubling information online. Until you see that your child's social skills are taking shape, it makes little sense to allow her to become immersed in technology that requires no need to look anybody in the eye. That's not to say that preadolescents shouldn't be able to use the Internet with supervision—exchanging photos on line with grandparents or a camp friend or using online video chats to talk to a parent in the military or away on business are great ways to stay connected. For young children, though, socializing should still be very much about being with family and playing with friends, and that should be done in person whenever possible.

For adolescents, the Internet can certainly strengthen connections by allowing them to keep up with their friends. Some shy kids might benefit from the ease of communication allowed by instant messaging and social-networking sites, and adolescents in a minority group (such as gay kids) may find it reassuring to connect with a community that is not part of their everyday circle. But this same connecting capacity can lead troubled kids to other troubled kids, perhaps ones with graphic information on how to cut or get high. That fundamental question of adolescence—"Am I normal?"—can lead young people to seek validation for troubling behavior or a dangerous idea, and the Internet can give a false sense about what's normal. The same antisocial idea that would be squashed when presented to local peers might get reinforced when isolated kids across the country get together online.

Adolescents also can compromise existing connections by making themselves socially vulnerable with comments they post. Part of being socially ready for going online is knowing what information is personal and what is okay for group consumption. What is written in an e-mail might be wildly misinterpreted, and even an innocent comment can come back to haunt. It's important for your child to get in the habit of not responding instantly to a bothersome IM or posting (the twenty-four-hour rule), because knee-jerk reactions are often regrettable. An exception: If your child feels a peer is ready to hurt himself or someone else, he should alert an adult immediately.

Competence and Confidence. Researchers are busy looking into all sorts of issues related to the impact that online technology has on children—

Does it enhance or diminish school performance? Does it worsen focus and increase impulsivity?—but only you can gauge whether being online is likely to improve or erode your child's sense of mastery over his world. Online competence involves being able to use technology in a way that allows you to find reliable information, explore ideas, and cultivate healthy, meaningful relationships.

Control. Parents often feel in control because they've installed software to block access to inappropriate sites or unknown people and monitor every keystroke their child makes. Such software does provide some peace of mind that your child will be shielded from pornography and sexual predators, but parents often overlook another danger that comes with being online: the possibility of being cyber-bullied or harassed by peers, or getting caught up in perpetrating the behavior. A study by the Pew Internet & American Life Project found that 32 percent of teens say they've been harassed online, by way of someone sending a threatening message to them, spreading malicious gossip, or posting an unauthorized photo.

Remember, though, the real control you want is for your child to gain their own control. You want him to do the right thing, whether you're looking over his shoulder or not. You can help that along by establishing clear expectations in a written parent-child computer contract. Some of the points to include in the contract: (a) location of computer (not in the bedroom is probably best, but that's tough to enforce with laptops); (b) established time limits; (c) a designated computer-free block of time; (d) what kind of monitoring you'll do; and (e) a promise that your child will come to you with concerns. Consequences also need to be spelled out in the contract. If you plan to use a monitoring device to see what sites your child has been to and what he has written in e-mails and IMs, you need to state what the consequence will be for unsuitable material. If you allow your child to create a social networking page with an understanding that you'll check on it occasionally, be clear on what you'll do if you find photos and comments you find offensive. (Ask her to remove them? Make her shut down the site for a given period of time?) The contract can be revisited every few months and open to renegotiation if your child demonstrates good judgment.

Character. The instant responses demanded by the online world can pose a real challenge for adolescents. It's so easy to get caught up in put-downs, gossip, and even outright bullying because there's a certain feeling of distance and anonymity that comes with online exchanges. A passing comment made to a best friend can be instantly turned into fodder for dozens of friends and frenemies to see. Remember, the "Am I normal?" question is often answered by, "Yes, I am because he's not."

Before your child enters the online world, he should be consistently demonstrating the admirable character traits you're striving to cultivate—such as kindness, restraint, tolerance, inclusiveness—because they will get tested. You need to be clear that "mean girl" behavior or bullying will not be tolerated in any form. An IM will disappear from the screen and a cruel posting can be removed, but they can do long-lasting damage to someone's spirit and reputation. In Jewish law, there's a prohibition called *lashon hara* (evil language/tongue), which forbids gossiping about someone else even if the information is true, because evil talk slays a person's reputation. It's a good concept to teach our kids. In this age of rapid-fire communication, we all need to hold our tongues.

Contribution. This generation of kids is as idealistic as they come, and surely the Internet has something to do with it. With a few clicks, they can see what's going on in remote corners of the planet and perhaps get motivated to do their own small part to help out people in need. The point to remember is that it's not simply what you're doing online that matters but also what you're not doing because you are online all the time. Remember, adolescents thrive when they hear "thank you" from people who are grateful for their help. Logging off and making in-person contact allows that to happen.

Coping. The Internet provides an excellent escape, taking you to exotic places and granting you instant access to music, videos, games, TV shows, and movies. But it can just as easily be a crutch to avoid schoolwork, relationship problems, and other stressors, perhaps even adding to depression or anxiety. You can help your child learn to use the Internet as a healthy distraction by setting parameters around time and place. There is an addictive quality to cruising the Internet and playing computer games, especially for some kids, and they can be highly stimulating, particularly right before bedtime. Bedrooms should be a place to sleep, not to be connected.

That leads to another C to add to the Seven Cs—Choice. Our kids need to learn that they have a choice in how much technology permeates their world. They can choose to log off, silence their phones, skip TV and video games, and do something else for a change. One of the problems with this generation of kids is they get "bored" so easily, perhaps because everything digital happens so fast. The sheer speed of stimulation and responsiveness might even be changing kids' brains. Your child needs to be able to fill space with the world around him, not just with space out in the cyber universe. That means play and family time.

You can set an example by establishing your own tech-free time—during dinner, perhaps an hour in the evening, or on part of your day of worship—and then invite your child to join in. If you want this to work, make those moments something to cherish rather than dread. Your child will appreciate the time to be part of a household and not out in the World Wide Web.

Bottom Line: Technology is here to stay. Your role is to be certain your child can exist in the real world as well as the virtual world.

CHAPTER TWELVE

~

GET A CELL PHONE?

GABBY BOUGHT HER son a cell phone when he was in the sixth grade without giving it much thought. It was easy to do (just add him to the "family plan"), not out of the norm (many of his friends had phones), and it seemed to offer both convenience and security. Max was off more and more on his own, attending sports practice and spending time with friends in the neighborhood.

"My thinking at first was that I wanted Max to be able to get in touch with me and me be able to get in touch with him at any time," Gabby explained.

But she began to second-guess her decision after Max dropped and broke his cell phone while skateboarding and then quickly lost the replacement. Her son's carelessness got Gabby thinking more about the rationale for the phone and whether there was any benefit in his having one. Their neighborhood was safe, and if Max said he was going to walk somewhere after school or be at a friend's house, Gabby either had to trust him or not let him go.

"A cell phone is no guarantee he is going to be okay no matter what," Gabby reasoned, and on top of that, Max hadn't exactly shown that he was ready for the responsibility of taking care of a phone. Gabby ended up telling her son that she wasn't paying for a second replacement. If a cell phone was something that he really wanted, he'd have to save up and buy it himself.

That Gabby, a thoughtful and involved parent, was rather casual in getting her son not one but two cell phones is not surprising given that phones are now seen as standard operating equipment for kids. It's so easy to get caught up in your child's "Everyone else has one" argument since that isn't far from the truth. But *When* to allow your child a cell phone should not be determined by "everyone else" because this decision is among the most consequential ones you'll make during adolescence. A cell phone will bring about fundamental changes in your child's world and yours—it will change the way your child interacts with peers, expand his horizons in unforeseen ways, and alter your access into your child's world. None of those changes are inherently bad, but you want to make sure your child, and you, are prepared. You need to carefully consider any number of factors—safety (always first), your child's existing social and communication skills, and the relationship between the two of you, not to mention a slew of practical matters, such as who pays. The goal is to minimize the many problems that can come with cell phones (including sky-high bills) so the technology enhances your adolescent's feelings of competency and control, not undercuts them.

∾ SAFETY

There are plenty of good reasons to have a cell phone. I thought it was wise for my girls to get phones when they started riding a city bus to school instead of being driven. I feel good knowing they can get hold of me or use a code word to reach out for help. The news is filled with examples of people who used their cells to summon help in an emergency.

But that same direct and instantaneous access can also lead to unhealthy relationships and even danger. A survey of teens by TRU (formerly Teen-age Research Unlimited) found that teens are frequently harassed, insulted, threatened, or sexually propositioned by their boyfriends or girlfriends via cell calls or text messages. Nearly one in four teens in a relationship said they communicated with their partners by cell phone *hourly* between mid-night and five A.M. Some teens said their partners checked as many as doz-ens of times a day to see where they were, what they were up to, and who they were with. Abusive relationships begin with jealousy and then slowly move to isolation and ultimately control. Adolescents are vulnerable to get-ting caught in this trap because jealousy seems so "cute" at first that it is welcomed. Cell phones may increase vulnerability because getting lots of calls and texts ups a teen's social profile, creating a blind spot to when atten-tion crosses the line to control. Before your teen enters this new frontier, you must have a discussion about how healthy relationships offer space and independence as well as loving attention.

Sexual predators are another concern, though in truth your adolescent is less likely to run into problems with a stranger than someone he knows. Child abuse experts say cell phones are ideally suited to predators because they can conduct a phone relationship, particularly via texting, without raising the suspicion of you or others in your child's life. Predators (who can be someone an adolescent is familiar with) also use the modus operandi of flattery and attention to hook adolescents. Remember that younger chil-dren see things as black or white and consider people good or bad. Your adolescent needs to have developed more sophisticated thinking skills to recognize that people in the virtual world aren't always who they appear to be. She also needs to have the confidence that she won't be dismissed or made to feel foolish by coming to you or another adult with a hunch that something's not right.

The most likely safety threat to your adolescent's emotional health is if he becomes the target of malicious text messages passed about by peers. Texts have become the number one way adolescents communicate with each other using technology, second to voice calls on their cells. These trun-cated messages are so easy to forward to a gang of people, setting in motion a chain of gossip or rumors that is nearly impossible to stop. Texts can be particularly biting in their brevity and they lack the nuance of the spoken word. If someone writes that you're a dork, it says you're a dork; in person, there could be body language that makes it clear the comment was made in jest.

The proliferation of "sexting"—sending nude or provocative photos of yourself or someone else—via cell phones is a big worry. Some teens may not consider this practice immoral or degrading to themselves, but getting caught up in sexting can have long-lasting repercussions. Some school administrators view this phenomenon as grounds for suspension or expulsion, and in a number of states there are laws that make it possible to criminally charge those involved in sexting with manufacturing, possessing, or distributing child pornography.

There are all sorts of technologies that parents can use to limit and monitor cell phone use. You can choose programmed phones that allow your child to dial or receive calls only from preapproved numbers, which seems like a good option for younger children who carry phones for safety reasons. There's also technology that allows you to monitor in almost real time the activity on your child's phone—calls, texts, photos. The sales pitches (which sometimes even use the word *spy*) appeal to that sense of wanting control over a treacherous world. But as with computer monitoring, you need to understand why you're monitoring your child's cell phone and what you'll do with the information. If a GPS (Global Positioning System) locator chip in your daughter's cell phone shows she's not where she's supposed to be, will you jump in the car and go get her? If your adolescent is sending malicious texts, are you prepared to take the phone away? Later in the chapter, we'll talk about how you can use a parent-child cell phone contract to spell out clear consequences before problems crop up.

∼ USE COMMON SENSE

There are many practical issues around cell phones, but I'll touch on just a few. Let's at least apply the commonsense test. You wouldn't give a nine-year-old a hundred-dollar bill to carry around, so why would you trust that an equally expensive phone won't end up at the bottom of the swimming pool? If your adolescent can't keep track of his assignment book, he'll probably lose his phone, too.

Not everyone defines *practical* the same way, of course. Anna bought her six-year-old daughter a programmable cell phone, and she's pleased with how it's working out. "She turned six and graduated from kindergarten and we decided to get her a phone. It was something she wanted and we gave in to her," said Anna, who works hard and is proud that she can give Janine things she didn't have as a child. Anna said the phone also gives her peace of mind because her daughter has asthma. "She goes away with her godmom every other weekend, so she can pick up her phone and call me or her dad." And sometimes Janine calls her at work to say, "Hi, Mommy, I just called to say I love you."

I can understand Anna's pride in providing for her daughter and her concern about the asthma, but I can't think of a reason why a six-year-old should have a phone. Young children should always be under an adult's eye, and they haven't yet developed the social skills and discernment needed to use a phone wisely. A cell phone is not a toy, even though there are some really cool games that come on them.

Financial issues fall into the practical column, too. Long before the first cell phone bill arrives, parents should have a firm agreement on who's footing the expense. With family plans that cover multiple people, often for a huge or unlimited number of call minutes and text messages, it's easy to take the attitude that the added phone isn't costing anything. I'm not going to dictate how to handle money issues with your child, but if the phone is primarily for his social convenience, I'd suggest coming up with a plan to make him responsible for at least part of the bill, perhaps using some of his allowance, and make it clear that your child is responsible for any additional costs if she goes over the time or text limits. I've heard parents of young adults say their kids are shocked by how much a cell phone costs them. Mom and Dad made it seem for years that talk was not only cheap, but free. Helping your child understand that everything costs money is a core lesson that prepares her to deal with the real world.

Parents also need to know where they stand on the "upgrade"

phenomenon before it presents itself. Cell phones have become such a status symbol for adolescents that a basic model doesn't quite cut it for many kids, who see their friends walking around with expensive smartphones. Cell phone companies are masters at tapping into our desire for the newest and the best by offering promotional offers that look like amazing deals in the moment but could end up costing you hundreds of dollars more a year in add-ons.

~ KNOWING AND PREPARING YOUR CHILD

Your child will enter a whole new world with a cell phone—one, for all practical purposes, that you're not part of. Taking stock of your child's maturity, social skills with peers, and overall temperament is extremely critical in the cell phone decision because there's so much potential for misuse or abuse of the technology. Most parents have a good starting reference point because their child already has spent time on the Internet. Just like with computers, cell phones can exacerbate tendencies in kids who are impulsive or easily swayed, and that's especially true of texting with its short-hand style and ability to elicit an immediate response.

It's also the seeming anonymity of cell phones that leads to insensitive or even destructive behavior. Adolescents will text things they wouldn't dream of saying to a person's face, and spreading mean comments via group texts might seem like an easy ticket to popularity for adolescents who aren't sure of themselves and want to be part of the "in" crowd. Camera phones also play into a child's impulsiveness or need to belong. A lasting record of an indiscreet moment gets quickly passed along or posted for all to see.

Adolescent culture seems to demand immediate responses. In truth, everyone tends to respond too quickly when angered, but the domino effect here is so real that you need to be sure, once again, that your adolescent knows the twenty-four-hour rule. When feeling most angry, that is precisely the time he or she is likely to say stupid, inflammatory things. If cyber-lies or cyber-gossip come across the airwaves, your child must turn the phone off and take a break. Otherwise, he'll be caught in the tension and likely make things worse for himself. This all needs to be part of a discussion that happens before a cell phone enters your child's life and also spelled out in your parent-child contract. There have to be clear consequences understood in advance if your child uses her phone to bully. Likewise, while you will be supportive of your child if she is the victim, she has to agree to discuss ways to minimize the likelihood that it will happen again. When parents have already established a constructive atmosphere of listening and talking, adolescents will be more likely to come to them if the cell phone causes trouble. Also, as we discussed earlier, if you position your concerns about cell phone use as safety issues, not friendship-based matters, your child may be more apt to disclose.

Some schools are introducing "cell phone etiquette" into classroom discussions, which helps bolster what parents say at home. An elementary school teacher I know took a break from the day's curriculum after she discovered that a disagreement between two students had spilled into an after-school fight using offensive text messages. The teacher had her class brainstorm strategies for being wise and kind users of technology. Cheating via texting is also getting the attention of teachers and principals, who have tightened rules on the presence of cell phones in the classroom, even if they are supposedly turned off. The list of potential abuses goes on and on, but I'm sure you get the point. Until your child has demonstrated good communication skills, responsibility, and positive relationships with peers in other aspects of her life, giving her a cell phone isn't really a gift.

~ CONNECTION: LET'S NOT FORGET FACE TIME

With a home phone, you have a pretty good idea of who's in your child's orbit. You can say hello to friends who call, and your child, likewise, is forced to talk to the parents of the friends he calls. Without a phone in the pocket, a kid will come to the door to get your child, not call from the street. Those are important connections, especially in adolescence. But with cell phones, kids can retreat to their bedrooms, or through texts, not talk at all. It's not that you eavesdrop on your kid's conversations, but you can sense quite a bit about how your child is doing by his demeanor. Knowing your child's friends is highly protective, but with cell phones in place you'll have to work harder to keep in touch with them.

Alex, the father of three, has watched the steady hold that cell phones have taken in his kids' lives in just a couple of years, and he's feeling frustrated. He remembers being shocked the time he opened his bill to see his daughter had sent or received twelve hundred texts in a month—but that's nothing compared to his latest bill, which showed that his son had logged three thousand texts, not at all outrageous by teen standards. With so much silent communication going on, Alex can't always keep track of who's who. "My kids have more acquaintances, as distinct from friends," he said. "It used to be their friends called on the phone and you had a quick conversation."

On the most basic level, a child needs to have mastered sufficient communication skills in face-to-face conversations before entering the cell-phone zone. While the world does revolve more and more around e-communication, I implore you to delay your child's entrance into it until her interpersonal social skills are well developed. Remember how as kids our parents taught us telephone manners and we practiced how to answer the phone and speak to our friends' parents? Knowing how to introduce yourself and look someone in the eye are still critical skills in the real world, and we're not helping our kids if we allow them to fall into the lingo of cell calls and texting before mastering real communication.

The frenetic pace of cell phone culture is not limited to kids. In truth, your own easy availability to the rest of the world may damage the most important connections of all, the connections within your family. When you talk on the phone during dinner, check messages in the middle of a conversation, or jump to take a call when you're stretched out on the beach, you're telling your kid that technology controls you.

Just as cell phones mean that we parents never get a needed break from work, cell phones can create stress in adolescents because they never truly get away from the posturing that is part of teen culture. As I said in the last chapter, you need to create a time in your home life when the rest of the world doesn't enter your relationships. Some parents I met in Dallas gave me the idea for establishing "cell-phone-free time," perhaps for an hour in the evening or on your day of worship to give everyone in the family a reason to disconnect and relax. Phones (including yours) should be out of reach during dinnertime, and adopt the "no calling after eleven" rule that many of us were raised on. You might think your child is asleep in her room, but she could be texting away. As part of your agreement in allowing your child to have a phone, she should agree to put it away at night. Dedicate a spot in the kitchen where all cells, including yours, are charged overnight.

～ YOU CAN'T TEXT YOUR WAY THROUGH LIFE

At the extreme of disconnection is communication solely by fingertip. There is something almost addictive about getting that shorter ring that says you have a message. Responding is so easy, and you don't have to invest too much thought. Texting makes a person even less present than talking on a cell. While teens brag that they can text without looking (amazing!), they are missing much of what goes on around them. Kenyetta told the story of how her daughters were showing a visiting cousin around town and the girl was so busy texting friends that she barely looked at the sights or said anything. Kenyetta and her girls felt slighted and sad about the lost opportunity to enjoy time with their cousin. Afterward, they got talking about how intrusive cell phones could be and how they shouldn't dominate every waking moment. Kenyetta came away from the conversation feeling that her daughters would approach phone use more thoughtfully than their cousin.

I recently spoke to a young man in his early twenties who shared with me how awkward he felt when he had to deal in person with people since so much of his social life growing up was conducted online and via texts. He said many of his friends felt the same way. His admission made me think of everything that's lost when communication becomes an exchange of abbreviated words. A teen who uses texting to ask a girl to the prom might think he'll protect himself from humiliation if she turns him down, but he'll more likely miss the excitement on her face when she says yes.

~ STAYING CONNECTED . . . NOT ATTACHED

In some ways, cell phones offer a closer connection than was ever possible before. Imagine hearing from your teen as he hikes up a mountain and wants to share the view at the top precisely as he experiences it. We so want to stay connected to our kids, and *Letting Go* challenges us deeply. The easy connection afforded by a cell phone can relieve anxiety about your teen's growing independence; she may be able to get around on her own, but at least you're still somewhat in the loop. But the positive aspect of this connection can be ruined if boundaries get crossed and the phone becomes a digital leash.

Some parents call their children incessantly and expect them to call all the time, too. In truth, this repeated checking in with the expectation that the phone will be answered immediately can pose a direct risk to your child. Your calls may come in at untimely and even dangerous times, when a teen is surrounded by friends or is driving. If you have already established an expectation with your adolescent that you will monitor her behavior—consistently using the check-in rule and an agreed-upon curfew—you should not have to resort to calling to see what your kid is up to. As Gabby wisely pointed out, parents put a lot of faith into cell calls. Parent: "Where are you?" Son: "I'm at Brent's house." Your kid could be at Brent's, or many other places.

There's also a danger that you will use a cell phone to insert yourself in an unhealthy way into your adolescent's world. Some parents fall into the habit of texting reminders and tidbits to their children while they're at school, but most things can and should wait for later. Kids in school should be focused on school. As for reminders, an adolescent should learn to plan his own day and take the consequences of forgetting something. Don't get me wrong; it should be part of your role to help your child develop organizational skills, but serving as the ever-present prompter undercuts that effort. A teen who finds it too easy to get instant answers won't learn to stand on her own. She will constantly "use a lifeline," like the contestants on the TV game show. Remember, the goal in all the *When*s and *How*s is to promote resilience—that inner strength to work through problems. Having a constant connection to Mom or Dad creates the sense that "I'm not capable, I'm not in charge, I can't possibly figure this out for myself." You need to resist the urge to call or text all the time, while making it clear that you're available to your child, should a dangerous situation come up.

Some parents say that their adolescents respond to their texts but not their calls, and that realization has made those parents turn even more to texting as a way to stay connected to their teens. They figure that at least their teen is sort of talking to them. I understand that reaction, but you don't want to slip into a habit of digital encounters that allow for none of that good listening and talking we discussed in Chapter 4. You can foster a stronger connection with your child by using in-person moments to catch up on each other's lives.

∼ WORKING IT OUT IN ADVANCE

There are three *When*s that can especially benefit from a formal parent-teen agreement—cell phone, Internet use, and driving. Drawing up a simple contract before you buy the phone will avoid fights down the road. The clearer your expectations are in advance, the more likely they will be followed. A kid listens better when he wants something. He wants the phone, so agreeing to ground rules and discussing your concerns are a small price to pay. I've included a sample contract at the end of this chapter that you can use to pattern yours after, but you still want to have some conversations ahead of time. Get the dialogue going with a statement like "For me to feel comfortable getting you a cell phone, I need to know you're willing to discuss some important issues, that you will follow some rules, and that you'll come to me if problems develop." It might be good to start with the easy stuff—your child's financial responsibilities for the phone and any time limitations you want in place. Request that your teen dock the phone at bedtime, continue to answer the home phone and take messages, and occasionally bring his friends into the house.

One way to approach the more sensitive topics might be to say, "I expect you to have good judgment, but I want to be sure you can protect yourself from getting into trouble with a cell phone." Then take the opportunity to discuss cyber-bullying; why to never send out group gossip or use the phone to embarrass peers with compromising photos; the twenty-four-hour rule to avoid quick, regrettable reactions; the danger of adults using the phone to lure a kid; and the trap a teen can fall into when she allows a boyfriend to keep too close tabs on her. I recommend, by the way, that you not barrage your adolescent with all of these topics at once; allow these pre-phone discussions to unfold over several weeks. Alternatively, if you want to surprise your child with a phone, as I did, then give it with the understanding that there are important topics you'll address in the coming days, though be sure to cover cyber-bullying right away because mistakes can happen quickly.

Still left is making sure that the cell phone won't end up undermining your child's evolving sense of independence. First, reiterate how you are always available in a crisis and will drop everything to help in an emergency. Next, set your rules on how you want to monitor her, and your expectations on how quickly she will respond to your calls. Never make the demand for an instant response, especially if she's driving. Finally, make clear that just as you will not check on him constantly, you expect that he will continue to make his own decisions and call you for the big stuff.

The last point to be hammered out is the question of what to do if your child breaks the agreed-upon rules. If your child behaves irresponsibly with a cell phone, the privilege that should be withdrawn is the phone. Similarly, the cell phone should not be used as a punishment for misbehavior in another area. The goal of discipline, remember, is to tie privileges to demonstrated responsibilities.

One thing for sure, just when you feel that you have this cell phone thing figured out, another technology will come along. But you'll be prepared.

CELL PHONE CONTRACT

~

Allison agrees to:

- Discuss with her parents ways the phone can be dangerous.
- Never use a cell phone while driving.
- Never use the phone to spread gossip or obscene comments or photos.
- Talk to parents if someone is bothering her via calls or texts.
- Keep it turned on when going out.
- Return calls or texts from parents within a reasonable amount of time.
- Use the phone to activate her "code word" to summon parents' help.
- Keep her phone in her backpack at school.
- Keep it away from the dinner table and turned off during designated family time or events.
- Place the phone in the charger in the kitchen before bedtime.
- Be reminded by her parents if the cell phone is consuming her time or getting in the way of her giving her full attention to a conversation.
- Pay $10 a month toward the cost of the phone, due the first of the month.
- Pay part of the replacement cost if the phone is damaged or lost.

Mom and Dad agree to:

- Respect Allison's privacy when talking on the phone.
- Not call or text more than twice an evening, unless something can't wait or it's an emergency.

- Return calls or texts from Allison within a reasonable amount of time.
- Always respond to a call to come get her.
- Not punish Allison for being in the wrong place or the wrong crowd if she uses the phone to get herself out of trouble.
- Pay the remaining cost of the phone.

If Allison breaks any point in this agreement, she will hand over her phone to her parents for one week, or longer depending on the severity of the problem. This contract will be renegotiated in six months.

_____

Allison's Signature   *Date*

_____

Parents' Signatures   *Date*

Bottom Line: Make certain your child can communicate well face-to-face before he talks mostly with his fingers.

CHAPTER THIRTEEN

~

MANAGE MONEY?

WHEN ALEX STARTED to think about what he wanted to teach his children about money, one thing kept coming to mind: "Don't spend all of your money on little stuff. Save it for what you really want."

It was a lesson Alex had learned, beginning when he was nine and started mowing his family's yard. Before long, neighbors hired him to cut their lawns and that was the start of a well-paying summer business. At his parents' urging, Alex became more of a saver than a spender, and he invested in a piece of land. Alex, a high school teacher, now lives on that property in a house he and his wife had built. Their home is a reminder that he didn't mow all those lawns for all those summers for nothing.

Alex doesn't expect his kids to follow in his exact path to financial security, but he does look for opportune moments to point out to his kids that what they want today might not be what they *really* want tomorrow. Also, their habit of mindlessly purchasing sodas and snacks means they won't have money when something better catches their eye.

"Even though you have the money right now, wait a few days and then if you still want it, fine," he advises his teens, and he sees signs that they are buying his logic. His college-age daughter banked most of her money from a summer job so she can study abroad next year. His older son passed on a couple of video games to save for software to upgrade his computer.

~ CULTIVATING THE RIGHT VALUES

Money frequently becomes a source of conflict between parents and their adolescents, and not just because kids seem to be forever asking for some. While parents will complain that their teens are spoiled or have a sense of entitlement, much of the tension, I think, stems from the fact that parents assume their teens should know how to be judicious about money when in fact they missed numerous opportunities along the way to teach them about financial decision making. We've all heard horror stories of college students who rack up thousands of dollars in credit-card bills and twenty-somethings with decent jobs who still count on their parents to pay the rent. It can be a shock how expensive car insurance is if you never were asked to contribute a dime.

Nothing magical happens when kids turn twenty-one to make them able to handle money. It's a skill that's gradually acquired through trial and error, and the sooner the lessons begin, the better. Money can be a difficult subject for so many of us, perhaps because we grew up in homes where parents always argued about it. Or, at the other extreme, maybe you were taught that it isn't polite to talk about money. But waving kids off with our parents' favorite comment, "Money doesn't grow on trees," doesn't get them thinking critically about setting priorities and making trade-offs. Neither does automatically opening our wallets to hand over yet another twenty.

Every family has its own way of budgeting money, and only you know what techniques work best for your circumstances. But no matter how tight or generous your family budget, the goal should be to cultivate in your child an attitude that values responsible spending and long-range planning, as well as generosity toward people or causes that could benefit from their help. A fundamental principal that children need to learn is that there's a difference between what you want and what you need. It's not that you shouldn't splurge sometimes, but when instant gratification is the norm, nothing feels special and even abundance doesn't seem like quite enough.

Young children shouldn't be drawn into financial discussions that might make them anxious—your pending salary cut or the drop in the stock market that decimated your retirement savings—or be privy to personal information such as your salary, but they can understand the reality that there's a limited pot of money that needs to pay for housing, food, gas, and other basics, and after all those come the frills.

Learning to recognize that distinction between wants and needs will serve your child throughout life. If we give our kids too much now, how will they learn to work with their own two hands or be satisfied down the road with a more frugal lifestyle? Even though our impulse is to shower our kids with happiness—and in kid language that translates into things—the goal is to raise an adult who is content with the life he makes for himself. If you buy a fancy car or all the latest designer labels for your teen, how will she feel when her starter salary doesn't cover high-end fashion or her spouse only makes enough to buy the family a used car?

Teaching your child to manage money will help cultivate many of the key ingredients of resilience. There's a sense of competence that comes with being good at the basics of finance—making a budget, balancing a checkbook, comparative shopping—and that's just the beginning. When children have their own small pot of money to manage—whether it's a weekly allowance, a clothing budget, or a set amount of spending money for vacation—they begin to gain a sense of control over their financial destiny. Character and contribution come into play, too, when children experience the satisfaction of using their money to help someone out—whether that entails patronizing a neighborhood shop or donating to a fund-raiser at school.

~ ALLOWANCE: GOOD OR BAD?

Parents can be very passionate on the topic of allowance. There's a camp that feels strongly that children should not be "paid" for doing what they should be doing as a member of a family. Another camp thinks that giving an allowance in exchange for chores—watering plants, feeding the dog, emptying the dryer—teaches kids responsibility and the benefits of work.

I agree that allowances are a great tool for teaching kids about money, but tying the granting of an allowance to routine chores can be problematic. For starters, if you set up such an arrangement, you need to stay on top of tracking whether your child holds up his end of the bargain. A chore chart is easily made and easily forgotten. One mom explained how she subtracts set amounts of money from her son's allowance if he slacks off, but keeping tabs like that requires focus and a resolve to stick to the ground rules. What if your child doesn't do his chores? Are you willing to stand firm when he starts pestering for money or presents a good explanation for why things didn't get done? Such arrangements will quickly fall apart if you hand over the money in the end anyway. Some parents tie allowance to behavior—you get your allowance if you're "good" or you get it taken away if you're "bad." Again, for discipline to be effective the consequences need to be directly related to the behavior at hand. It makes no sense to dock a kid on allowance because he talked back to you.

The better approach is to establish an expectation that everyone pitches in around the house; you don't get compensated for picking up after yourself. Go ahead and give a basic allowance, but let your child earn "extra pay" for bigger jobs, such as washing the car or cleaning the basement. Your adolescent has a goal to strive for if he knows three lawn cuts will buy a concert ticket.

I won't tell you how much allowance you should give your child, though some parents use the guide of $1 per year of age. That seems to make sense for younger children, who just enjoy having a little mad money, but when you consider that a movie and popcorn can be $15 or more these days, the formula might not work for older kids. You need to be clear what the allowance is expected to cover. It's one thing if it is totally for discretionary spending, such as eating out with friends. But it's a different matter if your child is expected to pay for school lunches, bus fare, weekend activities, or birthday gifts for friends or family members. Unless your adolescent has a job or gets monetary gifts from relatives, the allowance is everything. It's better to be a bit more generous in setting an amount than always be shelling out more money when your teen runs out. Having a little more money also ups the possibility that your child will learn to stash some away, though it's hard for kids to understand why they should save for something so far in the future as college.

Along with the allowance, take your child to set up a savings/checking account (online works, too) so she gets visible proof of how money can grow or evaporate. Once you set the expectations for your child's allowance, step back. You want your child to experience both the pleasure of spending well and the letdown from blowing money on something foolish.

Some parents try to control their kids' spending, with varying degrees of success. Isabelle liked to remind her kids of the "one-one-one" philosophy when they got money in their birthday cards: "If you have three dollars, spend one, save one, give one to charity." They were amenable to the idea. When Ling's son started working as a ref for youth soccer, her first instinct was to insist that he put a lot of his pay away for college. But the more she thought about why she wanted her son to have the ref job—not simply to earn money, but to learn responsibility—she decided to back off and let her son set goals. When control was no longer the issue, her son worked with enthusiasm and saved up to buy a laptop. He took pride in his accomplishment.

Parents certainly should encourage thriftiness and generosity, but children learn those qualities best when they see their parents forgo something because they want to put money aside for vacation or make a donation in a friend's memory.

∼ WHAT ABOUT CREDIT CARDS?

The allowance discussion inevitably leads to the next question: Should adolescents be given credit or debit cards? This is one where you have to think carefully about the temperament and maturity of your child, because there could be some expensive mistakes. Many adolescents would do quite well if you handed them a credit card and said, "This is only for emergencies," or "You can use this to buy two hundred dollars' worth of clothes, no more," but other kids are more prone to impulsive buying.

Given that credit card companies target young adults and much of business takes place online via credit cards, it makes sense to introduce your adolescent to the pros and cons of plastic before he falls for a sign-up offer as a college student.

By starting with the savings/checking account, you monitor how well your child is keeping track of how much he has. A next step would be to allow your child to have a debit card linked to that account—which reinforces the idea that you can (should) only spend what you have. Your teen will also learn about hidden fees that can accompany debit cards, such as when using ATMs not linked to your bank.

Monitoring is key if you decide to give your adolescent a credit card. Again, you need to spell out your expectations for use and be sure to show him the fine print about interest rates and how debt can balloon if you don't pay your bill in full. Tell your teen that you will review monthly statements as a basis for deciding whether the privilege should be extended. You want your teen to learn from poor choices—all those smoothies and burgers really do add up—but you don't want to be in the position of having to bail your teen out of debt. A reasonable in-between step would be to give your child a prepaid credit card, which puts a cap on spending, but such cards can also have hidden fees. You want your adolescent to learn that debit or credit cards aren't the means to a fatter budget, but rather are convenient tools to use in certain situations.

Ways to Help Your Child Become Money Wise

- **Let your child see your financial brain at work.** Show her how you come up with a household budget, write checks, pay bills online, make payments to your mortgage or student loan. Show her how you read sale circulars to look for bargains and use coupons for grocery shopping.

- **Use the Internet to teach comparative shopping skills.** When Liz's son needs a big-ticket item, like a new pair of basketball shoes, she encourages him to look around online and come back to her with a list of possibilities and prices. She's a stickler for free shipping, so her son has learned to never include a choice with a shipping fee and he's gotten good at finding bargains. After he's narrowed the choices, they either go store shopping or order online.

- **Give a clothes budget.** This saves a lot of haggling. Rather than debate every item of clothing your adolescent wants to buy, set an amount, say $300, and tell her that's what she has to spend for back-to-school clothes. Stephanie said she used to fight with her daughter over the sensibility of buying $100 jeans. Now, with a budget in place, her daughter can buy the jeans if she likes, but she knows that she won't have much left over for other items. A good way to phase in the budget idea is to start with a separate amount for every season, and eventually move to an annual or semi-annual chunk of money. If your teen spends it all in fall, spring's wardrobe won't have much new. Similarly, giving a weekly or monthly gas budget is a good idea if you have a teen driver—kick in a certain amount, but if the tank runs dry, the fill-up isn't on you. This budgeting strategy will promote the same goal as effective discipline—your teen will equate actions (careless spending) with consequences (I'm low on money and now I have to make it last for another week).

- **Make lists.** We all know what happens when we go to the store without a list. The cart gets loaded with stuff we don't really need, and we come home without an item needed for dinner. Teaching kids to make lists helps them to prioritize their spending. Before going back-to-school shopping, have your kids make a list of what they'd like to buy—how many pairs of pants, T-shirts, and so on—and then discuss what's a necessity and what's frivolous. Indulge a bit, but also encourage bargain hunting.

- **Set up a cafeteria account at school.** Rather than handing out dollar bills as your child runs for the bus, set up a prepaid account at your child's cafeteria with the understanding that it needs to last for a certain length of time, no exceptions. Your child will learn that the cafeteria account lasts if she packs lunch every couple of days instead of always buying it. It's a good habit to be in when you enter the workforce.

- **Use vacation planning to teach about money.** Tess and her family like to use their money to travel, but she wants her kids to not take for granted the cost of seeing the world. She has them get involved in searching the Internet for cheap airfares and hotel rates and they read online restaurant reviews ahead of time to see what meals would be worth the treat. You can use online vacation home rental sites to have your child find a beach house that's in your budget. You can also set a daily budget for traveling and get your child involved in creative ways to stick to it. Give your child a set amount of spending money before vacation begins with the understanding that he can spend it anytime on anything, but then be patient when on the last day he's still deciding what souvenir to buy.

- **Support causes as a family.** A home that commits to charity is a home that understands it has blessings. Giving is a responsibility and an act of righteousness. You can encourage your child to identify a cause she'd like you all to support—flood victims, an animal shelter, a homeless shelter—then find creative ways as a family to make a donation. Perhaps you skip pizza night once a month and set the $25 aside, or you all agree to dedicate a small percentage of your pay (or allowance) to the cause.

Bottom Line: If a person has to wait until adulthood to learn to manage money, she likely never will.

CHAPTER FOURTEEN

~

GO TO THE MALL?

HERE'S A HOMEWORK ASSIGNMENT for you: Go to the mall by yourself not to shop but simply to observe. For starters, linger in the clothing stores that are a magnet for young people and watch the shoppers frenetically going through the racks and bins. Check out the mannequins and gigantic posters of models—rail-thin women with full lips and well-placed curves, and young men with glistening abs, hairless chests, and jeans slung low. Take in the flashing lights, pulsating music, and store clerks wearing head-sets as if they're directing planes to land. Next, head into high-end bou-tiques and see if there's a price tag anywhere in plain sight. Don't miss the sports memorabilia store, where the autographed photos and game balls and "official" team gear can eat up several months of a kid's allowance. Finally, stroll around and see the clusters of teens who are trying to look nonchalant as they check out the other kids going by, but can't quite hide their anxiousness. They are all trying so hard to be normal; normal just as the posters and mannequins surrounding them define it.

I want you to take this field trip not so you'll come back ranting against malls, but so that you'll see for yourself that the mall serves up much more than a chance to shop. The mall is a case where it's easy to get so accustomed to the environment that you no longer pay attention to what's there. If you're like many parents, the mere mention of the mall makes you worry about worst-case scenarios—your daughter could be approached by a pervert or your son preyed upon in the men's room. But such qualms, though understandable, rarely are realized. By doing your own observing, you'll get reminded of the challenges that most definitely await. Think of that image of the little kid in the candy store; now think of being plunked down in the mall. The possibilities are endless, the seduction overpowering. The promise that you can be sexy, beautiful, thin, desirable, happy, fulfilled, popular (just fill in the blank) if you only had this item right now is everywhere you turn. Shopping with friends makes it even more appealing. Add in the social dynamics that take hold when a group of kids get together, and you can see why the mall is simultaneously an exciting and challenging place for adolescents.

∿ WHY THE MALL OR WHY NOT?

Going to the mall (or maybe in your community, the downtown district) is a ritual for many adolescents, and if your child hasn't already asked to go, he will. The social upsides of the mall need to be acknowledged. With so much online socializing going on, the mall at the very least provides a spot for kids to get together in person. It provides a setting for adolescents to expand their horizons outside parental supervision in a situation that's somewhat loose, but not devoid of rules and expectations for behavior. You can be kind of silly, but you can't act too outlandish. For adolescents intent on answering those two all-important developmental questions—"Who am I?" and "Am I normal?"—the mall also offers an opportunity to try out a new style of dress and forge connections outside of school. Younger adolescents often make their first forays into mixed-gender gatherings at the mall—a group of girls and a group of boys "just happen" to show up at the same time—again, a good thing when you consider that the mall is a fairly protected public place.

Many practical skills can be honed at the mall. Adolescents start to get competent at handling money, interpreting advertising and marketing messages, and prioritizing their needs versus desires. They gain a sense of control and confidence when they spend money earned babysitting or at a weekend job without getting a parental stamp of approval for what they buy. Even with small purchases, they get a taste for what it's like to be a smart consumer—shop around, compare prices. They also get a chance to work on character traits that will serve them well throughout life—how to treat clerks with respect, to put things back where they found them, to be mindful that they're not the only person in the room.

But the mall—as you certainly will see on your field trip—also has an edgy current running through it and you must consider whether your child has the social skills and temperament to handle a high-stimuli environment that offers so many choices. The mall by its very nature feeds off impulsivity and the need to be instantly gratified. Stores are masters at telling teens that the norm is to look thin or "ripped" and outfitted in certain logos. The steady promotion of hypersexuality is everywhere. There's also the unpredictability of the social scene going on—posturing, flirting, jostling, insulting, sometimes between kids who don't even know each other. The mall can be too much for an adolescent who hasn't yet learned how to rein himself in or avoid getting swept up in the emotionality of group dynamics. Your child needs to be able to think on her feet and activate a backup plan if she gets separated from a friend or something unexpected happens.

∼ MASTERING THE MALL STEP BY STEP

Almost every parent we talked to had strong opinions about the mall. A few went so far as to say they would *never* let their kid go by themselves—a position that seems shortsighted since their child probably will figure out how to get there sooner or later. Banning your adolescent from the mall might seem protective, but in doing so you're also denying him the chance to develop important competencies.

Fortunately, this is one of the *When*s that is conducive to the graduated, step-by-step approach to granting new privileges that we talked about earlier. The mall needn't be all or nothing. Taking into consideration adolescent development and some suggestions from parents, we came up with this approach that will allow your child to become mall savvy:

- Make a point to periodically take your young child to the mall or wherever kids like to shop and hang out in your community. The shopping trips will provide natural opportunities to talk about money, marketing, public behavior, treating people who are serving you, and other relevant topics. I'll give your some more detailed ideas later in the chapter.
- Right before adolescence, do your own observing at the mall. It will help refresh in your mind what skills you still need to stress.
- Start to encourage your child to invite a friend or two along on shopping trips with you. You'll get a sense of how they behave together.
- After you become comfortable that your child can handle more freedom, allow your child and a friend to go ahead, but keep them in sight.
- Next, still accompany them to the mall, but go off and do your own shopping or relax with a book at the food court. Have your child check in by cell phone at a designated time. You could also arrange to be called or meet up to discuss potential purchases.
- Eventually, start to drop off and pick up your child at a prearranged place and time, preferably during daytime hours. Begin by allowing your child just an hour or so on his own, and then increase the allotted time as he proves responsible. Two to three hours tops are plenty.
- Finally, your child can begin to take public transportation back and forth to the mall if that's an option.

~ CULTIVATE GOOD HABITS

There are many ways to use shopping excursions with your child to lay the groundwork for going to the mall with friends. Here are some key points:

- **Public behavior.** Your child must learn how to conduct himself in a public space. Seize on those teachable moments—ask your child what he thinks about kids cursing when there are older people or young children around and shoving each other in the middle of a walkway. Some malls have started to ban unaccompanied teens on weekend nights, fearing that their presence intimidates older shoppers. Instead of expecting the worst from teens, we would do everyone a favor by teaching our kids good manners and proper public behavior.

- **Shopping etiquette.** Young shoppers should be expected to put merchandise back where they found it, bring items out of the dressing room, wait patiently in line at the register, and be polite to clerks. If you leave your shopping cart in the middle of the parking lot or treat cashiers with condescension, your child will learn the same rude habits. Instead, teach your child that a smile and a thank-you go a long way with a frazzled clerk. Learning common courtesies will pay off in other ways down the road. Someday your child will be doing a job interview over lunch and the potential employer will be either impressed or turned off by the way your child treats the waiter. There are many businesspeople who intentionally take people out to see how they interact in the world. Everyone knows an interviewee is going to try to impress the interviewer, but what the employer is actually on the lookout for is a genuine demonstration of character. Civility is an acquired habit.

- **Shoplifting.** You can begin to educate your child on the dangers of shoplifting by pointing out the use of security tags on items and the presence of security cameras and guards. Adolescents might not set out for the mall to steal, but they can fall into it, sometimes because they want to impress their friends—the dare element at work—or because everyone else is moving on and the checkout line is long. Your child needs to understand the ramifications of shoplifting— which could vary from a store calling the parent, to the shoplifter being led away and later charged with a crime—not to mention the morality of taking something that isn't his. Your child needs to know to return quickly to the cashier if he discovers that he inadvertently took something without paying or if the security alarm sounds because the clerk forgot to remove the security tag. Your child also needs to know to remove himself from a group if he suspects someone of stealing. You might be right that your child would never shoplift, but she could get caught up in a scary situation. This is a good topic where you can reiterate the importance of your child activating the code word—your child can call you anytime if something feels funny.

- **Money smarts.** Stores that cater to youth know they often have plenty of money to spend and are skilled at luring them in with the promise of a bargain. Your adolescent needs to know how to calculate discounts (what does 30 percent off mean?) and read the fine print on sale signs to recognize gimmicks. There may indeed be "$20 off," but perhaps only on purchases over a certain amount. "Buy one, get one half off" sales aren't necessarily bargains because you end up buying two items instead of one. Another common tactic: asking customers to fill out a customer-satisfaction survey (the store now has your e-mail address to flood with promotional offers) or offering an application for an instant credit card in exchange for a discount. Such deals are meant to encourage customers to make impulsive purchases. One more thing—just because something costs more does not mean it's of superior quality.

- **Marketing awareness.** Stores use all sorts of tricks—lighting, color, smells, seductive words—to reel in shoppers. Manipulation is all part of the selling game. Sex particularly sells when it comes to adolescents, even if promotions are subtly presented under the guise of health and fitness. The model selling a sports drink or running bra lands the sale by pedaling sex. You can teach your child to recognize marketing come-ons—a skill that will come in handy in the dating world. Lingerie stores send customers out with tiny pink shopping bags because they know there's a certain cachet in broadcasting to other teens that you just bought a push-up bra. Expensive boutiques make a point to have smiling salesclerks greet you at the door because they know they'll hook you once they make you feel special. You can use the mall as a huge laboratory to teach your child that feeling good about yourself does not come from buying into the notion that you have to look a certain way to be lovable, desirable, and happy.

• **Body image.** Your child develops a sense of what's normal in large part by what he sees in his environment. At the mall, kids see mannequins shaped unlike real human beings, pictures of models who have to starve to stay thin, and racks of clothes where size 0 is a choice. Parents shopping with their kids sometimes play into this distorted sense of normal by telling their kids, "You look thin in that," or "It will fit perfectly if you lose a few pounds." The goal is to be healthy, not thin or built. You want your child to understand that their real value comes from who they are in the inside, not the shape of their body or what they wear on the outside.

Bottom Line: The mall is a highly charged place where teens have to be well prepared to deal with an atmosphere designed to get them to spend money. They have to be able to filter the subtle and not-so-subtle messages that may cause them to feel badly about who they are, what they can afford, or what they look like.

CHAPTER FIFTEEN

~

Travel Alone
Buses, Trains, and Planes?

People who take public transportation need to know how to put on a public persona. That involves projecting confidence, not cockiness. Being polite and respectful, but not chatty. Being able to look someone in the eye, but not staring or holding on to a person's gaze too long. It means knowing how to ask for directions without appearing flustered. It means being able to mentally size up those around you to identify someone you could turn to for help if something unexpected happened.

That sounds like a tall order even for adults, but I think most adolescents are quite capable of mastering the skills needed to travel safely and confidently. With extended families dispersed and divorced parents often living in different time zones, there are many practical reasons why you may want your child to become travel savvy. Sometimes, the reason is as basic as your child needs public transportation to get to school.

On a broader level, buses, trains, and planes provide a literal and figurative pathway to independence, just as walking without a parent to school does. Visiting a grandparent on their own gives kids the opportunity to build their own special memories. Taking the train to the city with a friend provides an adolescent with a sense of adventure and accomplishment. Public transportation might also allow your teen to stay connected with a friend who has moved, thus keeping one of those protective circles of friendship intact.

~ PLANES, TRAINS, AND OTHER THINGS

Air travel has become somewhat formulaic because airlines have so many rules regarding age requirements and the use of assigned escorts for minors who travel without an adult. Train and bus services also have guidelines, easily accessed on their Web sites. But just because children as young as five years old might be allowed to fly alone doesn't mean that even your much older child should. You need to read such policies carefully and then let your imagination run through your own list of "what-ifs." What would happen, for instance, if a flight is grounded because of weather and your adolescent, who has to make a flight connection, gets stuck? What if there's a lot of turbulence and your child gets scared? A bit of anxiety is a given with air travel, and you should be comfortable that your child is able to handle some uncertainty. Make sure your child knows that the flight attendant will give safety information at the start of the flight, but stress that emergencies are rare and adults are there to help if something does happen.

Perhaps even more of a challenge are municipal buses, subways, and trolleys because unpredictable things can routinely crop up. For starters, buses break down. If you have to change buses or subway lines to get where you're going, a delay on one leg of your trip can mean waiting around for your connection. Riders on public transportation also sometimes encounter people who are themselves unpredictable.

Cell phones provide some security because you know your child can reach you. You can have your child check in at departure and arrival and make sure she knows to use her code word to alert you to potential trouble. But while cell phones are important safety equipment, they aren't a replacement for good preparation. At the very least, some basic travels smarts need to be in place—the ability to keep track of tickets, tokens, or a transit pass, comprehend schedules, and activate a backup plan if the bus or train is late or breaks down.

Whether traveling across the country or to the next neighborhood, your child also has to understand the concept of "safe strangers." We talked in Chapter 7 about how not every stranger is to be feared and that police officers aren't the only people to be trusted. It's precisely strangers that we need to turn to if we're lost or feel uneasy or threatened. You can teach your child that when she gets on a plane or bus or train, to look around and spot someone who looks approachable—women and women with children are a good bet. Sitting near the front of the bus is a good idea because your child can ask the driver for help. One suggestion in *Protecting the Gift* is that parents start allowing their children to ask for directions when the need arises, just to get a sense of how they handle themselves.

Adolescents are quickly judged by adults, so make sure your adolescent knows basic etiquette—to give up seats to an elderly person or let an older person or a mother with a baby ahead in line. It's a courtesy that will make your teen feel good. Indoor voices and keeping hands to oneself are a must. While minding your own business is a good rule for the road, adolescents need to be aware that they can't get so immersed in their iPods or texting that they don't notice what's going on around them.

This is a *When* where role-playing through various scenarios is better than presenting your child with a list of dos and don'ts. What would you do if someone seemed to be following you when you got off the bus? What if someone gets in your face or picks on you? What would you do if you lose your transit pass? What if you miss your stop?

Because adolescents tend to have that awkward feeling of being onstage and don't like to draw attention to themselves, doing test runs with you to work out some of the kinks can help. Make sure your child knows how to buy a ticket or pay on board and doesn't just know his stop but the names of the ones that come right before and after.

One parent said that before her kids started taking a city bus to middle school, she rode the route with them multiple times to point out stops and introduced them to the driver. Another mother hired a college student to escort her elementary children back and forth from school on city transit as training to letting them ride on their own. Cathy started her adolescents out slowly—allowing them to take the bus a short way to the mall, and then, when that worked out okay, allowing them to take the local train line to the city on a Saturday.

No matter what the arrangement, teens who get comfortable with public transportation learn that there's an environmentally sound alternative to Mom or Dad always shuttling them about, and that's a good lesson for life.

Bottom Line: Taking public transportation requires knowing how to conduct yourself in public, and that's a skill most adolescents can master.

CHAPTER SIXTEEN

~

HELP WITH SIBLINGS
AND ELDERLY RELATIVES?

ROSE GREW UP on a farm in the Midwest and learned at a young age what was needed to keep things operating smoothly. Every single member of the family had a role, whether it was helping to milk the cows or sweep the barns.

"In a rural environment, even as a child you know you're an important contributor to the livelihood of the family," Rose said. "From the time you could walk, you had chores."

Rose moved to the city and became a nurse, but she never lost her farm-girl values as she went about raising her three kids. Her two daughters helped tend to their baby brother, feeding him and folding diapers, and they babysat him as they got older. When Rose's mother-in-law relocated to a retirement community near their home, her three kids pitched in to do laundry, driving, and whatever their grandmother needed.

"We always operated from the position that everyone is needed and everyone is able and reliable," Rose said.

Rose captured three excellent words in that thought—*needed, able,* and *reliable*. We live in such a child-centric society that we've forgotten that older children used to play a critical role in keeping families functioning. That's unfortunate because the home is an excellent training ground for teaching our kids about taking care of others. When given the chance to watch a younger sibling, adolescents feel what it's like to be a protective force—a prelude to what parenting is all about. When they spend a few hours sitting with a grandparent, they discover that even when people's bodies are frail, their minds are filled with wonderful stories and wisdom to share. Teens often say they don't feel appreciated, but you can help create moments where your child truly does feel needed in a very tangible way. This is one of those opportunities to learn that giving is the best way of receiving.

Of course, adolescents shouldn't be pushed into adult roles and siblings are still siblings. Ideally, a teen should have time to be with his friends on at least one night of the weekend and take part in sports and clubs instead of coming home after school to watch siblings. Also, avoid placing your teen in the job of nurse. Watching TV or playing cards with a grandparent who can't be left alone is one thing, but giving medications is an adult responsibility. Sometimes family finances or the inability to find a babysitter dictates that a teen must be enlisted to help. Just be clear about your expectations and, if possible, set a limit on how long your teen will be needed.

~ BABYSITTING

It's a compliment to put your older child in charge. You're essentially saying, "You're growing up. You're showing me that you're capable and trustworthy and I know you can take good care of someone else because you're taking good care of yourself." You're also presenting your adolescent with the opportunity to be a role model to his little brother or sister outside your shadow—part of that connection building that is so important. Teens also love the chance to play, though they won't admit it. Being "forced" to stage a battle with action figures or build a fort with blankets and chairs gives your adolescent a chance to straddle two worlds—"I'm a big kid because I'm in charge, but I still can act like a little kid."

It's hard to avoid an age discussion with this one. One mom told us she uses the headline rule when it comes to babysitters: "Ten-Year-Old Left Home Alone with Little Sisters." Doesn't sound good, does it? The point is that common sense, safety, and the comfort level of you and your children have to be your guide. All the many safety considerations we discussed in Chapter 8 ("Stay Home Alone?") apply and having your child complete a babysitting course is a good idea, too, though the babysitting certificate is not a substitute for your own judgment. Fifth graders can earn babysitting certificates, but most fifth graders probably aren't mature enough to babysit. By gradually introducing what's entailed in babysitting— starting with mother's helper, moving to a short daytime stretch and then on to nighttime—you get a chance to see that your adolescent follows through on instructions and is comfortable with the responsibility. One thing you may not be able to predict is the dynamic between or among your children. Kids will often behave beautifully for a neutral babysitter but be a terror for a brother or sister. You can help your older child establish his authority by making clear to your younger child that you won't take a slew of cell calls or texts complaining about what's going on, though an emergency is a different matter.

Babysitter is one of those extras for which I think adolescents should be paid. Add some professionalism to the arrangement by asking your teen if he's available, instead of assuming he'll do it, and state what you'll pay. Just like you do with an outside babysitter, hand over the cash when you get home rather than promising to pay later or bartering with something like, "Since you babysat, I'll buy your concert ticket." Your adolescent will feel good about earning money, even if he turns around and uses it to buy the ticket himself. Your teen, in turn, needs to do the same things she would do if she were babysitting for someone else. That means cleaning up before you come home and giving a quick rundown on how the night went.

~ HELPING OUT GRANDMA

Adolescents move in such peer-packed circles that their interactions with others generations are unfortunately often limited. Time spent helping care for a grandparent or other elderly relative can pay off in ways you might never imagine. Grandparents sometimes are more comfortable sharing family stories than parents are, and kids can come away with a better appreciation for their parents or perhaps a reassurance that their parents struggled in some of the very ways they are doing right now. An older person can bring out the tender side of even the most defensive teen. The same teen who complains as she loads the dishwasher at home will cheerfully clean up her grandma's kitchen. There's a potential benefit for you, too, besides getting a break from the demands of caring for an older person. Sometimes as parents we get so focused on what's annoying us or worrying us that we don't see that our teens are incredibly competent and kind. You might be surprised by the insight and reassurance your elderly parent passes on to you.

There is a point where contribution becomes a burden. It becomes a burden when helping out at home cuts into schoolwork or consistently keeps your teen from hanging out with friends. You want to avoid "parentification"—a dynamic where your child is forced into the role of adult. Adolescents who assume the job of caretaker can feel as though they have proven themselves as adults—fully independent—and no longer need adult supervision. But while parentified teens think they've earned the rights of full adulthood, they often resent that their teen years were taken away and may have spoken or unspoken tension with their parents because of that.

Bottom Line: Helping care for a sibling or elderly relative gives adolescents a chance to demonstrate they're responsible and to feel the rewards of being needed. Remember that the resilience of young people is enhanced when their contributions are noticed and appreciated.

CHAPTER SEVENTEEN

~

GO ON DATES, GO TO DANCES, HAVE A BOYFRIEND/GIRLFRIEND?

STEPHANIE WAS GOING through the drive-in window at the bank when her daughter asked if it was okay for her to start "going out" with a boy in her class. The question caught Stephanie by surprise because her daughter was only in the sixth grade, but she managed to squelch a knee-jerk response ("You've *got* to be kidding me!") and instead calmly asked what "going out" meant. Stephanie flashed back to the dating scene she had experienced as a teen—one-on-one arrangements, kissing, and more—and she knew her daughter was certainly not ready for that. But by her daughter's definition, "going out" meant that you declared your interest in a particular person to your friends and then sometimes went to a movie or school event as part of a group. Stephanie listened to the explanation and then summed up the essence of what she had heard. "If going out means no kissing, no touching except holding hands, it's fine," she said, using the no-beating-around-the-bush style her kids knew to expect.

Stephanie gets an A for that parenting moment because it could have ended with her daughter swearing to never talk to her mom again about boys. Stephanie could have sounded the parent alarm when her daughter uttered the words *go out* and descended into a dramatic lecture—dating leads to sex, leads to pregnancy, leads to no college, leads to life over. She could have belittled the idea, saying her daughter was too young or too boy-crazy. But instead she stayed calm and listened to what her daughter was saying—that she liked someone and he liked her and in middle school that meant they were going out even if they didn't ever go anyplace together. The chances are better that Stephanie's daughter won't sneak around with boys behind her mother's back because she knows she can go to her mom with concerns and be taken seriously.

∽ STAY CALM

Dating or its permutations can be a very emotional *When* for parents because it signals that your adolescent is not a baby anymore. The thought that your son or daughter might be sexually desirable or sees someone else as such is difficult to accept, in part because your child is always a child in your mind. The mere mention of dating, even in its earliest forms of hanging out or going to a school dance, can bring out powerful protective instincts as well as anxiety and fear as you ponder every conceivable worst-case scenario that could be coming along. Parents of daughters worry about pregnancy and date rape. Parents of sons worry their boys might not take a "no" for no, or will get a girl pregnant. Sexually transmitted diseases are on the worry list, too. There's also a fear that your child will get emotionally burned. We want our kids to find love, but our own experiences taught us how painful relationships can turn out to be.

If you think back to chapter on development (Chapter 5), as well as your own grade school days, having romantic interests is part of healthy, normal development. When I was in fifth grade, I found out I had a girlfriend when I came back to school after being sick to discover that she had pushed our desks together. Today's adolescents have at their disposal all sorts of gadgets to broadcast their romantic interests—some post on their social networking site how long they've been with somebody (two months, five days, thirty minutes!) as if wanting to make sure their relationship status is duly noted before it changes.

My aim in this chapter is to get you to think more like Stephanie—focusing on the facts instead of the fear of what might be, while still recognizing that there are physical and emotional risks that your child needs to be prepared for, even at the earliest stages of dating. As I've said before, I don't know your child or the social norms of her peers or the community in which you live, and the meaning of going out in your community might be different than in Stephanie's daughter's middle school. Dating comes in many forms depending where you live—from hanging out at a pizza shop with a group of kids, to showing up at a scheduled time at a girl's house to meet her parents to get approval for official dating, to hooking up casually. Social norms also change and what's considered typical or normal today could be quite different a few years from now.

No matter what, the answer to "When is my child ready to date?" should be nothing short of "When I have prepared her well."

∼ GETTING PREPARED

Ideally, you should read the *How* chapter on healthy sexuality (Chapter 29), before you read this chapter, but I'll go ahead and outline a few points to get you grounded. You might be surprised by what I say. For starters, dating (in its many forms) *is* sexual. You *want* your adolescent to be sexual. Being sexual is part of *healthy* development. But (you can resume breathing now) you want your child to be sexual *without* having sex. You'll be on the losing side of this battle if you deny your child's developing sexuality and allow him to receive only toxic messages about sex. You can tell your child that sex is evil or you can teach him, beginning when he is small, about what is involved in healthy, happy relationships.

Preparation for dating should entail:

- **Seeing good role models.** Children learn the good, the bad, and the ugly of relationships by observing. You can make a point (without being too sappy) to underscore the positives that are all around you—"Look how Pop-Pop lights up when Nana comes in the room! Your dad's been giving me roses every anniversary for twelve years." Remember, preadolescence and early adolescence are the times when your child is most likely to listen to what you say, so try to counter the negative portrayals of relationships on TV with real-life lessons on commitment. You won't have to bombard your teen with marching orders as he heads off on a date—"Open the door for her," "Be sure to treat her with respect"—if he's witnessed kindness and civility at home.

- **Understanding the human body.** No matter where you stand on the issue of premarital sex, your child needs to have the facts on how pregnancy occurs and how it can be prevented. As we discussed in the sleepover chapter (Chapter 9), this generation might not be into promiscuous sex, but in some communities it's considered okay to have sexual intercourse with a friend (friends with benefits) or for girls in middle school to perform oral sex on a romantic interest of the moment. Your child needs to understand that no sexual act is physically or emotionally risk-free. In the human sexuality chapter (Chapter 29), we'll talk about the importance of having a trusted health practitioner and other significant adults, such as an aunt or uncle or older cousin, in your child's life, so he can turn to them for relationship advice or accurate information on how to protect himself. No matter how close parents are to their adolescents, some kids simply find it too weird to talk with their parents about the details of sex.

- **Understanding the full range of sexuality.** You can't turn off your child's burgeoning sexuality, but you can have a big influence on what your child thinks is normal and acceptable sexual behavior. The media bombard our kids with the message that sex is all about "doing it," but they need to be reminded that sexuality involves a range of experiences. Talking on the bus or holding hands can be sexual. So, too, can exchanging comments on Facebook or hanging out with a group of boys and girls at someone's house. You want this low-risk stage of sexuality to last as long as possible. If your adolescent feels that having a crush is sexual and "normal," she might just stop there, but when sexuality is equated with heavy petting or intercourse, she might have to go further to feel normal. By forbidding mixed-sex gatherings in middle school, you might inadvertently push your adolescent toward an intense one-on-one relationship that involves sexual activity.

- **Having the needed social skills.** The three social skills that all adolescents should have (Chapter 6) are absolutely essential for dating: (a) Say "no," and mean it; (b) shift the blame to you ("My mom won't let me date until I'm sixteen"); and (c) activate your code word to get out of a tricky situation (on a date or otherwise). Teens, especially girls, must be on guard for come-on lines and manipulation. It's so easy to fall for compliments and charm if they don't understand that people can have underlying motives.

- **Being in control of body and mind.** Date rape and relationship abuse are significant problems among teens, particularly when alcohol is involved. Your adolescent needs to know what constitutes not just physical abuse, but verbal and emotional abuse as well. Your daughter, in particular, should understand how abuse progresses: It begins with flattery and attention, moves to being told how lucky she is to have the other person, and from there descends into jealousy, control, and isolation. Texting makes it easy for emotional abuse to occur.

- **Good connections with you.** You want your child to come to you if she gets caught in a bad situation or unhealthy relationship, but you also hope she'll share some positives. Put yourself in that role of active listener, not judge, and stay as low-key as possible. Some parents get personally invested in their children's relationships, wanting to hear every detail, or see their child's popularity as a validation of their own attractiveness. Posing questions like "What's she like?" "What do you like about her?" or "Why do you find that bothersome?" will help your adolescent develop the critical thinking skills involved in finding a suitable mate. You want your child to learn that there's no such thing as a "perfect match," but that a good relationship comes about when you get what you need from another person and feel good about what you can give in turn.

Two final issues: Does it make sense to have an age requirement for dating? And should you be worried if your child shows no interest whatsoever?

Age prescriptions on dating can be just the out some kids are looking for. Charlotte is typical of a number of parents we met who do set a minimum age on this privilege. It all started when her daughter was ten and she came home to announce her best friend had a boyfriend. "When can I have a boyfriend, too?" she asked her mom. They talked about what having a boyfriend entailed—from going to someone's house with a group of kids to play video games, to going to school dances (both perfectly okay in middle school by Charlotte's thinking), to full-fledged, exclusive dating (not okay!). Charlotte told her daughter, "I think sixteen would be the age I'd consider it okay to have a boyfriend." (Notice, she hedged a bit and left room to change her mind as the time approached.) Over the next few years, the "When can I date?" conversation was repeated in varying forms, including one time when Charlotte's daughter, then fifteen, admitted to her mother, "It's just easier if I can say I can't have a boyfriend until I'm sixteen." That's shifting the blame at work!

Parents sometimes worry that their teen isn't dating or showing any interest in anyone. Parents shouldn't pressure their adolescents to ask someone to the eighth-grade dance or even the junior or senior prom. For some kids, having a boyfriend or girlfriend is part of the healthy practice needed to ultimately establish a long-lasting relationship, but others just aren't socially or emotionally ready for a romantic interest, or they're busy with other things. Don't push. Your child will find romantic happiness when he or she is ready and open to it.

Remember: There is much more about sex and sexuality in Chapter 29. If this feels like a hot-button issue you are confronting now with your teen, go to that chapter right away!

Bottom Line: Sexuality is a normal part of adolescent development. Your goal is to have your adolescent feel good about this aspect of development and develop the insights needed to find a healthy relationship later. You want her to be knowledgeable about her body, but move slowly on the physical front.

CHAPTER EIGHTEEN

~

MANAGE OWN TIME AND SCHEDULE?

DAN FELT ALMOST panicky thinking of his son's first week of college. His son was scattered and forgetful, and Dan worried about what was going to happen when he wasn't there to help him keep things straight. Would his son oversleep? Remember his class schedule? Get to the campus bookstore to pick up the books that he had ordered online? Dan got so anxious that he called his son the night before classes started to ask, "You *do* know how to set your cell phone alarm to wake you up on time, don't you?"

Dan's story of angst might give us all a good laugh if it didn't hit quite so close to home. Think for a moment about your own child. She's probably used to your waking her up, coaxing her out the door to get to school on time, and reminding her to practice her clarinet. As a busy parent you might find it easier to keep track of your child's activities, logging them into your date book along with the rest of the family's schedules. You might not always remember what you have to do, but basketball and band practices are etched in your brain.

Many parents keep on micromanaging right on through the teen years, only to see things fall apart when their kids go off to college. Having your child gradually assume responsibility for her day is a key part of her achieving independence.

Managing time means knowing what to do both when you have too little of it and when you have too much. Managing a schedule involves not just keeping track of what you have to do, but making choices about what not to do. When you teach your child to manage his time and schedule, you want to emphasize both accountability and balance. You need to be focused and committed to what you have to do or have agreed to do, but you also have to allow some time to unwind, pursue creative interests or hobbies, and eat and sleep healthily. Learning those skills step-by-step seems all the more critical because our kids are growing up in a multitasking world where constant activity is seen as a sign of success. Who hasn't had this conversation lately: "How was your summer?" "Busy. I never sat still." "How was yours?" "Busy." Being overbooked and overextended are bragging rights, and our kids hear us talk as if constant craziness is a good thing. Wouldn't it be better if we instead replied, "I have a lot going on, but I'm still finding some time to relax."

∼ STEP BY STEP, STARTING EARLY

So much attention is given to teaching kids to tell time, but we also need to teach them about time. Here are some ways to do that:

- **Put in place visual reminders.** A watch or bedside clock keeps kids on top of what time it is, and a calendar helps them conceptualize how much time is left to get ready for something (piano recital, current-event presentation) or reach a much-anticipated event— "Only three weeks till my birthday!" Encourage your child to note important dates on a bedroom calendar.
- **Teach about the importance of being *on time.*** You can do this by referencing schedules—"The bus comes at seven twenty-one," "My shift starts at three sharp," "It takes us fifteen minutes, twenty in bad traffic, to drive to your guitar teacher's house." Children learn either punctuality or tardiness from their parents, and those habits

set in for life. Much better that your child learns that the world won't wait for her.

- **Assign deadlines and expect your child to meet them.** Give guidelines like "Be dressed and ready to go by ten" or "Set the table by five-thirty" to get your child in the habit of time-related accountability. It will prepare her for *When* she has a curfew, a topic coming up in the next chapter.

∼ MIDDLE SCHOOL

Middle school is a time when your child should be refining organization and time-management skills. Try these strategies:

- **Encourage your middle schooler to faithfully use a daily planner.** Many teachers start out the year requiring the use of planners to write down homework and test dates, but the practice falls by the wayside as the months go by. Have your child use the same book to write in extracurricular activities and special events so that he begins to see that with only so many hours in a day and days in a week, he has to both plan ahead and make choices. If a sleepover is on the agenda for Saturday and he has a big test on Monday, he should begin to recognize for himself that it makes sense to get some homework done on Friday afternoon. In Chapter 22, we'll talk about parental oversight of homework, but your goal as middle school progresses should be to move away from checking what's listed in the daily planner.
- **Try to set realistic expectations around how long it takes to do things.** Ask your child once in a while, "How long do you think it will take to get your math problems done?" Then have her time it. Your child might need only thirty minutes to complete homework, or she might need double that. Even adults often underestimate the time required for a task, and coming up short creates stress and can cause a mental block that gets in the way of finishing the job or taking on the next challenge. Having too much advance time can likewise lead to last-minute anxiety if you tend to procrastinate.

Knowing how long things take is especially important for children with attention issues or other learning difficulties.

- **Introduce the strategy of making to-do lists.** If your child learns to put a combination of easy tasks (feed hamster, clean baseball cleats) and hard ones (do lab report) on the list, he'll get a better sense of forward progress in his day. Lists are also a good tool for breaking big problems into little ones, a coping technique we'll talk about more in Chapter 26. Instead of writing, "Work on research report" (Panic!), write something like "Find two online sources. Do three note cards." Your child should keep the list realistic and cross things off as they get done.

- **Don't sign up your child for a lot of activities just because you want her to do them.** Talk to her about the time commitment and whether she thinks she can handle it. How many practices? Games? What time of day will they be? Will they cut into other things she's already doing or be held at a time when she's at her best for homework? So many parents create scheduling conflicts—running their kids from activity to activity or even signing them up for slightly overlapping activities—and then get upset when their child wants to quit or has a meltdown. This is a point on which it's critical to take into consideration your child's temperament. Some kids thrive on a lot of activity involving a lot of people, while others need more alone time and space.

- **Get in the habit of having your child give you a preview of what's coming up for the week.** For example, prepare your child by saying, "I have a busy week with lots of obligations. I need you to arrange a ride home from practice on Tuesday and Wednesday. Chelsea's parents are driving the other days." This teaches your child to look a few days ahead and also reinforces the fact that you have a life, too, so she needs to plan accordingly.

- **Keep your adolescent in a bedtime routine.** Don't assign a cut-and-dried bedtime in the same way you did when your child was younger, but encourage your adolescent to wind down the day around the same time each night by listening to music or reading. This practice encourages a lifelong appreciation for building some relaxation into the end of the day and teaches teens that they need downtime to promote getting a restful sleep. Adolescents' body clocks really do tell them to stay up later and sleep in, but they still need a good eight hours of sleep a night. Anything less can lead to focusing issues the next day, and chronic sleep deprivation can lead to a pattern of underperformance and stress.

~ HIGH SCHOOL

By the start of high school, your teen should be getting himself up and keeping track of his week. He should tell you whether there will be nights he's not home for dinner because of practice or work. Other considerations:

- **Let your older teen pick and choose.** While you can encourage your kids to be active and involved, older teens should have the final say in which specific extracurricular activities they sign up for. You shouldn't insist that your seventeen-year-old go out for football just because you'll miss chatting with parents in the bleachers.
- **Sometimes allow a bit of flexibility on school nights.** A "no socializing on school nights" policy is reasonable for younger teens, but as long as your older teen is on top of schoolwork and other obligations without experiencing stress or loss of sleep, she's probably ready to have a bit more freedom on both school days and the weekend.
- **Continue to honor family time.** Even as your teen's independence grows, don't abandon expectations that she be home for family dinners at least a couple of times a week and take part in some family activities. Those connections are more important than ever.
- **Make sure you stay in the loop.** No matter how good your teen gets at running her life, she should always be required to tell you where she'll be and agree to what time she'll be home. It's a habit she needs to develop for life—she will want her roommate or boss or spouse to be concerned if she doesn't show up as planned.

Bottom Line: Adolescents who learn to manage time learn how to be organized, efficient, punctual, and accountable. They also learn the importance of leading a balanced life.

CHAPTER NINETEEN

~

STAY OUT LATE, STRETCH A CURFEW?

CURFEW IS ONE of those words that adolescents seem programmed to hate because it's often interpreted as meaning "You just want to control me," "You don't trust me," or "You're trying to ruin my life."

There's no simple way around the word, at least I haven't thought of one, but you can make the concept far more palatable to your child by how you position it. Remember the discussion in Chapter 3 about how safety is on the "approved" list of topics adolescents believe their parents are allowed to focus on? (Issues dealing with friends and personal relationships are considered off-limits.) A curfew really is a reflection of your concern for your child's safety and well-being, so present it as such. Your teen no doubt will push back with a comment such as "I'm the only kid who has to be in at eleven" (which possibly isn't true, but don't go there), but you need to convey in whatever words you're comfortable with, "I love you, I care about you, I want to help keep you safe to the best of my ability." (Notice I didn't suggest you say, "Well, I must love or care more than your friends' parents.")

∼ GETTING USED TO CURFEWS

As we discussed in the previous chapter, children should be held to some time standard well before they're out and about on their own. Getting your child in the routine of being in from playing at five or turning his lights out at ten allows him to experience structure rather than a freewheeling approach to the day.

Nighttime curfews usually don't become an issue until later in middle school, when adolescents start going to friends' houses to watch a game or to the movies. Still, most kids at this age don't have a steady social life, so curfew is often easily dealt with on a case-by-case basis. These sporadic events are a good chance for you to see how your adolescent handles the responsibility of getting home at the designated time. Does he allow enough time to walk home from his friend's house? Are he and his friends waiting where promised when you come to pick them up? Does he call if something unforeseen comes up and is going to be a bit late? These middle years are also an ideal time to engage your child in discussions about problems linked with teens out late at night, such as vandalism and underage beer parties. But make sure not to make these seem like normal events because it will make your middle schooler fear getting older or could backfire into molding a "normal" picture of adolescence that is false and will be counterproductive. Health is closely aligned with safety, so don't forget to reinforce the idea of the importance of adequate sleep for school and sports performance.

The question of "How late can I stay out?" becomes a recurring theme as teens begin to regularly spend time away from home. Some parents prefer a set curfew, say ten P.M. for a fourteen-year-old or eleven P.M. for a sixteen-year-old. Margie, a mother of four who prefers cut-and-dried rules, took the position "Nothing good happens after midnight" and didn't allow her teens out any later. There's sensibility in her approach since teens are more likely to get in crashes late at night and certainly teens may be more apt to get caught up in risky activities as the night wears on. Other parents prefer to make curfew decisions depending on the circumstances:

One night ten-thirty makes sense; another night, midnight or even later is acceptable. I like some flexibility because it encourages a teen to demonstrate responsibility in exchange for expanded privileges. That's not to say that on any given night the agreed-upon curfew is open to interpretation by your child—tonight's eleven o'clock curfew *is* eleven o'clock—but that you give your child permission ahead of time to stretch the usual curfew on a particular night (after a concert or midnight movie premiere) because he's shown that he routinely can be counted on to get home on time. A flexible curfew, particularly in the last year of high school, allows a teen to prepare for the reality of college life, where it really will be up to him to decide when to head back to the dorm. You want your teen to learn to do some advance planning around social activities and make smart decisions for himself, rather than being dependent on what someone else tells him to do.

I can't tell you what your child's curfew should be. Some communities prohibit minors from being out after a certain time, and if that's the case, your child needs to follow the law. Neither should your teen violate state driving laws, which may forbid her from driving after a certain hour until she gets a senior license.

Keeping such given factors in mind, a good starting point is to ask your teen what she thinks a reasonable curfew should be. Remember, a curfew is not a punishment but rather a tool to help keep your child safe. Your comfort level, your teen's comfort level, and the reality of your community and your child's life should all be part of the discussion. In some communities, crime and violence are very real worries, and late-night driving is a hazard for young drivers, no matter where they live. But you also need to be reasonable so that curfew doesn't become a weekly battle. Do your teen's friends live nearby? Does he have a weekend job that keeps him from meeting up with his friends until later in the evening? Will he take public transportation or rely on a friend, factors that could dictate a certain schedule? You'll always be on the defensive if your child's curfew is decidedly earlier than his close friends' curfews. This is an instance where knowing other parents and discussing communal rules comes in handy—if your child's closest friends need to be home at eleven, your rule doesn't seem harsh.

~ MAKING CURFEWS WORK FOR YOU AND YOUR TEEN

No matter what time you agree upon, be clear that you will always enforce the check-in rule that we discussed in Chapter 6. Requiring your child to say good night when he comes in, even if that means waking you, gives you the peace of mind that she's home safe and gives her a face-saving out to avoid drinking or drugs.

Curfew works best when the expectations and consequences are clearly spelled out ahead of time. Any time is too late if it interferes with school-work. Homework must be completed and she must be able to get enough sleep to focus the next day in school and manage stress. You expect a call if your child is delayed because of traffic. You expect her to follow the check-in rule. You expect her to be respectful of others who have to get up early and not blast the TV when she gets in.

Parents often turn to grounding when a teen blows curfew, which is not a surprise because their adrenaline starts pumping when the clock hits midnight. As hard as it might be, do some deep breathing, tell your child calmly that you were worried but are relieved he's home safely, then tell him you'll talk to him in the morning. Late-night discussions in the heat of anger rarely lead any-where productive. The next day, apply what you learned in Chapter 4 about discipline: that you earn freedoms by demonstrating responsibility and you lose privileges when you demonstrate that you can't handle the freedom in question. Blowing curfew should not lead to grounding for a month (unless some truly troubling circumstances are involved) but instead to a measured rollback in privileges to the point that your teen was able to meet all of your requirements.

If your teen misses his expanded eleven-thirty curfew, your response should be something like "You did well when your curfew was eleven. We'll go back to eleven for a few weeks until I see that you're once again capable of keeping track of the time."

Bottom Line: Curfews are about safety, self-control, time management, and feeling fresh for the next day. Set clear expectations and consequences and stick to them, but also be willing to consider ahead of time your teen's reasons for wanting to stay out a bit later on a given night.

CHAPTER TWENTY

~

GET A DRIVER'S LICENSE—AND A CAR?

THIS CHAPTER HAS good news. Say what? You might very well be dreading the day your teen gets his license because in your mind cars and teens equal car accidents.

But this chapter isn't designed to make you fretful or paralyzed by fear because there's so much to be positive about. The first of the good news is that there are very few car *accidents,* though there are far too many car crashes. The next piece of good news is that crashes are preventable. There are a number of proven strategies that parents can follow to significantly reduce the chances of their teen getting into a crash. This is a *When* where thoughtful, active parenting really can save your child's life.

Teen driving is a particular research interest of mine because it overlaps with my interest in helping guide parents to be a proactive force in their adolescent's life. Unfortunately, driving is too often seen simply in terms of acquiring a set of skills that then leads to passing a licensing test. Parents often have a sense that fate takes over when their new driver grabs the keys, so the best they can do is cross their fingers or say a prayer.

But the reality is that we know from an extensive body of research what causes teen crashes and we know what works to prevent them. We know that inexperience plays a huge role. Having the basic driving skills needed to get a license is only a first step; driving maturity comes with lots of experience. We know teen crashes are more apt to happen after dark and that having other kids aboard increases the risk by as much as four-fold. We know that distractions such as cell phones are problematic.

Conversely, we know that placing restrictions on nighttime driving and the carrying of peer passengers works to prevent teen crashes. So, too, does having rules in place around seat belt use and cell phones. We know that being an involved parent who sets reasonable rules and provides appropriate supervision works. In fact, one of my studies found that teens who said their parents provided them with a mix of warmth, support, and monitoring—that desirable balanced (authoritative) style of parenting outlined in Chapter 4—were about half as likely to be in crashes than teens whose parents were less involved. They were also far more likely to wear seat belts, not drive while intoxicated, and put down the cell phone while driving.

As a parent, you're in a great position to make a difference by taking deliberate steps to ensure that your teen gradually and systematically gains the needed experience both before and *after* licensing. Keeping the lines of communication open with your teen also will pay off.

All the components of effective parenting that we've been talking about—active listening, no-lecture talking, the setting of reasonable rules and monitoring, the gradual granting of more freedom when competency is demonstrated, and discipline that ties consequences directly to the behavior at hand—will come together to help keep your teen safe and reduce the parent-child conflicts that frequently arise around driving. By positioning all your conversations about driving around safety issues, your teen is less likely to feel as though you're trying to clamp down and control him just as he's about to bust out in the world. Because a car truly can be deadly, you don't want the car to become the place where your child rebels against you or acts out his freedom fantasies. Instead, you want the car to be the means by which your teen demonstrates that he's capable and responsible and ready for even more privileges.

~ RITE OF PASSAGE

Getting a driver's license is one of those rites of passage that seem indelibly marked on our brains. You probably remember the details of whether you passed or flunked the test on your first try and what kind of car you drove. You might even remember that first night out with your friends. Seeing your teen heading down that same road toward independence no doubt triggers both pride and trepidation. "He really is growing up! Will I ever not worry when he takes the car?"

No matter how the statistics are sliced, there is no soft-pedaling the dangers that come with getting a driver's license. Per mile driven, teen drivers aged sixteen to nineteen are four times more likely to get in a fatal crash than older drivers, and crashes are the leading cause of teen death. In 2009, about 3,000 teens aged fifteen to nineteen died in vehicle crashes, and more than 350,000 were injured. Luckily, states have stepped up to address the hazards by enacting graduated driver's licensure laws, which put in place three stages: (a) a learner's permit; (b) a junior license that sets restrictions on nighttime driving and perhaps the number of passengers allowed; and (c) full licensing. As you consider whether your teen is ready to drive, you need to remember that state laws offer a *minimum* age of licensure. Your teen might be allowed under state law to get a learner's permit at age sixteen and a license six months later, but you need to be the ultimate judge of whether your teen is ready to take on this responsibility.

Driving a car is a complex process that involves paying attention, ignoring distractions, judging distances, and anticipating problems, as well as all the mechanical aspects of operating a car. Now think about what you know about adolescent development (Chapter 5). While teens are moving toward being abstract thinkers (as opposed to concrete ones), the area of the brain involved in organizing thoughts, weighing consequences, and keeping impulses in check does not fully mature until well into a person's twenties. Teens who show a proclivity for risk taking are probably going to take risks with driving.

This is a *When* where it's critical to consider your child's temperament—factors such as distractibility—and general level of maturity, as well as his social skills. Having good grades does not automatically translate into being a careful driver. The influence of peers is huge with driving, and chances are good your teen will drive differently with friends along. A driver needs to be in control of everything that's going on in his car while ignoring distractions, and that's not an easy thing even for adults. You may instruct your teen to take only one passenger, but if she's particularly susceptible to peer influences, it will be hard for her to say no when kids beg for a ride home. Another possible warning signal: If your teen uses alcohol or illicit drugs or has a short fuse that explodes into intense anger, she may not be able to keep those dangerous behaviors out of the car. If your judgment is that your teen isn't ready to drive, for whatever reason, you need to slow down the process.

Vickie, a nurse, and her husband, Thomas, a police officer, came to the driving issue as both parents and professionals who see the hazards. They worried that their son was still on the immature side socially and tended to get caught up in things without thinking. Their son, however, was also an enterprising young man who liked to work hard and earn money. The couple decided to offer their son $1,000 toward his savings account for each year he postponed driving—an amount equal to what he would have to pay for car insurance once he got a license.

"He was very money oriented, so we thought our plan would work," Vickie said. "We told him he could spend the money or save it up for his insurance." Their son accepted the offer for two years, so Vickie and her husband didn't have to put their foot down. When it came time for their daughter to get her permit, they felt she was ready for the responsibility, but they made the same offer anyhow. She turned the $1,000 down.

"We let both kids know that our concerns were all about safety. We weren't trying to keep them home or keep them away from their friends," Vickie said.

She and her husband put the emphasis on the right word—*safety*. Driving is a safety issue pure and simple, and safety always needs to be your number one priority. Your overriding message to your teen should be that while you share his excitement for this coming milestone, you're committed to doing everything you can to help him become a skilled and responsible driver when the time seems right.

~ START EARLY

Kids begin to learn to drive when they're still buckled in the backseat. They watch you put on your seat belt, slow down when the light turns yellow, come to a stop at stop signs, and sit patiently in traffic instead of getting all worked up. They watch as you put away your phone until your arrive at your destination, or pull off the road to make a call. At least that's what I hope they learn from watching you.

The next phase of driving lessons comes during early adolescence. Remember, kids pay attention to what their parents say in these preteen years, so it's a perfect time to point out confusing intersections, dangerous curves, and drivers chatting on their cells. Talking about your driving fitness is another good topic: "I'm not up for driving if I don't get a good night's sleep." Or "Can you adjust the dial because I can't take my eyes off the road?" There are also, sadly, plenty of headlines to provide grist for impromptu discussions—fatal crashes on prom night or a crash involving a carload of kids being driven by a newly minted driver. Remember what researcher Judith Smetana said about what topics adolescents consider "acceptable" for their parents to wade into (Chapter 3)? Safety is okay; most friendship issues are not. You're more apt to be heard if you keep focused on safety, as opposed to "See what can happen when you hang out with your friends?"

You need to start thinking about your teen's readiness to get a driver's permit before the allowable date rolls around. Teens see it as a huge deal to get their learner's permit, and it's best to get ahead of the conversation rather than pull a last-minute surprise. Let your adolescent know that learning to drive is a process and that you'll evaluate as you go—during the permit phase and after he gets his license. The pre-permit phase is a good time to float the idea of a parent-child driving contract, which will lay out ground rules for safe driving. You don't have to nail down the details quite yet, but if you introduce the concept of a contract now, your teen won't interpret it as your being a killjoy just as he is basking in the glow of passing his driver's test.

Use the contract to spell out the nonnegotiable aspects of driving behavior—no speeding, no cell phones, no drinking—and delineate the ways that you will monitor your teen's performance. Consequences for breaking the rules should also be included in the contract, including what will happen in the case of speeding or parking tickets. You should include a plan for increasing your teen's use of the car as he proves himself to be a responsible driver, because that's a good motivator. The contract can also save haggling by stating who pays how much for gas, car insurance, and maintenance.

Once your teen gets his permit, reiterate how seriously you take your responsibility of teaching him to drive. Remember, your state sets *minimum* requirements for the length of time a teen needs to hold a learner's permit as well as the number of hours a teen has to log behind the wheel before getting licensed. Let your teen know that you will gradually introduce him to varying driving conditions—traffic volume, time of day, weather, highway versus back roads and city streets—as you see him gain skill and confidence. It's recommended that teens get at least fifty hours of on-the-road experience before they get their license. More is better. Professional lessons can also be helpful because the instructor is trained to deal with novices and is a neutral person your teen is likely to listen to.

A license is merely the first step in the process of becoming a good driver. You should become familiar with your state's graduated driving laws. These laws slow down the licensing process and are designed to gradually expose teens to increasing complexity on the road. But you should institute your own restrictions because your state may not have all of the restrictions in place that are known to protect teens and prevent crashes. You might also make sure that other parents in your community are aware of all of the protections so your teen won't feel alone in having these measures enforced. Here is what I recommend based on expert recommendations and research:

- Unless it is necessary for your rural community and farming, do not get a learner's permit until sixteen at the earliest.
- Offer at least fifty hours of adult-supervised driving practice with a minimum of ten hours of nighttime driving.
- Allow at least six months of practice time from the time your teen gets a learner's permit to the time he can go for a license.
- No cell phone use in the car unless it is parked.
- No teen passengers for at least the first six months of driving after the license. No more than one teen passenger for at least the second six months of driving.
- No unsupervised driving between ten P.M. and five A.M.
- Continue with supervision and exposing your teen to new and varied driving conditions of increasing complexity after the license.
- Talk about substance use and driving and institute the Students Against Destructive Decisions Contract for Life (sadd.org/contract.htm). Add "code word" to the contract to make it easier for your teen to call you if he is in trouble.
- Consider getting professional on-the-road driver's education instruction. But even if your state says you can loosen any of the above restrictions because your teen has had driver's ed, do not take them away.

You should also control the keys at least for the first six months to get your teen in the habit of saying where he's driving and when he'll be back. Have him put the keys on a communal hook when he gets home. Under no circumstances should you allow your child to violate state rules—if the curfew for junior drivers is eleven P.M., that needs to be followed, and the same goes for passenger limits. Since most teen crashes are caused by rookie mistakes, remind your teen that experience only comes with time and that he'll need to demonstrate that he's good at the basic driving challenges before you trust him to handle even more. If you think back to the dilemma Steve had faced when his son had asked to drive his friends to an amusement park two and a half hours away, the problem wasn't that his son was a careless driver. Steve just hadn't given his son the chance to master highway driving. Once your teen gets his license, be the passenger as he takes on more challenging conditions.

Even with your focus on safety, be prepared for your teen to say, "You don't trust me," or "I always knew you hated my friends." Your responses should avoid defensiveness and reiterate your commitment to her safety: "More crashes happen after dark, and until you have more experience I just can't let you take that safety risk," or "I really love your friends and care about your safety, so please let me drive all of you to the concert."

It makes sense that how parents go about parenting—their parenting style—has an effect on their teen's driving habits, but even I was surprised just how much a difference it makes. When our research team at The Center for Injury Research and Prevention at The Children's Hospital of Philadelphia asked more than fifty-six hundred teens from across the nation to categorize their parents' approach to parenting, those who reported that their parents set rules in a helpful and supportive way and provided reasonable supervision (authoritative parents) were about half as likely to be in a crash. They were also 71 percent less likely to drink and drive and 29 percent less likely to use their cell phones to talk or text while driving, compared to those teens with less involved parents. Having authoritative or even stricter parents (authoritarian) also made it more likely that the teens used seat belts and avoided speeding.

Technology may fast be overtaking some of the monitoring parents do—such as checking the car for signs of drinking and watching periodically to check seat belt use. New tracking devices allow parents to keep tabs on where their teen driver goes, how fast she drives, and how long she stays at stopping points. Some GPS systems will even send an e-mail or text alert if the driver deviates from a certain route.

It will be up to you if you use these technologies to support your monitoring, but they should never replace open communication. Kids need to understand that your monitoring of their driving is an act of love and caring, not spying and control.

~ TO BUY A CAR?

Many teens ask their parents to buy them a car or, in some families, parents give their teens a car as a sixteenth birthday present. For families in rural areas with great driving distances or families where parents work, giving a teen a car might seem like a necessity. You need to think long and hard about that, however, because the research suggests that teens are more likely to be in a crash when they have their own car. Another study, which was done at Children's Hospital and included more than twenty-one hundred teen drivers, found that those who had "primary access" to a car were more than twice as likely to be in a crash and were about 25 percent more apt to use their cell phones and speed than teens who had to ask to take the car. Why that is the case isn't totally clear. It could be that when a teen drives his parent's car, there's a greater expectation that he'll be monitored, so he's less likely to drive recklessly or allow his passengers to get out of line.

If a family needs to buy an additional car so a child can get to work or practice, parents should be clear that the car is theirs and that they will allow their child to use it with permission as long as he follows agreed-upon rules. While your tendency may be to give your teen access to the oldest car in the family or to get the best bargain in a used car, it makes sense to be sure your new driver uses the car with the most up-to-date safety standards.

Some teens want to work so they can buy their own car. That is a tricky issue. You want your teen to have goals, and saving up for a big-ticket item such as a car takes hard work and a commitment to saving. Tell your teen that you admire his goal, but expect to be included in the final decision because, again, you care about his safety. By getting the conversation going around safety, you will have a say in whether he buys a flashy vehicle or one with a proven safety record.

Bottom Line: Driving presents a real risk to your teen's safety. The good news is that "accidents" are rare, crashes are preventable, and your involvement in both teaching and monitoring is key to your teen's driving safety. For more information visit The Center for Injury Research and Prevention's Web site at teendriversource.org.

CHAPTER TWENTY-ONE

~

GET A JOB?

THIS IS ANOTHER one of those topics, like allowance, that parents tend to divide philosophically into two camps. On the one side are parents who feel strongly that their kid's job is to go to school and nothing should interfere. On the other side are parents who believe that their teen will learn responsibility and financial savvy by holding a part-time job. There are plenty of valid points on both sides of the job argument, but the key is finding a reasonable balance that takes into consideration other aspects of your teen's life, including academics, extracurricular demands, and leisure time. A job should help promote healthy development—socially, emotionally, physically—not stymie it.

I can't give you a formula to say that adolescents should devote X number of hours to school, X number of hours to sports or other activities, and X number to work. Temple University psychology professor Laurence Steinberg has research indicating that grades suffer when teens work more than twenty hours a week. He and other researchers who have looked at the impact of teen employment see other potential downsides, too—studies suggest that teens who work long hours are more prone to risky behavior, including delinquency, smoking, drinking, and drug use. Such findings are alarming at first glance and are worthy of your consideration, but please don't overinterpret them. There could be multiple reasons to explain the findings. A teen might seek out a job because he wants money for cigarettes and alcohol, or it's possible that working in an environment with older people provides access to those very items. It might also be that teens who already feel disenfranchised with school or are drawn to risky activities are more likely to seek employment. None of those points may describe your teen at all. Also, for some kids, a job provides an excuse to stay away from drinking parties or gang activity, and for a kid who is floundering at school, a job could provide a needed spark.

Keep in mind that work can take varying forms—it can be a paying job with set hours, but it can also entail a regular volunteer position, or something occasional such as babysitting or shoveling snow. No matter what, teens need time to play, just like small children do. While your teen probably no longer hangs out on your backyard swing set, he needs unstructured time to unwind and let his imagination run wild. Any job should leave time left over to be with friends and take part in family activities, because those familiar connections provide a protective effect.

～ WHY WORK?

All those caveats aside, jobs no doubt can provide teens with important lessons that will stay with them long after they turn in their badge. It's always interesting to listen to a group of adults talk about their first jobs—they reminisce about how little they got paid or their crazy boss, but they almost always say that stocking shelves or answering phones taught them something that still pays off in what they do today. In some cases, a job at a summer camp or hospital or other place pointed them down a career path. And we must not forget that in today's economy, most families appreciate a teen earning spending money, and in some families it's an absolute necessity that everyone pulls their weight. Either way, the ability to contribute holds value.

We also must not forget that every kid needs the experience of being successful. It is critical to their sense of self-worth, their resilience, and their capacity to thrive. Not every teen is destined to go to college, and not all will thrive in school. Of course, we must first give them the opportunity to succeed in school by offering a wide variety of curricula so each can feel engaged and find an area in which to excel. But then we have to look at our children and acknowledge that the world of work may be the place they will get a confidence boost by discovering their competencies. I am not suggesting this as an alternative to school and still suggest limiting work hours. Instead I am hoping that a teen who has gained confidence will also feel better in school.

Teens who work learn to keep track of a schedule and be punctual, follow workplace rules, and interact with people of different ages and backgrounds. In many cases, they get proficient at money transactions and master the art of being polite when feeling harried or put upon. It's a confidence booster to hear you're doing a good job from someone other than Mom or Dad. For some kids with time management problems, having more to do can be better than having lots of time to fritter away, though there is a tipping point where it is impossible to do it all and education has to be top priority.

Getting a paycheck gives teens a sense of accomplishment and independence because they no longer have to hit up their parents for money for every little thing, and money means more when you earn it yourself. A paycheck can be a real eye opener because teens see evidence of how much work it takes to pay for things they take for granted—ten hours of work won't even buy a pair of basketball shoes!—and how much goes toward taxes.

Lynn, the mother of three children, said she expects her kids to have jobs in their nonsports seasons not because they need the money but because they get experience with demands that are different from those found in the classroom or on the playing field.

"I'm adamant that my kids have jobs, but I'm shocked at how much they like them," Lynn said. Her high school senior, an honors student who works at a garden center, came home proud as could be when she was named "top cashier" for the month—a recognition that she was a dependable, efficient, and a pleasant worker. Lynn notices that her son, who is quiet and introspective, shows more confidence since he began working. She likes that he experiences the "hard part of low-paying jobs," such as sweeping floors at closing time, because he doesn't see much of that side of life in the affluent community where they live.

Lynn's attitude is refreshing because so many parents view their adolescents' jobs mostly as a means to build a résumé that will catch the attention of college admissions officers. That attitude can lead parents to nix the idea of working as a waitress or playground helper, instead steering their teen toward every conceivable extracurricular activity and volunteer position. Teens more and more are arriving at college with thick portfolios of experiences—and in some cases an accompanying air of entitlement—but have never learned the basics of the workplace, such as properly filling out paperwork, showing up on time, dressing neatly, and giving the boss as much notice as possible when you need a day off. Sometimes it's the very routine of work that teens find appealing—so much is required of them at school, but at work they might have a very specific task to tend to. Don't belittle a job because it doesn't sound impressive. A budding musician might enjoy working in a deli precisely because it is so different from her other focus.

Adolescents should learn to respect hard, honest work, and you want them to appreciate workers at all levels of the economy. Anyone who's manned the grill at a fast-food restaurant probably is less apt to bark at a worker when an order comes out wrong. I worked painting houses beginning at fourteen, and the experience has given me lasting respect for laborers.

~ THINK THINGS THROUGH

Here are some points to consider with your adolescent:

- **Talk with your teen about why he wants to work.** Is it for spending money? To buy a car or other big-ticket item? To save up for college or car insurance? To pursue a particular interest? To gain a certain skill or type of experience? Because all of his friends are working? There's no right or wrong answer to this question, but knowing your child's motives or goals will help you guide his decision making.

- **Take stock of how she's handling what's already on her plate.** How are her grades? What are the expectations of the sports, clubs, or other activities she participates in? If your teen is already feeling overbooked, a job will only add to the stress. It's hard for a kid to constantly split loyalties—cutting out of practice early to get to work or having to constantly take off work because of sports.
- **Consider the specific demands of the job.** Are a set number of hours required? How about time off? Is the employer a known entity in the community and is the working environment safe? Working close to home not only saves commuting time and gas, it can strengthen your child's sense of connection to his community.
- **Don't forget good nutrition and sleep.** Many part-time jobs start right around dinnertime, making it impossible to eat a decent meal. Teens need eight to nine hours of sleep, and long work hours piled on top of schoolwork can cut into that.
- **Look at how the job would affect the overall functioning of your family.** Does your teen expect you to drive him back and forth? Would that fit with your schedule? Would a job mean you could no longer count on him in a bind to watch a younger sibling after school?

Looking at each of those issues might lead you and your adolescent to conclude that a job isn't a good idea for the time being or that a better strategy to earn some money would be to put out flyers around the neighborhood that she's available for babysitting or dog walking. It's better for your adolescent to start out slowly with work (remember the step-by-step strategy) than to drown in anxiety.

If your teen decides to seek employment, establish clear expectations around existing commitments. You expect her to keep up her grades, be accountable to teams or clubs, and join in a reasonable number of family events. Let her know that you care deeply about her health and well-being and that you reserve the right to put a stop to the job if concerns arise. Potential worry signs would be if grades fall, your child takes "easy" classes to have more time to work, or old friends start fading from the picture.

Also establish expectations for what she'll do with the money. Do you expect your teen to bank a chunk of each paycheck to help pay for college or car insurance? Can she spend her money however she wants, or do you expect to be asked for advice or approval on major purchases, such as a car?

If you can, drop into your child's workplace from time to time, not to mortify her with a gushy hello, but to just get a sense of things. Sadly, some employers will take advantage of young people, so your teen needs to keep track of his hours and pay and speak up if there's confusion. Knowing how to say *no* confidently and respectfully is important for the workplace, because it can be hard for a kid to turn down a request to take an extra shift. Girls especially must understand the many variations of sexual harassment. The boss will probably not offer a raise or promotion in exchange for sexual favors, but bosses and coworkers might make your teen uncomfortable with references to her clothes or body shape.

This is a *When* where it's important to reassess with your teen how the job is working out in the bigger scheme of things. Tell your teen that you applaud his hardworking nature, but you want to make sure the job is not taking over his life. An after-school job might be manageable in tenth grade, but when the crush of studying for SATs or ACTS and doing college visits and applications begins, it may be too much. Later in senior year, a job might be just what your teen needs to keep busy and away from trouble when the social frenzy of approaching graduation takes hold.

Bottom Line: There's a lot be learned from working, but a job should help, not harm, your teen's development.

CHAPTER TWENTY-TWO

~

MAKE EDUCATIONAL CHOICES?

FINDING THE RIGHT BALANCE of involvement in your child's education can be tough because we all want to help our kids succeed. We know that getting a good education and doing well in school matters in a competitive world, and we don't want our kids to be left behind. When your child was young, you might have obsessed over finding the right day care, quizzed him on spelling words and multiplication tables, and helped him build a display for the science fair. Your latest worry might be over whether he takes regular or honors math, or maybe you're already deep into the college search.

This chapter will address some key educational issues on the way from middle school to college, all of them situations that challenge parents to decide how much room to give their adolescents to work things through by themselves. Research clearly shows that kids do better in school when their parents are engaged in education, and parents should be interested in what their kids are learning and experiencing in school. If it's possible in your life, be involved in your child's school, whether as a volunteer or PTA member, and do your best to attend parent-teacher conferences and school events. You want your adolescent to know you care that he does well in school. No one should condone slacking off.

But what we're going to talk about here is your approach. Do you continue to manage every detail—homework, test scores, teacher encounters, college applications—right on through the day you kiss your kid good-bye? Or do you encourage your adolescent to start to troubleshoot for himself and arrive at his own thoughtful decisions about courses and school selection? Do you push or step back?

The answers aren't necessarily easy for parents. Perhaps you regret your own underperformance in school or know from your experiences what can happen when the goal of getting into the "right college" takes over a kid's life and then fails to materialize. Or perhaps you realize that you owe much to the educational opportunities that were presented to you, and you want the same good fortune for your child.

If hovering and micromanaging every aspect of your child's academic life was best for your child's success, I absolutely would be recommending it here. But since the ultimate goal of parenting is to foster your child's resilience, I'll focus on ways you can gradually let go and allow your adolescent to feel more competent, confident, and in control of his own destiny as he moves along in school. Coming up in the *How* section, Chapter 25 is devoted to what it means for a teen to be "authentically successful." The cultivation of healthy attitudes around success and failure is key to raising adolescents who not only thrive in the classroom but develop a lifelong desire for learning. We'll also talk some more in that chapter about your use of praise and criticism, and why you want your child be a high achiever who values effort, not a perfectionist who only focuses on the grade.

I'm not asking you to choose between resilience and success for your child, or happiness and success, because I know that resilient, happy children are successful. Let's get started toward that aim by considering some specific academic issues that you're sure to wrestle with during adolescence:

Homework. At a recent back-to-school night, two high school teachers used a word to describe homework that really made sense. They said homework was "practice." It's a good concept because our kids spend a lot of time practicing sports or an instrument or video games, and they know what it takes to become competent: putting in the time, focus, consistency, a willingness to look at what didn't go as expected and either redouble efforts or come up with a new game plan. If you look at homework through the lens of resilience, the goal is to encourage that competence. Homework can become a nightly battle when your child feels as though you're trying to control what he does, as opposed to supporting his desire to be a successful student who can cope with the increasing demands of his education.

It might have made sense to have your young child do his work at the kitchen table while you made dinner, but by middle school adolescents should be comfortable doing homework pretty much on their own. Checking homework is okay with young children (some schools require a parent's signature), but if you continue to insist on doing it into middle school or even high school, you will establish the perfect setup for homework to become a control issue. You want your adolescent to be a self-starter and experience satisfaction in sticking to it. Instead, use homework assignments as a springboard to talk with your child about what he is learning in school and what particularly interests him or where he might need added help. Establish expectations—"I expect you to do your homework, be prepared for class and tests, and to come to me if you need help or are feeling overwhelmed or offtrack"—but then back off on a day-to-day basis.

Because many middle school and high school teachers now routinely post assignments online, it's easy for parents to fall into the habit of double-checking what needs to get done, but I urge you to resist unless your child has a particular learning issue that can interfere with his school performance. Instead of checking homework, try something like, "Let me know if there's anything you want me to look over or brainstorm with you tonight." That signals that you care about your child's school performance, but you trust him to buckle down. Don't be surprised if your young teen still asks you to quiz him. Make it fun and acknowledge that his study efforts seem to be paying off.

Some parents make it their habit to read every book their child is assigned to read as a way to help their child shape ideas for classroom discussions and papers. It seems like a harmless strategy, but think again of the message you're sending: "I'm worried you can't come to your own good conclusions about this book." Wouldn't it be better for your teen to see that you love reading for the sake of reading and then you swap ideas on the books each of you enjoys?

Middle school usually marks the beginning of students' having multiple teachers, so help your adolescent to get organized with colored folders, binders, and a daily planner. Adolescents should have more leeway on where and when they study, though in front of the TV should not be an option. Some research suggests that varying studying locations might actually lead to better learning. It makes sense that you might get refreshed and refocused by switching from your usual study base periodically. This is a good example of when consideration of your child's temperament (attention, distractibility) comes into play. You might no longer insist that homework be started at four P.M., but you can set the expectation that your teen wrap things up by a certain time in the evening.

Some parents insist that their adolescent study a certain amount of time each night, regardless of assigned homework. Telling your adolescent how much she has to study can be shortsighted because study needs change all the time. In the real world of work, demands ebb and flow, allowing opportunities to slow down and refresh so you're charged for the next big push.

Troubleshooting. E-mail makes it easy to communicate with teachers, but it can also lead to a tendency to intervene with every little thing. Try to follow the twenty-four-hour rule when it comes to e-mails, unless it's something of immediate consequence. You may react to something in the moment—"Why did you assign one hundred pages to read over break?!"— that really is inconsequential in the great scheme of things. Teachers want to know if there are circumstances affecting your child's school performance, but you also want the benefit of a teacher viewing your child through her own eyes, rather than relying on your interpretation all the time.

By middle school, you want to encourage your child to begin troubleshooting for himself, though you'll probably still need to lend some support. Asking for makeup work for the days he was home sick is not taxing for many kids, but asking a teacher to explain a grade can be scary. Speaking up for himself requires an adolescent to be assertive but respectful with adults—a skill that comes with practice. You can get your adolescent launched by gradually phasing out your involvement: Talk about how he wants you to word your queries to the teacher; then, as issues come up, role-play with him how to strike the right tone—confident but not aggressive to the point the teacher becomes defensive. Your adolescent might decide he's ready to handle something, or wants you present or to be available to the teacher afterward as a backup. Eventually, your teen should know to how to handle concerns himself, with the assurance that you'll help out if things remain unresolved. Teachers will often say that parents today are too quick to jump in on disciplinary matters, perhaps because of that societal attitude that no one should be able to correct other people's children. I urge you not to step in to try to stop disciplinary action unless something is truly out of line. Teachers and schools have rules, and though your child, and you, might not agree with all of them, your child needs to face the consequences for breaking them and then move on.

Adapting to teachers. Some schools have grown so weary of parents trying to switch their child's teacher assignments that they wait until the last moment, or, in the case of high schools, hand out schedules on opening day. The notion that you need to find the "perfect teacher" for your child, or that your child needs to avoid a certain teacher, is problematic. Remember, your job as parent is not to pave a smooth path for your adolescent or to make her life easy, but to help her adapt and thrive in challenging situations. In the real world, you can't really pick your boss, but you can figure out how to make the most of whatever boss you have and the position you hold. The very teacher you find dull might turn out to inspire your child, and the very teacher your older child loved might not be as comfortable a fit for your younger child. Many of us have had to admit that a crusty English teacher did indeed teach us how to write. While you are no doubt the best advocate for your child, a better approach is to help your child find ways to adapt to a teacher's style, whether it's keeping a super-neat binder or being on top of last-minute assignments. You want your child to respect his teachers and forge those protective connections that are part of resilience, and you undermine that process when you criticize teachers in your child's presence or make it seem that you, not the teacher or school, always know best. If your high schooler wants a teacher or schedule switch, for whatever reason, he should be the one making the request, with your backup if needed. It's good practice for college.

Online grade reports. Many schools have adopted online tools that allow parents to check grades and see if homework assignments are complete. Such tools are a blessing and a curse for parents. On the plus side, you can see if your child is struggling or slacking off. On the downside, the ability to continually monitor your child's performance can drive you crazy. The program only tells about grades, not anything about learning or effort, so you're getting an incomplete picture.

As with any monitoring program, you need to be clear with your child on how you are going to use the technology and what you are going to do with the information you get. Will you check on grades once a week, twice a week, every other week? If grades are low or homework is missing, what will your response be? Screaming? Criticizing? Punishing? If you use this online tool to merely to react in the moment, you'll end up with just another source of tension between your child and you.

The less you treat this technology like spyware, the better. If you see the tool as something that allows your child the chance to give you a peek at what's going on in his world, you're more likely to draw him into meaningful discussions about what classes challenge or interest him the most, how to better organize his week or seek out extra help from a teacher, and whether he's feeling stressed because he's juggling too much.

Consider coming up with an agreement with your child about how the two of you will utilize the grade-reporting tool throughout the year. For instance, you will check the grade site together every Thursday evening and if work is incomplete or tests scores show more studying is needed, your adolescent will be expected to stay in one night of the weekend to catch up. If you're not prone to doing things on a set schedule, consider the approach of one mother who gives her kids a heads-up before she goes online as a way to make it less confrontational. She tells them, "I'm going to check the school site in a bit. Is there anything you want to talk about?"

Your goal should always be to stimulate conversation around what your child is learning. I don't believe in rewards or punishments for grades. The real danger with having a grade-reporting tool at your ready disposal is that your child starts viewing his worth by what the computer is telling you. Try to keep both your praise and criticism in check, because one week's worth of As or Cs does not a person make. Also remember that it's the rare human being who excels at everything. Expect your child to be better in some subjects than others, but if grades in one given subject are all over the board or all grades are heading south, that could be a sign that your child is being inconsistent with homework and studying, feeling overwhelmed, or perhaps even subconsciously decided to take herself off the academic playing field. We'll talk more about that phenomenon in the *How* chapter on success (Chapter 25).

Course selection. After years of being told precisely what subjects they have to study, adolescents usually are excited to take their first elective course. Often in middle school they can select a language or choose from electives such as cooking or shop to fill a free period. Unfortunately, the enthusiasm is often quickly squashed by parents who are ten steps ahead and thinking about what their child's college applications should look like. A teen wants to take French and his parents tell him Spanish is the only way to go in today's global world. Or the parent nixes the idea of a woodworking or songwriting class because it doesn't seem serious enough for a kid with college aspirations. (Never mind that being good with your hands and having a 3-D visual ability is a must for so many professions and trades.) Kids need creative time, both at school and at home, and not every class needs to be of the same intensity.

Many parents step up the managing of their children's academics come high school because the pressure is on to produce the right package for college admissions. It's a message that schools reinforce, too, often beginning from the first semester of freshman year. Packing schedules with every conceivable course is routine now, sometime to the point that students don't even have a set time for lunch. Guiding your teen through these high-pressure years involves a balancing act. Your teen needs to take the courses that are expected for the type of college or course of study he hopes to pursue, but he also needs time for rest and socializing and to explore a creative interest, such as music or art. When teens are pushed into taking all AP and honors courses, it implies that they are expected to not only be good but outstanding at everything. Overmanaged, overscheduled adolescents tend toward perfectionism, which isn't a good thing because it gets in the way of a student's creativity, innovation, and willingness to think outside the box and take risks. Perfectionists will do anything to get the grade. There will be a lot more about this in the *How* section.

Picking a school. High school choice may not be a possibility where you live. But if there are school options to consider—public, charter, magnet, vocational, single sex, private, even boarding school—you want to focus on the place that will give your kid an opportunity to experience success, whether that's academically or through the arts or sports. Look at the school's culture and compare it with your child's style and learning experience so far. Is it test heavy? Big on project learning? Nurturing or competitive? Will it make your bright kid feel average? Or your struggling student to feel more enthused about school? Project-based learning, for instance, might force a shy kid to come out of herself a bit, or a super-competitive school might push a perfectionist even further to that extreme.

Picking the right high school can become a bigger-than-life deal for families who are intent on gaining the edge they think will allow their children to stand out from the pack in college admissions as opposed to finding a school where their kids can find their own ways to shine. You have to ask yourself if a certain school is *your* dream or your child's? Whether you're pushing too much or too little? Whether the school will allow your child to grow in new ways or settle into a familiar routine? Many kids really do reinvent themselves in high school and sometimes, but certainly not always, that happens best in a new setting. Listen to what your child is saying about academics, friendships, and extracurricular interests and then be confident that she'll make the most of the choice you make together.

∿ COLLEGE ADMISSIONS

Parents' involvement in their child's academics gets really put to a test when college starts to loom on the horizon. The college admissions process is many teens' rite of passage into the adult world but, unfortunately, parents more and more are seizing control of it. They are taking what should be an exciting time of self-reflection and exploration for their teens and turning it into a high-stakes game in which the end point is either success or failure.

I can understand why parents get wrapped up in the college hunt. The competition can be tough for college entrance and getting a scholarship requires even more diligence. Also, let's face it: You can't be casual about such a big-ticket expenditure. With an economy that is never predictable, it makes sense that parents want their kids to get as good an education as possible so they can land a decent job.

The problem comes when parents take charge of the college search and selection process as if it were their own. Think of how jarring that seems to a teen. Here, you've been showing your appreciation that your teen is thinking wisely and acting responsibly by granting him more freedom, and now you're jamming on the brakes and signaling, "I'm at the wheel."

If you focus on one or two schools and your child doesn't get fat acceptance envelopes from those places, then your child has "failed" on his rite of passage into adulthood. The process gets all the more confusing and frightening to teens because they're also hearing, perhaps from their parents, friends, and schools, that there's a "perfect school" somewhere out there for them ("Yikes! How in the world do you find it?") and that they better pick carefully because the rest of their life rides on their decision.

One mother told us that when her daughter was in the eighth grade she printed out the application for a certain top-shelf school so that her daughter knew "what she had to do to get in." You could argue that the girl now had a good goal to shoot for, but in doing so she might be closing her eyes to numerous opportunities that her mother couldn't imagine.

You need to curb that sort of one-directional thinking. There is no "perfect school," though every kid can find a number of schools that would be a good fit. What matters in the long haul in the workplace is that you value hard work, have good interpersonal skills that enable you to be collaborative, keep your skills sharp and up-to-date, and have the confidence to take risks and tackle challenges rather than being content with what's easy and familiar. Those qualities will get nurtured when your child is in a college environment that makes it possible for her to grow academically, as well as emotionally, socially, and morally. If you think of all the many traits you hope your child will have going into the adult world, then that narrow list of colleges you have planted in your brain suddenly grows quite long.

So what should a parent do or not do? We'll look some more at the college admissions process in Chapter 25 when we talk about the meaning of authentic success, but let's briefly consider a few points here:

- **Be a stable force in a shifting world.** We've talked about this concept earlier in the book. Your job as a parent is to provide guidance as your teen gets comfortable charting his own course. Your teen might very well look to you for advice on meeting deadlines for college applications so there's not as much last-minute scramble, but just knowing you're nearby as a constant, unwavering support is the best help of all.
- **Don't write the essay.** If you tell your teen what to write in his college essay, it's tantamount to saying, "You're not good enough the way you are so you need to beef things up." Of course, encourage your teen to seek out an English teacher to review his essay and be willing to give your own constructive feedback if asked.
- **Don't take over on college visits.** Your teen might not say much, or even a word, as you go around on a college tour, but that could be because he's feeling anxious and is busy taking everything in. Resist the urge to jump in and ask the tour guide your own questions. Limit your comments and watch your teen's reactions as you go around the campus. Afterward, draw him into a conversation about his impressions instead of rendering your opinion off the top.

- **Be honest but not heavy-handed about practical issues.** Finances and location need to be strong considerations, but try not to limit your child's college exploration too much at first. Go easy on pushing your alma mater. Debbie, who works in the financial field, and Rich discovered the benefits of using Excel spreadsheets with their kids as they faced college choices because it allowed them to take some of the emotion out of the process. Together with their kids they created spreadsheets with categories such as size, major, location, tuition costs, and available loans and scholarships, and then used the information to ask good questions: "What added value would come with the more expensive choice?" "How much of a loan would you need for this school?" "Do you want to be within easy driving distance of home?" They wanted their kids to own their decision in every possible way, not to blame them for forcing them into a choice. Spreadsheets are great, but remind your teen to check his gut, too.

- **Watch your emotions.** Much of your child's anxiety around the college search could be coming from you. You're probably anxious about how things will turn out, but also at the thought that this it— you really are *Letting Go.* Seeing your kid filling out college applications is a reminder that he's about to leave home, and that can stir those conflicting feelings of pending loss.

  Don't let the application process become a fight or so all-consuming that you can't enjoy the many pleasures of your child's last year at home. A lot of the anxiety about the college search is that everyone is talking about it. Try not to talk with other parents about where your child is looking because you're going to end up with a lot of opinions that are just that. You need to respect your teen's privacy by keeping personal details such as SAT scores and her GPA to yourself. You're under no obligation to reveal where your child stands in the application process. A friendly comment such as "We'll let you know when she makes her final choice" is all you need to say.

- **Help your teen manage his emotions.** Teens can likewise minimize the anxiety they're feeling by not getting caught up in conversations with their friends about where they're applying and how it's going. While completing applications and getting all the needed documentation in place takes time and focus, it's also important for your teen to pay attention to sleep, nutrition, and exercise when feeling under the gun.

- **Be genuinely excited for your teen.** You've arrived at an incredible moment with your teen. Through college visits, essays, and applications, he's taking stock of where he's at, what he wants to do next, and where he ultimately might want to head in life. Be proud that he knows how to size himself up, but still wants to have you as a sounding board. Take delight that at this moment in time your teen's world is filled with possibilities and so much promise. If you steer the ship too much, your teen will feel like he has to satisfy you, rather than charting his own course. Charting new waters. Owning choices. That's what education is all about.

Bottom Line: Be interested in what your child is learning and the effort he shows, not simply what he's producing. Education is about learning. The more your adolescent navigates his own educational course, the more he'll learn about life.

CHAPTER TWENTY-THREE

~

Stop Going to Religious Services?

If your family's rituals include going to religious services, your worship day could turn into a weekly battle during adolescence. Your teen might have dutifully been by your side from the time he was small, but suddenly start balking.

This can be an emotionally tough dilemma for parents. Your family may have strong traditions and tenets around worship, and there's something comforting in knowing that on a set schedule every week there's a chance to come together to reflect or pray. You might also feel hurt, as though your values and identity are being disrespected, when your adolescent refuses to go to services or mouths off the entire way there.

I certainly can't tell you what your family rules should be. Spirituality and faith are such personal things. But if I could pick one theme to be front and center to religious discussions with your teen, it would be respect. Your faith may teach tolerance for religious diversity in the world, yet you might be failing to tolerate differing points of view within your own family.

Parents and teens need to listen respectfully to each other so they can find common ground.

~ WHY TEENS OFTEN FIGHT RELIGION

There are many reasons why teens frequently start resisting religious services. Parents often call it being lazy, and there may be some truth to that, but teens really do relish, and perhaps need, the chance to sleep in one morning a week.

Simple rebellion is another possibility. If the answer to "Who am I?" has to be in part, "I am not my parents," then thumbing your nose at your parents' religious practices, at least for the time being, is an obvious (and quite frankly safe) way to rebel.

But aside from any tendency to rebel, pondering the big questions of life is also part of every teen's development. Your adolescent is going through the transition from concrete thinker to abstract thinker, an exciting process that allows him to consider more deeply the complexities and mysteries of life. Being told by your parents what to believe and what to do because of those beliefs works perfectly well for a concrete thinker. But as your adolescent grows into an abstract thinker, things that he might have never considered become possibilities. Your teen might develop nagging doubts about the existence of God or the tenets of the faith he was raised in, and no matter what, he starts to realize that not all questions have easy answers. "Why do bad things happen to good people? If there's a God, why is there war or hunger?"

By way of reading, class work, exposure to media, and the growing circle of people he interacts with—with you most definitely the most influential person—your teen's intellectual and moral fabrics are taking shape. Adolescents, especially as they get into high school, often embrace a broader definition of what it means to be spiritual. They may view spirituality in terms of how they treat other people or can fix a wrong in the world, rather than worshipping at a certain time or place.

If your response to your teen's beliefs is to brush him off, condemn him, or tell him, "This is what you have to believe because I believe it," your teen probably will rebel, perhaps for the long haul, against what you believe and hold dear. It's better to create an atmosphere of mutual respect in your home that allows your teen to arrive eventually at her own truth while being held to the expectation that she stay part of your family's rituals as much as possible. Teens might look like unwilling participants at times, but they take comfort in the rhythms and predictability of family life—certain rituals, traditions, celebrations of holidays.

Betty faces lots of complaining, but she is standing firm that her sixteen-year-old daughter continue to participate in church services by being in the choir. Going to church is on the list of the family's nonnegotiables—which means you can grumble but not win. "I told her that if she can go out there and spring cartwheels and cheer for the team, she can find time to sing in the choir," Betty said. "I told her you have to show 'Him' some love, too."

A good approach is to turn the conversation around. Instead of telling your teen what she should believe, tell her what your faith and religious practices mean to you: "I get a lot of comfort from my faith when things are tough. From the time I was little, my faith has been my rock in life. My desire to help other people comes from what I believe."

Be sure to also tell her what it means to you to have her be part of family rituals. "I feel that my worship is so much better when I'm with my family. I treasure the time we spend together each week."

Cheryl watched all three of her girls go through various stages of rebelling against organized religion. While she didn't budge from her rule that as long as they were in high school they had to go to church, she acknowledged the legitimacy of her girls' questioning. If they complained that the sermon was boring or pointless, she drew them into a discussion about why they felt that way and what they would have focused on. She also stressed the community aspect of faith.

"We wanted our girls to realize that when you're sick, you're dying, you lose your job, or your kid is struggling with health issues, your faith community is there to support you if you choose to reach out," Cheryl said.

Debbie and Rich took a different approach, but not after thinking a lot about it. While they felt strongly that one of their jobs as parents was to provide their children with spiritual enrichment, in the same way they provided them with educational opportunities, they also sensed that it wouldn't be a bad thing if their teens had some leeway. They came to an agreement with their older teens that if they didn't go to Sunday Mass, they needed to do something else during the week that allowed them time to get in touch with a cause bigger than themselves. One possibility was to volunteer at a local soup kitchen.

~ SOME TEENS DRAW CLOSER TO FAITH

Adolescence is a time where there is an almost obligatory search for answers to some of the most fundamental and troubling questions about existence. Many adolescents find that faith offers solutions. Their spiritual journey may make them more deeply religious, and exposure to new ideas and friends can sometimes lead them to turn toward a faith different from that of their parents. But in the end, most grown children end up embracing values and beliefs very similar to those held by their parents. If you respect your teen's expanding views on religion, he'll likely respect yours.

Bottom Line: Faith is about something bigger. Adolescence is a time when people begin thinking about things they never imagined before. It is a natural time to struggle and then arrive at one's own spiritual beliefs.

CHAPTER TWENTY-FOUR

~

SEE THE DOCTOR ALONE?

THE FIRST TIME the pediatrician asked Liz if she could go sit out in the waiting room, she felt almost like she was being asked to give up her first-born child. She had been coming to the doctor's office for years and had watched with pride each time her three sons got weighed and measured and were pronounced to be in good health. Taking her boys for their checkups was something she actually looked forward to because the visits reinforced that she was doing a good job. Now she felt as though the doctor was saying she wasn't quite needed anymore.

As an adolescent medicine doctor, I routinely deal with the touchy issue of telling parents I prefer that they wait outside for a bit. I can understand why it's hard for parents who have held their kids' hands through immunizations and earaches to be on the other side of the examining room door, but there are good reasons for your adolescent to be on his own for least part of the appointment. Think about these:

- **You want your adolescent to experience the full potential of a doctor's visit.** It's not just about getting checked when you're sick—the doctor's office also is a place to seek out reliable information and get emotional support when needed. Your teen should feel as if the appointment is for him, not you, and feel empowered to set the agenda. Your teen can ask questions at a health care visit that he might be afraid or embarrassed to ask elsewhere and expect to be taken seriously.
- **Your want your adolescent to develop a connection with the provider.** Teens who get regular checkups have more opportunities to be assessed for issues such as nutrition, sleep habits, stress, exercise, and alcohol and drug use that have a bearing on whether they'll go on to a healthy and successful future. Parents are undeniably the most important people in their children's lives when it comes to health, and ideally teens will tell their parents if they're feeling overwhelmed or heading down the wrong road. But adolescents often are willing to reveal things— about stress, school, girlfriends or boyfriends, drugs—to a health professional that they wouldn't to their parents because there isn't the fear of punishment or of disappointing someone they love.
- **Your adolescent must learn to be his own health advocate and a savvy health care consumer for life.** You don't want to end up kissing your twenty-five-year-old's owies or accompanying him to the orthodontist. Adolescents need to become competent at describing symptoms, family history, and what medicines they take. They also need to be familiar with the insurance side of health care—referrals, co-pays, generics versus name-brand drugs. Teens who learn how to take charge of their health care won't be clueless the first time they show up at the college student health center feeling lousy.

∼ KEEPING THE CONNECTION GOING

Most parents are faithful about taking their child for regular checkups when they're little—there are shots to be gotten and there's something reassuring about being told that your child is growing normally. But somewhere between early elementary school and adolescence, health care visits may become less frequent, in part because older kids get fewer bugs. Parents will take their adolescent for a physical required for school or camp, but regular checkups might fall by the wayside.

You're doing your adolescent a long-lasting favor by keeping the connection going with a health care provider. As you help your adolescent transition toward being her own health advocate, be assured that the doctor is not a stranger out to keep secrets from you, but rather is another caring adult there to guide your child safely through adolescence.

Part of my research has involved studying what makes for a worthwhile encounter between adolescents and health care providers, and trust is an essential ingredient. When I meet families for the first time, I begin with a brief conversation with both the parent and the child to explain that my office is a trustworthy place where no one is going to be judged or condemned, and that information is kept private. I explain that I will focus on medical and behavioral issues because both sides of the equation are essential to good health. I assure my patients that what they tell me is private unless their life is in immediate danger, and I explain to parents that aside from a life-and-death issue, what their child tells me is kept private as a strategy to create a dynamic where an adolescent is more likely to disclose problems. But I also tell parents that my goal is always open communication and that if we agree beforehand to work together to address their child's problems—to move forward without punishment—kids often use my office as a place to talk candidly without fear of getting into trouble.

Laying out these ground rules helps adolescents feel more in control of the situation, which in turn makes them more comfortable with talking, and gives parents the confidence they need to let go of managing every moment of their child's health care encounters. It is a common experience for me to be working with a very loving, highly functional family, and the parents leave the room assuring me that they know their teen is making safe choices around sex and drugs. Within three minutes, I find out that the information the parents have is not complete. I then have the opportunity to become another responsible adult—another "connection"—in their child's life who can provide education about safe and wise decision making and, I hope, help prevent further risky behavior. I get kids talking not because I'm smarter or more empathetic or cooler than their parents, but because I'm a neutral person whom they can hold at a distance and not worry about making upset or sad. It's often precisely because a kid loves his parents so much that he'll make the mistake of hiding things rather than revealing that he needs help. Teens also can use the setting of a doctor's office to talk about the most important relationship in their lives—the one they have with their parents. The bottom line here is that I want you to view the private time afforded to your child not as a sign that you are being excluded, judged, or marginalized. To the contrary, it's a time to take a breath, relax with a magazine, and know that a well-trained adult is reinforcing good choices and addressing any mistakes your teen might be making.

∼ RAISING A CONFIDENT HEALTH CARE CONSUMER

You prepare your adolescent to begin to take charge of her health care. Here are some suggestions for phasing in this responsibility:

- **Approach going to the doctor with a positive attitude.** It will help your child to know that you likewise schedule regular checkups with your doctor. I like the tradition of some parents who cap off their child's yearly checkup with an outing to a movie or favorite lunch spot. It underscores the point that good health is to be celebrated.
- **Let your child know what to expect at a medical checkup.** Explain that the doctor or nurse will take a health history, ask about any problems or worries, and do a physical exam. Your adolescent should be able to sum up her health status—I had a lot of ear infections when I was little; I'm allergic to penicillin—and have a general knowledge of the health of close relatives. I don't expect teens to provide a lot of details on what ails their parents or grandparents, but they should know whether heart disease or diabetes runs in the

family. Talk to your child about why the doctor or nurse will ask questions about diet, sleeping habits, and stress and whether she smokes cigarettes or drinks. Explain that all those things impact on health and the doctor cares about her staying healthy.

- **Let even your young child explain to the doctor or nurse why she's there.** Most health providers who deal with children direct questions at the patients, but anxious parents often jump in with their version of what's happening. Children should be able to explain their symptoms and whether they're getting better or worse. This early interaction with a doctor or nurse will start building your child's confidence in a setting that can be intimidating.

- **Beginning at a young age, tell your child what shots are for and why they're taking medicine.** There's no need yet for detailed medical explanations, but children should understand that shots prevent serious sickness and that antibiotics help the body fight infection. I tell kids they should always ask two questions when given a shot or prescribed a pill: What's it for and what are the side effects?

- **Make sure your young adolescent knows the names and rationale for any medication he takes.** He also needs to know what time of day to take the medicine, whether to take it with food or on an empty stomach, what the side effects are (drowsiness, trouble sleeping, stomach cramps), and whether there's a danger in taking the drug with other medications or alcohol. This is especially important information for your teen as he spends more time away from you and begins to drive, an activity that requires alertness.

- **Have your adolescent gradually assume responsibility for any daily medication.** Your teen should ideally be taking medicine unprompted by you, though some kids set their cell phones to remind them. Darleene, whose daughter has a seizure disorder, got her middle school daughter into the habit of filling her pill organizer every week and keeping track of when refills were needed. You might even have your teen place the refill order. Your teen is less likely to call you from college in a panic because he only has a pill or two left if he learns early on to pay attention to his medication supply. Darleene still worries every day about her daughter, but when she packed her off to college on the other side of the country, she was pretty confident she had taught her why she needed to stay on top of her medicine.

- **Even if the doctor or nurse hasn't asked you to step outside, you can suggest that perhaps you should.** That will give your adolescent a chance to discuss anything that's on her mind. Your child has the security of knowing you're close by and will be back, but he also starts to get comfortable with the idea that he can handle things. Eventually, let your adolescent go back to the examining room on his own, saying you'll join him later in the appointment if needed. Many doctors like parents to be present at the both the start and conclusion of the visit so the parent can supply missing information, express any concerns initially, and then be clear on the follow-up plan.

- **Let your teen have some say in doctor choice.** Some teens want to select their own doctor, seeing it as babyish that they're going to the same office that their little brother or sister goes to. This might be an inconvenience, but it's also an opportunity to teach your teen how to use online resources to find a doctor, ask around for recommendations, and research whether a given practice accepts your family's insurance. Of course, you stay involved in the process, but your teen gets a taste for navigating what can be a very complicated health care system.

- **Don't pry.** Eventually the day will come when your older teen or young adult goes alone to an appointment. Ask how it went, but don't pepper your teen with too many questions, because that sends the message, "I don't think you're really ready to take charge of your health." You need to respect your older teen's privacy, in the same way she respects yours.

By systematically expanding your child's role in his health care, he'll become confident that he has the knowledge needed to stay on top of his health and you'll be confident that he can take care of himself when you're not around. That's precisely what happened to Francine when her teenage daughter came down with swine flu while studying in South America and had to rely on her host family and unfamiliar doctors. As luck had it, Francine's family had hosted exchange students over the years and she had made a point to have her daughter go along when the visitors needed to see a doctor.

"She had seen that when we had young women in our house who got sick that we took care of them, so she had learned that she could trust people herself when she was put in that situation," Francine recalled.

See, trust is everything.

Bottom Line: Adolescents need to learn to navigate the health care system on their own. They also need to understand that healthy people attend to both their physical needs and emotional concerns and make wise behavioral choices. Health providers can reinforce all of these points, and can do this best when they have some private time with your teen.

SECTION III

~

HOW TO TALK . . . ABOUT THE REALLY TOUGH STUFF

INTRODUCTION

~

Why How?

I HOPE YOU'VE PICKED UP some ideas and gained confidence to deal with the *When* questions. You see that the *When*s—cell phones, driver's licenses, going to the mall—don't have to be so daunting if your child, and you, are prepared. Now let's turn to some issues that deserve some added attention. I call these the *How*s because all of us parents ask ourselves "How in the world am I going to talk to my kid about this?" The first topic we'll explore is at the core of parenting: "How can I raise my child to be successful?" Other topics are particularly difficult for many parents to address, but they are the challenges through which teens all need to navigate—peer pressure, sex, drinking, and drugs. Your teen can make it through relatively unscathed with your loving support and continued guidance.

I'm not going to give you word-for-word scripts for talking your way through these topics, but I will give you reliable information and a resilience-based philosophy that you can adapt to fit your conversational style and your child's needs. You'll also learn about how to help your teen manage stress. This is a particularly important chapter because stress impedes success and can drive teens to worrisome behaviors. In another chapter, we'll talk about *How* to turn for help when your instinct says your teen needs additional professional guidance.

Parents really do matter. Although some of these topics may seem overwhelming, your involvement makes an immeasurable difference. I hope this section will empower you to tackle difficult topics with insight, openness, and skill. Rather than shying away them, you'll know how to get started.

CHAPTER TWENTY-FIVE

~

Authentic Success

WITHOUT A DOUBT, the topic of success is one that gives most parents a reason to doubt themselves. Settle into the bleachers or linger in the grocery store aisles and listen to the conversations that unfold. There's a lot of anxiety flying about as parents trade talk regarding teachers and tests scores and team tryouts. Even if parents aren't coming out and saying, "I'm worried," their inner questions are undeniable: Am I pushing my kid too hard, or not enough? Am I making the "right" decision now to ensure success down the road? Is my child keeping up with her peers? Is she too competitive or not competitive enough? Is her school expecting too much or too little? Is she participating in the "right" mix of activities that will allow her to stand out?

Wherever I go around the country—small towns, suburban communities, urban centers, public schools, private schools—parents seem more worried than ever that their kids' future might not turn out to be as bright as they had hoped for. They sense that the competition to succeed might be tougher than ever. There's a feeling that success is a game to be won and that parents need to make sure their children ultimately capture the prize by making every move of childhood count.

The parents I meet know there is something distasteful and even a bit crazy about how society seems to be increasingly narrowing the definition of success for kids—putting more and more emphasis on grades, honors courses, SAT and ACT scores, and thick résumés for college applications. But they also are somewhat ambivalent because they don't want their own kids to be left behind in the rush or later regret that they missed out on some golden opportunities.

At one neighborhood parent gathering held to inform this book, the topic of success and its flip side, failure, kept coming up even when the parents weren't directly talking about it. It surfaced in discussions about school, dating, sports, even sleepovers. Listen to these snippets:

"The moment my daughters stepped into the building for ninth grade, they started talking about college."

"I read a study that having a girlfriend or boyfriend can affect your grades by one letter grade."

"Not everyone wants to be number one, but I told my son, 'I'd never push you to do something you're not capable of doing.' I just want him to leave his mark in college. He did not leave it in high school."

"The repercussions of sleepovers are so great. . . . You did all this to get ready for the game. Worked hard at practice. Why blow it due to sleep deprivation?"

"Sometimes you see kids and it seems like fire is coming out of them. I have busy kids, and a couple of things have caught fire with them on their own."

"Is it good we micromanage everything? What's the worst that could happen?"

"Way too much is expected of them. If they're in a sport they have to practice six hours a day. You can't go on a family vacation or your kid gets benched."

"I'm struggling with whether to let him fail when the stakes are low. My husband said, 'Let him fail. This is not us. He has to crash and burn so he knows how to recover.' But it's a terrible thing to watch."

"We're all kind of watching a movie of our own kids that we've already seen. They're in eighth grade and you know what tenth grade is like. They're in tenth grade and you know what's coming in twelfth grade. You tell the kids, 'This is the plot that's coming on,' but the more you say it, the more they want to do it their way."

The parents, when directly asked about their feelings about success, were very clear that they believed happiness was a vital part of being successful and they acknowledged the importance of family and connection and contribution to community in achieving lifelong satisfaction. But they couldn't quite shake the reality that for so many teens, success has become tantamount to "the pressure to succeed." They worried about kids being so performance-driven, but also wanted to be sure their kids, whom they loved more than anything, didn't "fail."

This chapter will introduce you to another way to think about success. I call it *authentic success,* but it could just as easily be called *genuine success* or *real success*. There's no simple, one-size-fits-all definition for the brand of success I'm talking about, but there are some key qualities that contribute to it, including happiness, an ability to make and maintain meaningful relationships, generosity, compassion, a desire to contribute, creativity and innovation, and, of course, resilience.

This philosophy of success:

- Puts the emphasis on high achievement, not on performance.
- Acknowledges that the ultimate sign of whether a child has learned well isn't a high GPA or letters of acceptance from certain colleges, but rather that he has developed an appreciation for learning and a curiosity about the world.
- Celebrates kids' academic accomplishments, but acknowledges that kids are so much more than their report cards or standardized test scores.
- Discourages the commonly accepted notion that kids need to be good at everything to succeed, and recognizes that we all have areas where we shine and others where we are adequate or struggle. Being well rounded is good as long as it is not interpreted as having to be adept in every category.

- Recognizes that successful people usually just excel at one or two things, but are interested in many things.
- Sets the bar high for every kid, but the bar is set on high effort, not on performance-driven standards such as grades or test scores.
- Recognizes that children are most apt to achieve when they are given the opportunity to discover what makes them passionate.
- Recognizes that we need a highly educated populace, but college isn't for everyone. Our society needs well-prepared people in all vocations, and education might look different depending on your goals. Some kids shine in the classroom, others in vocational settings, others when given service opportunities.
- Provides a broader range of "heroes" for kids to aspire to be like, not just the sports stars, celebrities, and CEOs typically placed on a pedestal. Teachers, nurses, social workers, men and women in the military, police officers, and the man down the street caring for his wife with cancer all offer proof that society couldn't function without people willing to serve.
- Recognizes that each child can thrive. Rejects the idea that only the superstars deserve attention. Expects every young person to contribute to the fabric of society.
- Recognizes that some kids receive dispiriting messages about their potential due to their gender, race, ethnic background, or socioeconomic status that undermine achievement. These messages are rarely given intentionally, but still need to be addressed square on and eliminated.
- Minimizes the risk of developing perfectionism, a potentially self-destructive way of thinking that makes people feel unacceptable with anything less than the highest level of recognition. Rather than actually leading to excellence, perfectionism can stifle out-of-the-box thinking as kids take the easy way out for fear of not receiving guaranteed praise. It can lead other teens to get off the playing field altogether because of fear of failure.
- Promotes creativity and innovation, both core attributes of high-achieving people.

- Builds on the well-targeted use of praise and criticism, rather than effusive praise or labeling, to spur kids to try harder.
- Values participation in sports, the arts, volunteerism, and other activities because it builds complete human beings, but doesn't promote the padding of résumés simply to look good for college admissions officers.
- Does not require parents to choose between happiness today and success tomorrow. It understands that happy children who are driven by curiosity and a love of learning are precisely those who will be successful tomorrow.

This chapter will give you ideas for how best to promote *authentic success* in your child. The aim is to encourage hard work and high achievement, instead of pushing your child into a frenzied mode that might leave him joyless and burned out. It will introduce strategies for immunizing your child against the forces that can lead to self-doubt and paralyzing perfectionism. I'll teach you how to praise and criticize in a way that will make your child want to try harder. We'll talk about the dangers of overscheduling your child and turning sports and volunteerism into just more things for your kid to worry about. No discussion on success would be complete without some reflection on the college admissions process.

First, though, I'll encourage you to look at your own views of success and failure. That isn't always an easy thing to do because we all come to this topic with hard-earned experience in the school of life. What I hope to do is challenge you to think more broadly about what it means to succeed so that you create an environment where your child is likely to achieve *authentic success*.

∼ HOW DO YOU DEFINE SUCCESS?

I have never met a parent who doesn't want his child to succeed, and that is certainly my goal for my girls. Most parents would say that they want their kids to grow up to get a good education, engage in fulfilling work, not have to worry all the time about money, find someone to love, and contribute in some way to the world. Those are admirable goals that we should encourage all young people to attain.

So now think about how limiting the definition of success has become for our kids. They're bombarded with messages that being successful means having money, nice things, and power, and that they can attain all that by getting straight As, earning high scores on standardized tests, loading up on lots of AP courses, bulking up their résumés with activities, and applying to top-tier schools. Children more and more are being told what they need to do to succeed rather than being allowed to discover what makes them excited to learn. They've come to dread the B+ and assume they'll be disappointed in their college search unless they somehow can document on paper that they are unusually smart, artistic, musical, athletic, creative, compassionate, experienced in the workplace, and, oh yes, a leader, too.

Those misguided messages of what defines a kid's current worth and future potential are coming from all directions—your child's school, the media, their friends, and possibly you. Don't get me wrong. I'm sure nothing you may have done was motivated by bad intentions, but the best of intentions can backfire. In some cases, what one child in a family views as helpful encouragement by his parents might be viewed by another child as way too much pressure. Even if you're not part of the problem, you can most definitely be part of the solution. Stick with me as we talk about the toxic messages coming at your child and how you can better frame your success-focused messages so he doesn't become driven by anxiety or the fear of disappointing you.

Whether we realize it or not, we're constantly sending our kids messages about what we think it means to succeed and what we think about people who fall short. We might tell them that we want nothing more than for them to be happy, but act happiest ourselves when they bring home good grades. We might tell them they can be anything they want to be in life, yet we gush over people with high-paying jobs. We might tell our kids that we just want them to do their best, but what they're really hearing is that we can't stand for them to fail. Yes, we want happiness and all those good things, but deep down inside we worry that if we don't push and then push some more, our kids will be bound for mediocrity—a particularly scary thought given what we know about the economy.

But in trying to shore up our kids' standing, we might be undercutting their real potential. In pushing kids to be well rounded, we might be prohibiting them from having the time and focus to dig in and get really good at something. Perfectly packaged kids who have every category on a résumé accounted for might appeal to college admissions committees but feel so stressed that they lose the love of learning that will help them thrive in life.

The broad goal for every parent should be to raise children who work hard, have insight to recognize what they enjoy and are good at, and have the confidence to set and achieve challenging goals, not just safe ones. As a starting point in that process, take a few minutes to consider your own feelings about success and failure:

- Do you consider yourself a success? Why or why not?
- Why do you value what you do?
- How do you define a successful child or teen? Is it being ranked at the top of the class? Good at sports? Talented in music or art? A class leader? Compassionate? Good character? A people person? Popular?
- Do you make a huge deal about grades? Do you give rewards for As or punishments for low grades?
- How do you praise? Do you tell your child she's smart when she gets a 100, or do you tell her that her hard work paid off?
- How do you criticize? Do you tell your child he's becoming a slacker when he earns a bad grade, or do you talk to him about what he's done in the past that worked well? For that matter, what do you define as a bad grade?
- Do you drive around with bumper stickers or car decals—PROUD PARENT OF AN HONORS STUDENT!—advertising your kid's academic accomplishment or where older siblings go to school?
- Do you compare your child's achievements to those of a sibling?

- Do you insist she sign up for every conceivable activity? Do you allow her to decline or drop out of activities if she wants to focus elsewhere?
- Do you consider downtime a waste of time? Do you appreciate that your child needs time to reboot?
- Do you come up with volunteer activities for your teen because "they'll look good" to colleges, or do you allow his genuine goodness to bubble up?
- Do you encourage sports because they offer kids opportunities to be committed, make friends, and stay healthy, or are you dreaming of a college scholarship?
- Are you envisioning your teen at a certain college and on a given career path? Or do you take delight when you see glimpses of what he might become?

The point in asking these questions isn't to label you a pushy parent or a lackadaisical one. In fact, most of us would find some inherent contradictions in our answers because ambivalence about these questions is normal. Having done some self-reflection, however, I hope you'll be open to readjusting your thinking a bit so you truly do promote success.

~ PERFECTIONISM: THE DOWNSIDE OF "SUCCESS"

Parents often seem confused when I start talking about perfectionism as a worrisome fallout of the success craze. After all, most of us know perfectionists or maybe even consider ourselves one. We knew the girl in high school who headed every club and always had an answer for the teacher. Or we sit in the next cubicle over from someone who doggedly works and reworks a proposal long after we go home. Wouldn't it be nice if we were all more perfect?

But don't confuse perfectionism with high achievement. You want your child to be a high achiever who makes the most of her talents and feels good about it, but you don't want her to veer into perfectionism because perfectionists tend to worry so much about the possibility of failing that they avoid challenges that could allow their talents to really shine. Perfectionists never are satisfied with themselves.

Let's be clear on how perfectionism can be born of a skewed view of success. When we tell kids, overtly or in a roundabout way, that what it takes to be successful is to make the top team, be chosen captain, win a blue ribbon at the state fair, earn first chair in orchestra, make the honor roll, or take multiple AP classes, we hope we are motivating them to work hard. But that can boomerang. Reaching the end goal—good grades, a solo performance, the lead in the play, a stack of acceptances from top colleges— might become everything, and soon your teen can't even consider thinking outside the box or taking on anything that doesn't have a guaranteed positive outcome. The perfectionist, so intent on not flubbing up, starts to play it safe, even though it might appear to the outside world that she's running on all cylinders. The message "Here's what you need to do to succeed" ends up producing a kid who doesn't succeed nearly enough.

You want your child to be a high achiever, not a perfectionist. The world is run by high achievers—people who genuinely enjoy sweating over a problem or bringing a task to completion, whether it's a landscaping project, the development of a new drug, or the redesign of computer software. High achievers know how to turn on just enough anxiety so they have the energy to work hard and complete a job on time. Perfectionists worry so much about turning out a "product" that they can't take pleasure in the process that gets them there, and they can become immobilized by the fear that they will be discovered to be an imposter. Even when the perfectionist delivers a sterling performance—the winning touchdown, a well-researched debate presentation, a moving rendition of a concerto—it isn't ever quite to his liking. "I messed up but they didn't notice . . . this time. I should have been so much better!"

There are other differences, too. High achievers take pride in their work, but accept criticism because they see setbacks as opportunities to learn and move forward. That spirit of wanting to do things better makes people want to work with them. Perfectionists have a hard time with critiques because they worry that less than glowing reviews chip away at their perfect veneer. Perfectionists get defensive and embarrassed at criticism, and may be ungracious with compliments because how could they possibly be true? Perfectionists can give off a lot of nervous, unproductive energy. That's not surprising because they are riddled with anxiety over the possibility that they might lose their image.

The thinking that ruin is just one mistake away is not totally off base since kids see example after example in the media of celebrities, sports stars, and politicians who are idolized only to be dragged down by some revelation or another. They clearly absorb the message that to earn recognition you have to be on top, but to stay there, human frailty is not an option.

The need to always play it safe can mean that perfectionists have to be conformists and not attract too much attention. Proposing a new idea could lead to criticism or even failure, so forget about thinking differently from everyone else in the room. You can see why perfectionism is the death of innovation and creativity—two qualities essential for success in the twenty-first century.

Carol Dweck, the Stanford University psychologist who studies the effect that praise, and conversely criticism, has on students' performance, adds tremendous insight into what it takes to build high achievers and likewise some of the major factors that produce perfectionists. In her book *Mindset: The New Psychology of Success,* she talks about a "growth mindset" compared to a "fixed mindset" and explains how the two different ways of thinking can influence performance.

Kids with a "growth mindset" (budding high achievers) believe that their intellectual skills can be cultivated with effort on their part, so they put in the work needed to achieve the desired result. Even when they come up short, they don't view themselves as failures, but as learners. She notes that people with a "growth mindset" want to get reliable feedback on how they're doing because they understand they need accurate assessments if they are going to learn to do things better.

"The passion for stretching yourself and sticking to it, even (or especially) when it's not going well, is the hallmark of the growth mindset,"

Dweck writes. In other words, effort is what builds intelligence, and talent is demonstrated through hard work—effort leads to success.

People with a "fixed mindset" (the grouping includes perfectionists and others) see things much differently: You're either smart or you're not; failure means you're not. In fact, hard work suggests you don't have natural intelligence, and therefore may be viewed negatively. Their goal becomes to avoid mistakes, struggles, and failure at all costs since every situation needs to confirm that they're smart. Dweck explains that the person with the "fixed mindset" sizes up every situation with calculated thoughts such as "Will I succeed or fail?" "Will I look smart or dumb?" "Will I win or lose?"

People with a "growth mindset" say they feel smart when they learn to do something they couldn't do before. People with "fixed mindsets" say they feel smart when they don't make mistakes. They find criticism hard to swallow and instead seek out information to confirm their view, "I'm smart."

So where does perfectionism come from? Certainly, some of it is internally generated—some people seem born to please and pay attention to every detail—but your child is feeling the pressure to perform from so many outside sources, too. Perfectionists often are the very type of kids adults rely on because they can be counted on to get the job done. Teachers or coaches or even peers might turn too often to them to run things or take the lead, and perfectionists might have trouble saying no because it could look bad. The people who rely on perfectionists are usually not aware that the other person's anxiety is building for fear of disappointing if every request is not delivered to a tee.

Mariel grew concerned when her perfectionist high schooler added more and more to her list of activities. She decided some creative brainstorming was needed when her daughter got asked by a teacher to be an editor of the school paper, even though she didn't enjoy that kind of writing. Rather than advising her daughter to simply turn the teacher down, a suggestion that would have generated too much anxiety, Mariel helped her come up with the strategy that she would write the teacher a letter to nominate a student who had a real interest in journalism. Her daughter ended up feeling helpful, not as though she was slacking off.

Sometimes perfectionism is a reaction to a child wanting to shield a parent from added disappointment during a time of change or hardship, or to control a situation that feels out of control. It hurts a kid to see a parent consumed by the death of a close relative, reeling from a job loss, or going through the struggles of a divorce. The child reacts by trying to do everything right and making no demands on the parent. She only wants to please—to be the "perfect little girl." The problem is that this desire to spare her parents may make her withhold information even when she really needs them.

If you're facing a period of change, be attuned to such a possibility. It might be best to address the issue head-on by saying something like: "I know you want to protect me from more worries and I appreciate that. But the one thing I want to do right now is be your dad. Please allow me to do that."

∽ ARE LAZY KIDS REALLY LAZY?

It's seems counterintuitive that perfectionists or kids with "fixed mindsets" who care most about a positive label could be underperformers in the classroom, but not if you think about what you've just read. Because everything is about proving that they're smart (i.e., successful), students with these tendencies might start bypassing situations that require a lot of effort because that would make it seem as though they don't have natural talent. They might play it safe in course selection and in classroom discussions because it's all about getting good grades, not about learning for the satisfaction of it. It can even cloud their sports performance. They want to win but not have the game hinge on them. Risks aren't worth taking. Perfectionists are often procrastinators, too, because they are so afraid of messing up that they can't even get started. The anxiety of thinking of possible failure becomes paralyzing.

When taken to an extreme, perfectionism can cause kids to burn out to the point that they might turn to alcohol or drugs to self-medicate their stress. They might also find relief from all the pressure they feel by "getting off the playing field." They worry so much about the possibility of not doing everything well—it's so exhausting—that they assume an air that they just don't care much about anything. They may actually work hard at putting on a slacker image.

If your child has gone from being a high performer to an under-achiever or consistently seems to sell herself short, laziness might not be at the root of what's going on. It could be that your child cares too much—that she is so afraid of not living up to her reputation and disappointing you, her teachers, or her coach that she decides that the best solution is to stop trying. She is so overwhelmed by people's expectations, or thinks it's impossible to live up to her older sibling's performance, that she becomes determined to forge a different kind of reputation—one of a kid who is just too cool to care about all of that "stupid stuff."

I've had numerous experiences in my practice where parents who have been butting heads with their kids over being lazy end up realizing just how fragile their children feel. Healing happens when kids are able to say the truth—"It's not that I don't care, it's that I care too much. I just couldn't bear always hearing that I was not living up to my potential."

In the next section, I'll talk to you about some changes you might want to make to ensure your child is getting the message you intend. Children, as I've said multiple times in this book, become resilient and thrive in the long haul when they know they are loved unconditionally. While parents certainly don't intend to imply conditional love when they overfocus on grades and test scores, children can interpret the situation as meaning, "If I bring home good grades, you'll love me even more." Children should never fear being loved less or being a disappointment because of how they per-form at school or sports or other activities. They need to know you love them, As, Bs, Cs, and all. You cherish them whether they're on the A team, B team, C team—or not on any team.

Your kid needs to hear from you that you believe that experiencing happiness and a sense of fulfillment are essential to being ultimately suc-cessful, and that not everyone achieves those things in the same way or on the same schedule.

~ ALL KIDS CAN SUCCEED

If our society is going to readjust the narrow definition of success, we need to support educational models that give all kids a chance to become engaged in learning. We need to value curricula that offer variety and options for different styles of students but establish high expectations for everyone, whether they're taking a remedial, regular, honors, or AP course. Vocational programs should not be considered a dumping ground, but rather a place where kids can thrive in a setting other than the classroom. If you think back to the Seven Cs of Resilience, Confidence flows from being Competent. When kids feel they can do something well, they're more likely to take on even more challenges.

We also need to offer up more examples of real achievers in our midst. It's easy to point to the player who drove in the winning run in the World Series or the singer who took home multiple Grammy Awards. But achievers are everywhere. They generate scientific advances, run plumbing businesses and auto body shops, and work the night shift at your local emergency room. Sometimes they drive expensive new cars, and sometimes they keep their older car in fine shape. Our kids are looking to see whom we value, not just whom in our dreams we wouldn't mind trading places with for a day. It is critical that kids see the ordinary heroes in our midst so they have realistic role models to emulate.

As I travel the country and spend some time in schools, I often worry most about the average kids. Their parents come up to me at the end of a talk and speak of how their B and C students feel like failures. They are pained as they witness their children giving up on themselves. First, I ask them what makes their child sparkle and I listen as their love pours out. Then I ask them to remain committed to the belief that their child will succeed. I ask them whom they would rather hire: the person whose jeans are worn out at the knees because of how he digs into tasks and works hard, or someone with a worn-out seat because he's waiting for things to come to him? Who would they rather have as a colleague: the collaborator who helps them stretch or the person who needs to do everything on her own for fear of losing control? I urge these parents to teach their children that the most successful people in the real world are those who work hard for their As, Bs, or Cs.

The bottom line is that kids succeed when the people around them believe they can. Jed Michael, a stress-reduction specialist at Covenant House Pennsylvania—a homeless shelter for older teens and young adults where I serve as health services director—uses a strategy that speaks to overcoming the paralysis of self-doubt and to the power of having someone believe in your potential. Many of the kids have repeatedly received messages over the years that suggest they are incapable of success. When a young person seems defeated or hopeless and says something like "I can't" or "I won't be able to do it," Jed just asks them to add the word *yet* to the sentence. "I can't yet. I won't be able to do it yet." It changes the meaning of the sentence—it now says, "Yes, I can succeed." Effort, tenacity, and perhaps a little more time will get you there. I have repeatedly witnessed a palpable change in a teen's mood with this simple intervention that forces him to reframe the expectation he sets for himself.

∼ PRAISING WELL

This is a good place to say that broadening the definition of success does not mean we shouldn't celebrate kids' successes. Kids *should* be recognized when they work hard to achieve an exceptional result. We should celebrate when a teen gets selected for her school's Honor Society. We should celebrate when a kid has such an exceptional aptitude for math that he lands a top SAT score and is named a National Merit Finalist. We should celebrate when a kid earns a spot in the state orchestra, or gets his poem published in a literary magazine. But go back and carefully reread those sentences and you'll notice that I didn't say we should celebrate a kid because he's smart or a musical genius or the next Great American Writer. The point is that kids should be recognized for specific accomplishments and the hard work that got them there, whether they're medal-worthy or not, rather than being lavished with praise for being an intellectual genius or a child prodigy.

Parents used to be told that they should do whatever they could to build their kids' self-esteem, so parents got in the habit of piling on the compliments. Thanks to the self-esteem movement, kindergarten art projects became worthy of hanging in the Louvre and a soccer goal was greeted as if it were a World Cup victory. Yes, parents should celebrate their kids' specific accomplishments, but if you're the kid who's forever being told, "You're so bright," imagine the devastating feeling when you run into trouble with algebra? If you hear constantly that you're a star, what happens if you don't make the top-level travel team? If you're supposed to feel special as a butterfly all the time, how much worse does it feel when you are emotionally down?

Research by Dweck offers some clues into how to praise effectively. Remember the experiment she did in which children were given math puzzle tests and then were either praised for their intelligence or their effort? Then she had them repeat the puzzle test. She found that those students who were told they were smart actually did worse or took the easy way out on subsequent tests compared to children who were noticed for working hard. In other words, recognizing effort spurs children to work harder, and hard work leads to high achievement. Kids can control effort, but they can't control "intelligence." When the emphasis is placed on "being smart," kids feel they can't control the outcome and might try to avoid the task altogether for fear of losing the positive label.

The bottom line is that effusive, nonspecific praise can end up undermining success. Dweck noted another disturbing possibility: Frequently praised children might become so caught up in competition that they prop up their position at the top of the heap by tearing others down.

Parents should get excited when their kids win a game or competition, but the emphasis used when acknowledging an accomplishment can make a difference. "I am so proud of you for scoring that basket or getting that ribbon" inadvertently says, "I wouldn't be as proud if you hadn't come home with the prize."

You might have to retrain yourself to notice effort. We were so good at that when our kids were little—we noticed when they buttoned their sweater for themselves, even if all the holes weren't lined up right. As children grow, parents tend to focus on the outcome—was it a success of failure?—rather than the process involved in getting there. It's important to always acknowledge preparation and effort, no matter what the final result.

A lot of this has to do with the words you use. Instead of telling your second grader she's smart because she got a gold star on her spelling test, tell her it's great that her studying paid off. It will encourage her to put the same effort into next week's list of words instead of becoming anxious that she won't bring you a star again. Instead of telling your tenth grader that his PowerPoint presentation is sure to land an A, tell him that you noticed he worked hard to find just the right photos and graphics. He'll appreciate your recognizing that he cared a lot about the assignment.

How you criticize matters, too. Your goal should always be to keep it specific. A low grade should be met with open-ended comments such as "What do you think happened?" or "Why do you think things turned out better on the last exam?" None of that diminishes your expectation that your child will do well in school, but it once again shines the spotlight on effort.

Please let me reiterate that point—I'm not asking you to ignore bad grades or a halfhearted effort, but to shift the conversation so your child comes up with a plan on how he can do things differently. I also don't want you to minimize how your child might be feeling. Kids often feel quite bad about getting a low mark or critical comments on a paper, even when they act as if they don't care. Try something like, "I notice you're upset about the remarks Mrs. Brown put on your report. Want to talk about it?"

Start looking for opportunities to notice effort and use praise well. Dan found himself always greeting his three kids at the end of the day with comments such as "How'd you do on your test today?" After he became tuned in to how his children felt pressured, he tried a different approach: "How did your day go?" Dan's neutral, wide-open question brought out an interesting range of responses from his kids and he learned more about their day than merely whether they aced or bombed a test. In doing that, he gave them more opportunities to show how they're succeeding.

INSTEAD OF SAYING THAT . . . TRY THIS

~

What do think you got on your history test? . . . How did you feel about your studying?

You're a math whiz. . . . What strategy worked to help you figure out all those equations?

How many points did you score? . . . Tell me about the game. Did you have fun? Did you play hard?

Wow, you really bombed that one! . . . You did well on other tests, so I know you can do it. How will you study differently next time?

Did Mr. Lee like your presentation? . . . Did your presentation go as you wanted it to?

Wow, you got a lot of playing time! . . . What did you like about the game today?

Colleges will be begging for you with those SAT scores. . . . You must feel good your studying paid off.

You're an incredible musician. . . . You really played that song with feeling.

Practice makes perfect. . . . Good preparation always makes me feel more confident.

You dominated at the game today. . . . You really worked well with your team.

You make me so proud. . . . I'm so happy to see *you* happy about your accomplishments.

~ DISAPPOINTMENT AND FAILURE

Of course, criticizing well requires that we get in touch with how we feel about disappointment and failure. When our kids were little, we got the fact that setbacks were part of a child's learning curve. They fell when they started to walk. They wobbled and crashed their bikes the first times out without training wheels. You didn't react with disappointment or searing criticism. Instead, you praised the effort and encouraged your child to try again.

Parents have a tougher time adopting a similar attitude about setbacks as their children grow, maybe because the potential repercussions seem much greater. Or maybe your own experiences have taught you how rotten disappointment can feel. Many of us were raised to thrive on competition, and competitive people can have difficulty dealing with failure.

Sometimes parents tend to brush off a child's disappointment or struggles, or interject their own feelings before their child has time to process what happened, because they don't want their child to feel even worse. Another common reaction to a child's disappointment, whether over school or sports or a friendship, is to say something like, "Don't worry," and then to swoop in to fix it. That says, "I don't think you're capable on your own of improving this situation." Being resilient means knowing what needs to be done to turn around an unfavorable situation. That's learned through experience.

Sometimes a parent's toughest call is to give a go-ahead or keep their mouth shut even though they suspect their child will end up disappointed or outright failing. It might be easier for you to say, "No, I wouldn't try out" for an all-county travel team because you know from seeing the competition at games that the chances are slim that your teen will make the squad. But kids need to experience that feeling of stretching as long as the failure won't put them in a dangerous situation. Otherwise they'll miss out on many of life's best opportunities and most valuable lessons.

Our own attitudes about failure rub off on our kids, just as our view of success does. When you beat yourself up over something at work, your child is hearing, "It's bad to fail." When you're critical of people, your child hears, "I better not mess up or I'll get labeled a failure, too." Curb your harsh or inpatient words.

Parents sometimes make the mistake of making everything seem so easy. Let your child know it's not always a breeze for you—that you don't necessarily nail the report on the first draft or get the promotion. Let her know that you don't always do justice to Grandma's recipes, but that you still get tremendous pleasure from baking.

Make it clear to your child that your definition of success includes taking chances. Reinforce that you like it when they take a different tack instead of the predictable route or come up with an idea that never occurred to you. Let her know that creativity is one of the greatest predictors of success. Help her understand that innovative ideas are often rejected at first and that even superstars fail sometimes, but that successful people learn how to do better next time.

In being more accepting of others and yourself, you teach your child an essential component of *authentic success*—that no one is good at everything but successful people grow from their mistakes.

~ OVERSCHEDULED KIDS (AND OVERBOOKED PARENTS)

Somewhere in this march toward success, the collective wisdom became that the more kids do, the better they'll do. Maybe it had to do with playing the odds—if you try this and that and that, you'll end up standing out at something. There's some sense in that thinking, quite frankly. Parents also rallied around the idea that busy kids are happy kids. We used to play from morning until dark, or at least until our parents sent someone to find us, but some neighborhoods nowadays look like ghost towns even on weekend afternoons. We assume that keeping kids busy with sports, lessons, Scouts, and other enrichment activities helps keep them out of trouble and away from too much TV or video games.

Some high-energy kids flourish with a full plate, and in some communities organized activities might be the only outlet for kids to play safely or congregate with friends. But overstretched kids can also be stressed-out kids. They skip meals and eat snacks on the run. They might feel exhausted, but can't go to bed on time because homework needs to get done. They always have to be "on" because an adult is watching what they do. There's not the spontaneity that comes with unstructured play. Even teens need time to play, because it gives them a chance to decompress and discover who they are. Being overbooked can have the opposite effect of what you first intended—instead of finding something she really enjoys, your child does a lot of different things with not much enthusiasm at all. Overscheduled kids might have trouble simply going with the flow because they're so used to having people tell them what to do.

Even if the intent of scheduling lots of enrichment activities starts out noble enough, parents can easily get caught up in "If everyone else's kids are doing it, I better make mine do it, too." The pressure mounts quickly— if you settle for the more casual demands of rec-league soccer instead of the fifth-grade travel team, your child won't have the stuff needed to make the high school team. Parents might also worry that their kids could become socially on the outs, and having lots of friends is seen as another measure of success. Ballet, gymnastics, judo—you don't want your kid to miss out on friendship opportunities. It's easy to see how the craziness snowballs, perhaps setting in motion the dynamic that leads to résumé packing as college approaches. Taking it easy becomes not an option.

None of this might seem unusual to a parent who has a high-demand job that requires constant attention to productivity. Also, parents who have taken time off from work for child rearing might continue with the same standards of efficiency and productivity that served them well on the job. A hectic, stressful day is a sign that you've gotten a lot done.

Another possibility is that parents become overinvolved in their kids' activities—they pace the sidelines at practice, watch every rehearsal, coordinate every team, and run the fund-raisers with the same strategic planning used in closing a business deal. It's a good thing for kids to see their parents involved and attending activities whenever possible, and certainly school teams and clubs couldn't function without parents' help. But sometimes too much parental involvement can put even more pressure on kids to perform because they know their parents are always close by and they don't want to disappoint you. Every game or show becomes a high-stakes performance.

Kids need some breathing room, to sometimes be able to come home and tell you *their* version of how things went. Maybe in their eyes they didn't mess up their lines or let the goal in. So often, we jump in and give our own play-by-play and that becomes a kid's reality.

I can't tell you how many activities are too many, or too few, for your child. But I urge you to be on the lookout for signs your child or teen might be taking on too much—exhaustion, headaches, stomachaches, or trouble falling asleep. Take a look at yourself, too. If you're feeing stressed or resentful from driving her to all her activities, there's a good chance she's stressed out, too.

~ THE YEAR-ROUND ATHLETE

In so many communities today, success is defined as being good at sports. Without a doubt, sports are a terrific outlet for young people. But where kids used to hang up their uniforms at the end of the season, the year-round athlete has become the ideal. The regular season is over, but kids continue to play the same sport throughout the off-season, taking part in travel teams, select teams, club teams, elite teams—there are all sorts of names to signal that playing sports is serious business.

For some kids who have a real passion and talent for a given sport, playing year-round offers the opportunity to improve skills and compete against other athletes who are similarly gifted. But the move to professionalize youth sports can have some unintended effects:

- Kids pick up the message at a young age that if they want to succeed at a sport, they need to get serious about it quickly. They hear that rec-league teams are for the not so athletic. Travel teams are where you need to be.
- Some kids drop out of sports early (and lose a terrific outlet for relieving stress) because they think sports are only for the most talented.

- Year-round sports require a lot of time and commitment: weekend tournaments, evening practices, summer camps, perhaps frequent workouts in the weight room. For some kids, it becomes too much to handle. Kids who might have eventually thrived at a sport sometimes drop out.

- The intensity required for year-round sports can make it hard to participate in other activities and sports. Some kids get pleasure from being a standout on one team and in the middle of the pack with another sport, or they like the variety that comes from doing multiple sports. But with youth and high school sports becoming so outcome-oriented, it's hard to do a sport just for fun. Kids end up missing out on the important social aspects of being on a team.

- Year-round sports are not good for young bodies because it creates repetitive stress and wear and tear on the same bones, ligaments, and joints. When kids vary sports during the year, this is less likely to be a problem.

- The sports intensity is fueled by the tantalizing thought that if you get serious about a sport at a young age, a college scholarship awaits. The truth is, it's the rare high school athlete who lands a full ride to college. The greatest payoffs are physical fitness and stress reduction.

Your role as a parent needs to be as fan, not personal coach or manager. Sports is an area where you need to do a self-check on whether you're living vicariously through your child, because that puts an awful lot of pressure on him to please you. Applaud your child's participation in sports, take lots of pictures, and enjoy your days in the cheering section, but don't imply that his ultimate success depends on it.

~ THE COLLEGE ADMISSIONS PROCESS (OR MESS)

Beginning at age fourteen or fifteen, kids hear day in and day out that every activity they do, every choice they make, every test they take and grade they earn has a profound effect on what will happen to them—four years and more from now. Then we wonder why they're anxious?

The adult world is telling teens very clearly what it takes to truly succeed—good grades, high SAT or ACT scores, acceptance to certain colleges—at the same time that teens are grappling with those all-important development questions, "Who am I?" and "Am I normal?" Talk about having a lot to manage.

It would be easy at this point to go into a diatribe against the college admissions process, but I want to keep the focus on what's going on between you and your teen.

YOUR GOAL NEEDS to be to avoid getting caught up in the warped message, and instead keep the focus on the attributes you believe are needed for *your* child's success. It's easy when everyone is talking about SAT prep courses and college rankings to forget why you so admire your child and the core traits that have served him well to date—he's compassionate, sensitive, witty, insightful, tenacious, an independent thinker, a consensus builder, or whatever.

One mom, sizing up her son's academic potential, confessed, "The problem with my son is that he's average." She failed to mention that her son was charismatic and a loyal friend—the kind of positive person other people gravitate toward. Another mom lamented that her daughter didn't get into her top college choice because "she lacked evidence of leadership," yet that same mom talked about how her daughter served as such a fine role model for her brother.

The skewed messages your child is getting from school (to be fair, school administrators are responding to parental pressure to push kids to make sure they get into good colleges), peers, college ranking guides, and Web sites won't go away, but you can provide needed balance to the two predominant myths that have taken hold:

Myth 1: Your score on a given test on a given day—the SAT or ACT—will determine the rest of your life.
That's a breathtaking statement. On one hand, it suggests that a good test score is *all* you need to be successful. Forget about the ongoing effort, willingness to take chances, and passion that we've been talking about. On the other

hand, it suggests that you can't possibly be successful if you don't have what it takes to land a high mark on a standardized test. That notion is demoralizing. Try to tell your kid to relax on test day after she's absorbed these messages.

Of course, it's true, for better or worse, that certain scores make students attractive candidates for certain colleges. And I'm not knocking the potential value of test-prep courses or the opportunities that high-profile universities and colleges can offer some kids. But when teens and parents buy into the notion that a high score will open up the gates to success, it puts all the focus on the endgame instead of allowing teens time to explore their emerging interests.

Despite the catchy titles of college ranking guides, there really is no college that can magically transform your life. Finding a life that makes you happy and satisfied comes about through hard work, trying out different experiences, and recognizing what it is that turns you on. The higher-profile colleges might help land your first job, but nowadays most people stay at their first job only a few years. It's your performance at that job, especially how you interact with your coworkers, that gets you to the next step.

If the pressure to produce a perfect résumé—perfect enough to get into the best college—ends up stifling creativity and innovative spirit and interferes with the development of good interpersonal skills and a capacity to rebound from setbacks, long-term chances for success in the work world are undermined.

Myth 2: To get into a decent college, you have to be able to document that you're good at everything.
This one is somewhat baffling because we've all heard truly successful people say that they're actually *not good* at any number of things. Successful people usually excel in one or two areas, but what makes them interesting is that they have hobbies unrelated to their work or are willing to take on new challenges.

The myth that you need to be well-balanced and brilliant in every way is driving kids to beef up their résumés like never before—sports, countless clubs, summer courses, camps, unpaid internships, and volunteer positions. Our kids are doing things we never dreamed of, and that can be a good thing. It's the overdrive and calculated planning that are troubling. Volunteering at the local soup kitchen, for instance, might be seen as a so-so activity; better to stand out more in the pile of college applicants by spending your vacation building a health clinic in a foreign country. I'm all in favor of volunteerism—it brings out the best in kids and opens their eyes to people whose lives might not be as comfortable as theirs. But I worry whether résumé building is making kids a bit jaded about the real meaning of contribution—you help out because someone needs you. You can't document kindness on a résumé. Also, sometimes the best things in life are discovered on a whim, not through deliberate planning.

As you approach the college application process with your teen, don't forget that while your teen is getting ever closer to independence, she continues to look to you for guidance and support. The values and attitudes you convey still really matter. You can't change what her peers, teachers, or guidance counselor tell her about *what it takes to succeed,* but you can remind her of the many qualities you see that make you certain she *will be successful.* You can help her see that there is so much life to be lived both before and after college apps are history—there's no need to sacrifice happiness and healthy balance in order to achieve.

If you knock anything less than the "perfect product" in preparation for the college hunt, you're going to kindle perfectionism, which will squash creativity and innovation. If you urge your child to beef up his activities, you're saying that you don't think he's good enough as he is. If you write your senior's essay, you will be saying, "I don't think your own story as you see it is impressive enough." (On the other hand, if you're not available to hear her ideas, you may be communicating that you don't care about how she presents herself.) If you treat your teen's rejection to her first-choice school as a disaster, you are saying, "It's impossible to be happy with a second choice." Remember, this is your child's initiation rite into adulthood; it is imperative he or she feels successful. Life is filled with wonderful second, third, and fourth choices. Life works out just as it is supposed to if you take full advantage of every moment.

People who are *authentically successful* find opportunities to shine in unexpected ways and places.

CHAPTER TWENTY-SIX

~

MANAGING STRESS IN HEALTHY WAYS

STRESS IS EVERYWHERE. Just hear the chat all around us: "I'm so stressed out." "My job is stressing me out." "I'm *really, Really, REALLY* stressing."

Sometimes it seems as if people are wearing stress like fashion—being busy and overwhelmed and perhaps even close to their breaking point is considered a sign that they're important or needed. Badge of honor or not, too much stress can damage both emotional and physical health.

Adults often assume that children and teens don't really stress. Kids don't have to worry about paying the mortgage, dodging layoffs, or juggling family demands. If you're one of those adults who believes kids don't have stress, it's time to take another listening tour. Go back to the mall or to a school parking lot at the end of the day. Listen to the conversations your kids are having with their friends as you drive them. Look at your child's face as she talks about school, her peers, violence in the neighborhood. Pay attention to the physical symptoms that might signal that her body is awash in stress.

Teens sometimes behave as though they are made of steel to mask their real thoughts and feelings, but they worry about all the things that adults worry about, including the economy, crime, wars, and the environment. They worry about their education and their future. They worry about school performance and how well their family is getting along. They worry about their parents' happiness. They have a heightened sense of worry about what their peers think of them. Their biggest source of stress is trying to answer those fundamental developmental questions—"Who am I?" and "Am I normal?"

TEENS SOMETIMES HAVE catastrophic thinking about things that we know from experience do not really affect life in the long run. They fear a B+ with all of the intensity that we fear losing our jobs. They are certain their future is over if they get a critique that is less than glowing. They agonize over the loss of a friendship with almost the same level of emotional energy we would react to a divorce.

I consider this chapter one of the most important in the book, because if you can guide your teen to manage everyday stress as well as extraordinary pressures in healthy ways, you will be taking a huge leap toward creating that well-balanced thirty-five-year-old we're all hoping for. This chapter is strategically placed before we discuss *How* to deal with drinking, drugs, and sex because your teen is more apt to steer clear of those behaviors if equipped with a repertoire of healthy coping skills. I am going to teach you my Ten-Point Stress-Management Plan that you can, in turn, share with your teen.

The ten points are:

1. Identify the problem and break it into small pieces.
2. Avoid things that bring you down.
3. Let some things go.
4. Exercise.
5. Relax your body.
6. Eat well.
7. Get enough sleep.
8. Take "instant vacations."

9. Release emotional tensions.
10. Get outside yourself and contribute to the world.

Before we delve into each of those, let's take a look at what stress is and why it can ruin our health.

~ STRESS IS A SURVIVAL TOOL THAT CAN HELP US OR HARM US

For our ancestors roaming the jungle or grassy plains eons ago, stress was a survival tool. Stress mounted a biological response that readied all their body systems—nervous, hormonal, sensory, circulatory, muscular, digestive—to flee a tiger or other threat, or to dig in and fight. Stress also helped our ancestors stay alive by keeping them on guard, just in case a tiger leaped from the bushes or enemy villagers attacked. A danger they faced one day made them alert the next day for similar signs of trouble.

FLASH FORWARD and that same stress helps us today. When our surroundings dictate that we should be vigilant, fearful, or even hostile, our bodies transform nearly instantly to meet our needs. The adrenaline that spurred our ancestors into action and kept them from getting eaten helps us to run into the street to grab a child or make a snap decision in an emergency. Lower-level stress sharpens our thinking as a deadline bears down or the big game gets under way. It gives us energy to go one more round in practicing a presentation so we're polished and prepared for any questions that come up. It allows us to mobilize all our forces in an ongoing crisis.

The problem occurs when your body gets in the habit of mounting a full-blown stress response to rather ordinary events. You're primed for fight or flight, but in reality there's nothing to kill or run from. Without a physical outlet that makes you feel like you're escaping, the stress locks in and takes hold, ultimately keeping you from the physical and mental relaxation that's needed to get you refreshed for the next challenge to come along.

Similarly, a trauma or frightening experience can leave you in a constant state of worry, just waiting for another disaster. Your emotions no longer are capable of giving you an accurate picture of what's going on. You might begin to view rather ordinary circumstances as outright catastrophes.

Although stress can be the fuel that gets us through a tough situation, it can also be destructive to our bodies and minds. Ongoing stress generates hormones that over time contribute to obesity and chronic diseases, such as high blood pressure, heart disease, and stroke. For teens, stress can be so uncomfortable that it drives them to risky behaviors, such as smoking or drinking, that lessen their discomfort for the moment but may severely harm them in the long term.

There are two keys to preventing destructive stress. The first is to be able to take a realistic assessment of whether a given situation is worthy of an all-out stress response or heightened vigilance. The second is to have a set of coping strategies in place that deal with stress in a healthy way.

For our ancestors, stress was an innate response essential for *surviving,* but for your teen, knowing how to manage stress is the key to *thriving.* Some parents think the best way to help their kids manage stress is to protect them from anything that's upsetting or to assume their kids' problems as their own, but that doesn't promote resilience in a stress-filled world. When adolescents have effective coping skills, they don't just try to survive for the moment by doing shots or popping pills to dull their worries. They develop healthy habits that allow them to view challenges not as catastrophes (tigers) about to descend, but as problems that can be figured out. They see disappointments not as permanent setbacks but as lessons to learn from. They know how to take the steps needed to thrive.

∼ WHAT HAPPENS TO THE BODY DURING STRESS

To better understand why effective stress management methods involve both the body and mind, it is helpful to know how the body functions during a stressful event and how our thoughts can transform our body into a relaxed state. Consider what happens:

- All of the bodily changes needed to take on an emergency are triggered instantly by the nervous system and then hormones serve as messengers to keep the body in a prepared state. The brain controls the nerves but is heavily influenced by emotion and passion. So how we think about a situation or perceive a crisis has a huge bearing on how strongly and for how long the body reacts. This is why how we think about or experience stress and what we choose to do about it are critical to our health. Blood pressure, for example, can fluctuate in a fraction of a second so the blood quickly shifts in a way that allows you to jump up and run. If you are worried that an emergency could be coming at any time, blood pressure might remain elevated, preparing for that looming crisis.

- Some hormones help the body burst into action. Additional hormones replenish the body after a crisis or sustain it in a vigilant state to prepare it to launch into full-blown crisis mode at any time. These "replenishment" hormones drive both your thirst and your appetite. They guide you to eat salty foods to keep that blood pressure up. The hormones associated with chronic stress are tightly linked to chronic disease.

- As soon as the body senses peril, either through our thoughts or our "gut instinct," it rapidly prepares itself to escape the danger or fight it head on. The first thing that happens is that the blood shifts from the stomach and intestines—where it has been absorbing nutrients—to the muscles that will propel us toward safety. (This partly explains that sinking feeling or butterflies you get in your gut as a first reaction to stress.) Then the heart beats rapidly to pump the blood through the muscles and lungs. Breathing intensifies so the body can absorb as much oxygen as possible to nourish the muscles. Sweat cools the body as it works on its escape. Pupils dilate so any obstacles in the escape path will be noticed, even in the dark. Thinking is focused only on escape because now is not the time to stop and negotiate.

- A set of hormones is released that works with our nervous system to act in an extreme crisis. These hormones scream *Ruuuuuuuuuuuuuuuuun!* When they are surging through a body that is standing still, the body is confused. But when exercise is used as a response to stress, the body feels as if it has successfully dealt with the emergency. This largely explains why exercise has such a calming effect on stress.

- Just as there is a crisis mode, there is a relaxed mode. These modes do not operate simultaneously; either the body is functioning calmly or reacting to stress. This means that one of the keys to transforming our bodies into a state of relaxation is by "flipping a switch," and that can be done by doing the opposite of what the body does in crisis. It's not so easy to shrink your pupils, reverse your blood flow back into your gut, or calm racing thoughts in a state of panic. However, each of us can control our breathing with ease and thereby switch our bodies into relaxed mode. Breathing is the portal to relaxation.

~ GOOD FIXES, BAD FIXES

Stress sometimes stems from true life-or-death issues, in which case it is a necessity to mount every bit of our stress response. But sometimes we experience something as if it is an emergency, even though it couldn't actually harm us. Whether genuinely life-threatening or just deeply disturbing because of how we perceive a situation, stress makes us physically uncomfortable and emotionally fragile, often triggering irritability, anger, and shortsightedness.

To avoid that discomfort, we'll look for anything that will banish those feelings. We all have positive and negative ways of coping, and both approaches work, at least temporarily. With stress bearing down, we might go out for a walk, pet the dog, or do gardening. But stress, if left to fester, can be wearying and even paralyzing, and it can lead us to grab on to quick fixes to quiet our inner turmoil. The fix might be a few glasses of wine or a junk food pig-out or perhaps a night of channel surfing. The fixes are effective in the moment, and then the gnawing of stress returns.

For teens, the fixes might be the very things parents worry the most about—drinking, drug use, anorexia or bulimia, self-mutilation, sex outside the context of a healthy relationship, truancy, running away. Other negative coping strategies involve avoidance. Procrastination and immersion in the cyber world are less worrisome than drinking or drugs, but they still interfere with success. All those fixes offer some fleeting relief, but soon a troubling pattern takes hold. First, stress leads to an unhealthy fix. Then the unhealthy fix leads to educational and social failures. Judgments and condemnations come from all directions and stress rises. These added pressures lead to ever more reliance on the unhealthy fix. This pattern can be the birth of addictions.

So how can we break that troubling cycle or keep it from happening at all? Parents can have a tremendous impact on whether their teens avoid negativity and dangerous behaviors by guiding them toward healthy ways to relieve and reduce stress. Please let this point really sink in: Your greatest opportunity to steer your child away from the behaviors that frighten you the most could be to point him toward positive coping strategies.

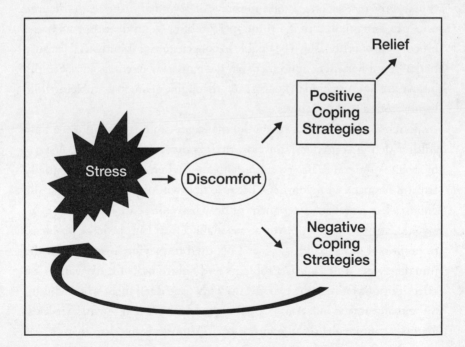

The diagram on page 249 helps explain what you're aiming for. Some stress is a given in life, but the response to it can be managed. Negative strategies, as you can see in the drawing, end up causing harm because they perpetuate and intensify the cycle of stress. Positive coping strategies, on the other hand, enhance well-being because they lead to at least some relief. As a parent, you want the path to positive coping strategies to be so familiar and well paved for your teen that it makes much more sense for her to follow a healthy strategy than to reach for a dangerous quick fix.

∼ SIZING UP STRESS

A first step to effective stress management is to be able to separate the real tigers from the paper ones. People who are good at coping can distinguish an actual crisis from a challenge. A bear attacking us on a hiking trail is an undeniable crisis. A tornado forecast mobilizes us to quickly take shelter. Milder stressors, such as a job interview or tryouts for the team, deserve some extra attention. But if a young person blows a mild stressor such as a test out of proportion, she'll be unable to concentrate and study well because she has all of her energy and focus on facing down an emergency. Simply put, we are not supposed to be working through a geometry problem while fleeing from a pack of wolves.

Parents' subtle (or not-so-subtle) messages can heavily influence how children define a crisis, and thus how their bodies respond to stress. A starting point is for you to have a calm demeanor when something potentially stressful happens with your teen because that will up the chances that she will arrive at a realistic assessment of how bad things are or aren't. Try to have the attitude that if time or a reasonable effort can solve the problem, it's not a real crisis. Sandy got her kids used to playing a game from the time they were little called "Problems and Solutions." "I can't wait to see what solution you're going to come up with," she'd tell them when a bump in the road came along. Another parent made it her habit to ask her kids, "Is this a catastrophe or an annoyance?" Almost always, the answer was annoyance, a recognition that it wasn't worth getting all worked up over.

It is beyond the scope of this chapter to teach fully how to transform someone's thinking into a healthier pattern so that stress can be assessed realistically. If you are concerned about your teen's doomsday attitude, speak to your teen's guidance counselor or health care provider about how best to help her develop healthier thinking patterns. I also suggest two books that you may find helpful: Dweck's book *Mindset: The New Psychology of Success* and *The Resilience Factor: 7 Essential Skills for Overcoming Life's Inevitable Obstacles* by Karen Reivich and Andrew Shatté (Broadway, 2003).

ANOTHER GOOD FIRST step in helping your child learn to handle stress is for you to model good coping strategies. Our kids are constantly seeing how we cope, or don't. They hear us blow up at minor irritations and complain about the same things day after day. They hear us say we skipped lunch for the umpteenth time because we had too much to get done. They see us constantly check our e-mails and texts, looking anxious when something isn't there. They see us go outside for a smoke instead of talking through a family issue. How you wear stress plays a big role in how your child learns to manage it. This gives me one more opportunity to tell you to put on your oxygen mask first—taking care of yourself really is the most effective way to care for your family. Many of us were raised to think it's best to keep our emotions bottled up and forge on with the attitude "Don't worry. Everything will work out just fine." A suck-it-up strategy is okay in some circumstances, but if chronic stress is ignored, it eats at us and can lead to depression or anxiety that interferes with our ability to sleep, think clearly, and get things done. Relationships can suffer.

When you take time to relax, pursue a hobby or creative interest, or spend time with your spouse or friends, you soothe your stress and you show your teen ways to achieve good emotional health. It's a powerful statement to say, "I had a hard day at work. I'm going for a run before starting dinner," or "Taking care of Grandpa wore me out today. I'm heading to bed early." When you live a balanced life, you show your teen what he needs to do to be healthy and happy.

～ HOW THE STRESS-MANAGEMENT PLAN WAS CREATED

I see teens all the time who somehow manage to thrive in spite of an incredible amount of stress in their lives. Their parents are divorced and not speaking to each other. Their neighborhood has gangs and drug dealers. Their high school expects them to carry a load of courses suited for a college kid. They feel pressure from their families to stand out at sports so they can land a scholarship, but feel pressured by their friends to kick back and party.

I have consistently noticed two things that seem to make a difference in who thrives and who turns to the dangerous escapes. The first is that kids who rise above adversity have that adult who believes in them unconditionally and never wavers in holding them to high expectations. The second is that young people who participate in activities that offer a positive peer group and support healthy coping tend to thrive. These positive activities include volunteer opportunities that allow kids the satisfaction of contributing to their community; organized or pickup sports; outdoors groups, such as hiking clubs and Scouts that allow for physical releases and emotional escapes; and programs that provide an outlet for kids to express themselves creatively.

I studied the scientific literature to see what coping techniques have been proven to be effective. I've also made a habit over the years of asking teens and their parents what works for them in managing stress. I have used stress-reduction strategies over the last two decades with young people from age eleven to twenty-five. I've seen the payoff both at the shelter where I care for homeless and traumatized youth and my medical practice, where I more typically see young people who are thriving in many ways but need to overcome day-to-day challenges. All of that led me to formalize my approach into a research-informed, yet practical Ten-Point Stress-Management Plan. It is an integral part of my overall strategy for building resilience in teens and is presented in great detail in my book, *Building Resilience in Children and Teens*.

∼ THE PRINCIPLES BEHIND THE PLAN

Everyone responds to challenge differently. Researchers often describe different coping styles as falling into one of three categories: (a) problem-focused engagement, (b) emotion-focused engagement, and (c) disengagement or withdrawal. In plain English, some people cope by dealing with the problem directly and fixing what they can. Others focus more on the emotions associated with the problems; they work at making themselves feel better. Still other people choose to avoid the problem; they deny it, withdraw from it, or escape from it using any means possible.

A great deal of research has gone into the relative benefits of problem-focused versus emotion-focused strategies. People who use problem-focused coping strategies to reduce stressors rather than just deal with the uncomfortable emotions they produce usually fare better because if only the emotions are dealt with, the problem remains to strike another day. Nevertheless, emotion-focused strategies are useful because they often involve seeking support from others and that allows people to forge connections that are supportive through good times and bad. It is generally agreed that people who engage a problem (by focusing on either the problem or the emotions) do better than those who avoid it altogether.

It would be a mistake; however, to believe that we should rise to meet every challenge life throws our way. Avoidance will never address the problem, but a problem can be so overwhelming that it might be wise to say, "I really don't care; it doesn't bother me," at least for a little while. We shouldn't expect people to face every struggle or dilemma immediately because sometimes time and space allow for skills to be developed and strategies to be formed.

Resilient people are able to address problems while managing the physical and emotional discomfort created by stress. They also can strategically avoid problems so they can conserve energy to address issues truly worthy of attention. A comprehensive stress-reduction plan has to include a wide array of strategies that prepare us to problem-solve effectively, deal with emotions in a healthy way, and use safe, thoughtful means to avoid other problems.

∽ APPROACHING THE PLAN FOR DIFFERENT AGES

Some of the stress-management strategies included in my plan can benefit children as young as two and all are useful for teens. But your role in guiding your child to use it will vary dramatically depending on her age:

- **Young children.** Stress reduction is too abstract a concept to teach to young children. Just offer them opportunities to learn how to feel emotionally healthy and physically strong. Let them notice that they feel better after exercise and lighter after they have expressed themselves through art. Use blowing bubbles to teach them about controlled and relaxing breathing. Offer even the youngest child a listening ear so she can learn how much better it feels to talk. Let her learn about escape through play, fantasy, and reading.
- **Preadolescents and early adolescents** will listen attentively as you teach them stress-management strategies. Offer them opportunities to practice what you have taught them.
- **Mid and late adolescents** probably don't want to hear about stress reduction from you. (But remember that they are watching you!) Let them read this book or go to my Web site FosteringResilience .com, to further their understanding of stress and allow them to devise a personalized coping plan.

All children and adolescents will learn from what you do. It really is true that sometimes our actions speak so loudly that our kids can't hear the words we say. Your child will better embrace safe and productive coping strategies if he sees you taking care of yourself and not spinning out of control.

∼ THE TEN-POINT STRESS-MANAGEMENT PLAN

Each of the ten points in my Stress-Management Plan includes a variety of strategies that you and your child can try out and tinker with as needed. Managing stress is about finding out what works best for you—not everyone responds to a given strategy in the same way, and what is helpful at one point may be less effective later on. That said, if you were to pick only a few of these strategies to focus on with your young adolescent, I'd suggest exercise, good nutrition, and sleep. They're very tangible strategies and the payoffs are often quickly visible.

Don't try to implement all the points at once. Pick an item or two from each category to see which ones fit best. For example, the creative arts provide outlets for expression, but you don't have to be a concert pianist, master sculptor, *and* world-class photographer. There's a good chance simply tinkering on the keys or getting your hands covered with pottery clay will work pretty well. It's nice to be the quarterback, but the guy running alongside you gets the same stress-reduction benefits of exercise. Personal tastes have to come into play, too. Some people like to go fishing to relax; others prefer to sit beside the stream and watch the water ripple over rocks. I'm trying to say, "Don't stress about the stress plan."

THE PLAN IS a ten-*point* plan, not a ten-*step* plan. Draw from its wisdom to match what is needed at the moment. Sometimes problem-solving is the last thing a person can do; only a run or playing outside will relieve stress. At other times, there is a burning need to conquer the problem, and taking a moment off feels unimaginable.

The plan has a five-pronged approach. (a) It helps adolescents identify the problem at hand and go after it in a doable way. (b) It teaches adolescents ways to take care of their body so stress is lowered. (c) It provides techniques for managing and releasing potentially damaging emotions. (d) It acknowledges that there are healthy ways to escape feelings sometimes.

(e) It recognizes that young people who contribute to the world feel better themselves.

Finally, even though I designed the plan for teens, the approach should work wonders for you, too.

~ TEN STRESS-BUSTING STRATEGIES

TACKLE THE PROBLEM

1. Identify the problem and break it into small parts.
The first step in dealing with a problem is identifying it and then focusing on realistic ways to resolve it. When we see a problem as bigger than we are, we begin to view it figuratively as an insurmountable mountain. We cannot imagine climbing to the top. We give up before we begin, get anxious, or, maybe as a defense, decide to ignore the problem or deal with it later. But ignoring problems doesn't make them disappear, and procrastination is usually a prescription for anxiety because challenges loom larger when they remain in the background. When they finally are faced, there are often new tasks that need to be dealt with simultaneously, and the cycle of stress deepens.

A good strategy is to break a problem into little pieces. It means visualizing that mountain differently, viewing it as a series of hills that lead to the summit. As each hill is climbed, the height seems less imposing. It's helpful to also remember that each hill is made up of rocks or dirt and that if you are equipped with the right shovel, you can get to work whittling down the hills.

When problems are divided into clearly defined parts, it becomes easier to see some way to begin to take action. Accomplishing that first step then gives you encouragement to go on to the next one. Forward movement builds momentum. Making lists can help kids see how a problem that seems gigantic can, in fact, be manageable. The thought of having to complete five college applications is daunting, but the various components needed to get to that goal aren't quite so scary: (a) Do outline of essay. (b) Work on Application A. (c) Ask English teacher for letter of recommendation. (d) Do rough draft of essay. (e) Work on Application B, and so forth. Even better would be if you make a time line because it offers more assurance that if you deal with the problem one step at a time, you can accomplish a task larger than you imagined you could handle. You might even end up ahead of schedule.

Social situations that seem catastrophic to a teen can also be managed better when broken down. "I got in a fight with Shanae and now everybody hates me" is a social nightmare in the life of a teenager. Panic will set in and your teen cannot imagine ever living a normal life again. But with some active listening you can help her find the inroads that can repair relationships. "Everybody" suddenly turns into a few girls, and maybe even two or three friends understand the situation and can help her find the right words to deescalate the social crisis.

2. Avoid things that bring you down.

Sometimes confronting problems isn't the best strategy. In fact, sometimes even just being exposed to a problem is all it takes to trigger bad behavior or unwise choices. When a person with an addiction problem returns to her community after rehabilitation, she is strongly counseled to avoid her "triggers." Triggers are those people, places, or things that either influence you negatively or push one of your buttons so that you make bad decisions. Why would we use this wisdom only to help someone recover from an addiction? We should use it to prevent problems because much of stress can be avoided with a little bit of foresight.

There's no reason to confront every challenge. Sometimes it makes more sense to stay away from people, places, or things that bring on stress. Sometimes it's not so obvious who or what drags us down, but usually it is. You can avoid a route home from school that brings you into contact with the neighborhood tough-guy or walk away from conversations about who's applying where for college. If you want to break a bad habit, such as smoking, you can try to steer clear of kids who do it, at least for now. Sometimes turning off your cell phone or logging off your laptop is the best way to avoid things that pull you down.

3. Let some things go.

An essential part of coping or dealing with problems is to sometimes mount a direct response. That takes energy and focus. It is vitally important that you have that energy when you need it. This means that it's best to conserve energy by focusing on things you realistically think you can influence and let go of the things you can't. Optimists are sometimes not the best at coping because they may expend energy trying to fix things that can't change. Don't get me wrong here; hope is incredibly important, as are a can-do attitude and tenacity. But people who handle problems well also have a realistic assessment of a challenge.

In some cases, there really is nothing you can do to fix a situation. The problem is what it is, so you need to focus your energy on what you can control. Perhaps your chemistry teacher demands that you memorize the entire periodic table of elements. You can mount a class campaign to try to get the teacher to change her mind, which she won't, or buckle down and make note cards to help you study.

The serenity prayer most often attributed to the theologian Reinhold Niebuhr captures the essence of this coping strategy: Grant me the serenity to accept the things I cannot change; courage to change the things I can; and wisdom to know the difference.

TAKE CARE OF YOUR BODY

4. Exercise.

Of any of the ten stress-busting strategies, exercise is the most important. Research has shown the power of exercise not only to lower stress but also to enhance concentration and focus, which are key to learning and performance. Exercise can be an essential component of treatment plans for kids with ADHD, depression, and anxiety. A good book that explains more about that is *Spark: The Revolutionary New Science of Exercise and the Brain,* by John J. Ratey, M.D. (Little, Brown and Co., 2008).

If you think back to the role of stress in our ancestors' lives, it makes perfect sense why exercise remains so important to physical and mental health. When you're stressed, your body is programmed to say "Fight!" Or

"Run for your life!" Modern-day exercise helps modulate the stress-related hormones involved in those age-old responses. But if you don't exercise—if you don't run or fight—the stress hormones remain unused and become confused. You feel jittery, edgy, unfocused, perhaps tired or even somewhat paralyzed by worry.

By listening to the signals your body is giving off, you can determine what type of exercise is best for the feelings you're having at the moment. Are you scared and want to take off? Are you angry and ready to take someone on? Are you nervous and in need of calming down? A run or bike ride might mimic the feeling of "Run for your life!" Shadowboxing or a workout with a punching bag can release anger ("Fight!"). Weight lifting can allow time to refocus and give a sense of power and control needed to deal with ongoing stress. Exercising also makes the body strong and fit—which can make you feel more confident during tough times. Try to encourage your child to participate in both team and individual exercise. Team sports offer lots of added benefits like collaboration and healthy competition, skills that will carry into the workplace. Individual sports become the lifelong sports that busy people can manage on their own time. No matter what, exercise is usually enjoyable, and by mixing it up, you don't get bored.

Timing of exercise is important, too. Late-night exercise can make you too wired for sleep, so it's better to do it in the late afternoon or just after dinner. For some kids, exercise has an especially strong focusing effect, so early-morning exercise is beneficial. Kids who say they don't have time to exercise—especially those who run high on anxiety—need to be told that they don't have time not to exercise. The payoff in efficiency, reduced anxiety, and better sleep will be clear very quickly.

5. Relax your body.

Relaxation is not just the absence of external stressors. It's a state that can be actively achieved if you understand how the body and mind are connected. Earlier in this chapter, I explained all that happens to the body when it senses that trouble is afoot and the fact that the body has two nervous systems—one relaxed and one poised for crisis. Because those systems cannot act simultaneously, it is helpful to know how to flip the switch to relaxation. You can learn to slow your breathing and relax your muscles by shifting your posture and purposefully going through a self checklist: "Unclench my teeth, relax my jaw, drop my shoulders," and so on. People who practice yoga and meditation know the mental transformation that can occur when breathing slows and muscle tension fades. A good way to teach kids to slow down their breathing is to blow bubbles. Taking a warm bath is another way to work on slowing your breathing and relaxing your muscles. As you lie on your back and submerge your ears under the water, you can hear yourself breathe. As you take deep breaths you float higher, and as you exhale you gently sink. This repeated rhythmic action can help bring you to a state of deep relaxation. In number 7, below, I'll tell you about another particularly useful breathing technique.

6. Eat right.

Good nourishment improves concentration and contributes to an even temper, both helpful for managing stress. It's beyond the scope of this book to offer a detailed nutrition plan for your teen, but the basic thing to remember is that the brain functions best throughout the day with a relatively stable supply of sugar. Simple carbohydrates—sugary drinks, candy, and other sweets—cause a spike and then a quick drop-off in blood sugar, while complex carbohydrates—fruits, vegetables, whole grains—keep the brain nourished with a steady sugar supply. Caffeinated drinks likewise provide a quick boost, only to be followed by a drop in energy and focus.

It's not just about what you eat, it's also about how you eat. Research has shown the powerful protective effect that family meals can have on teens. A good meal shared with family or friends creates an opportunity for meaningful conversation and for a connection, an important part of building resilience in teens. It can be difficult to keep teens on a regular eating schedule because of practices, jobs, and other commitments, but eating together should be a family priority as you strive to lower everyone's stress at the end of a busy day.

7. Get enough sleep.

Being tired exacerbates stress; stress causes sleeplessness. The cycle can be broken by adopting good sleep habits. Many parents concede defeat on this one. What can you do if homework and texting keep kids up at all hours of the night? And adolescents' body clocks really do tell them to stay up later, even though they still have to get up early for school. Nonetheless, teens need at least eight hours of sleep to function well. Encouraging more sleep, along with exercise, is one wellness routine for which I guarantee you'll notice a change.

A good starting point is to draw your teen into conversations about what happens when he doesn't get enough sleep—you drift off in class, get into arguments—and what happens when he does. "I felt great in the game today!" Teens sometimes don't realize how exhausted they are. Taking stock of their sleeping environment is also key. A bedroom should be a soothing spot, not a high-stimulation zone. The American Academy of Pediatrics recommends no TVs in bedrooms, and we've already talked about how to institute a family policy that requires all cell phones to be charged in the kitchen overnight so sleep is not disturbed.

Research shows that exercise should be completed by about five hours before sleep, or else the body will still be overheated, and we fall asleep best when we are cooling down. If bedtime is at eleven, that means exercise needs to be done by six. Because exercise is a terrific focusing agent, homework should soon follow. That still leaves time afterward for a little TV, downloading music, or whatever your teen enjoys.

About an hour before bed, your teen should begin to actively work on getting into a relaxed state. A hot bath or a cup of warm milk or herbal tea is helpful, as is reading a book or listening to music. Your teen can symbolically sign off on the day and any of its worries by loading his backpack, making a preliminary list of what needs to get done the next day, and placing her phone in the charger so that late-breaking calls or texts don't send her into a fit. The goal is to not take worries to bed because that will cause the adrenaline to keep pumping, making sleep hard to come by.

It's important not to turn your bed into your counselor. Some people are so busy or distracted during the day that they save all their planning or worries for when their head hits the pillow. Their heard starts spinning with excitement or anxiety and they can't get into the calm mode needed to fall asleep. Instead, your teen should deal with her emotions in a positive way before turning out the light—to release them, so to speak (see number 9, page 263)—so the bed is associated only with sleep.

Having a calming routine leading up to bedtime should help your teen arrive in bed relaxed and ready to sleep. If he still feels a bit wired or has trouble falling asleep, he can use the "4-8" breathing technique, which is far better than counting sheep because it distracts you from what's on your mind and gets you physically into a relaxed state. It works like this: Interlock your fingers loosely across your belly. Take a full breath, expanding first your belly and then your entire chest. As you breathe in slowly, notice that your fingers are moving apart. Breathe in for four seconds, hold it, and then release the air slowly, counting to eight. Notice your fingers coming back together. Repeat several times, focusing fully on the timing and depth of your breathing and on the sensation of your fingers spreading apart and coming together. Soon you'll be fast asleep.

Manage Your Emotions

8. Take an "instant vacation."

You can consciously choose to take a break from the emotions that are controlling you. When children are small, play serves as a powerful release for their pent-up energy and emotions—they exercise their bodies almost to the point of collapse and let their imaginations run wild. Sadly, as our kids grow, we sometimes forget the benefits of play, seeing hanging out as a waste of time. But often the best way to escape stress is to be immersed in something else. Call it healthy disengagement, play, or simply giving yourself a needed break. You can go on an instant vacation from your emotions by visualizing a beautiful spot you discovered on a real vacation, immersing yourself in a hobby, or shooting some baskets with a friend. One of the best ways to achieve an instant vacation is to read a book. Reading takes you somewhere new and requires all your senses as you imagine how things look, taste, sound, feel, and smell. The problem will still be there when you return from your instant vacation, but often a mental break allows a fresh perspective or even a solution to begin to take shape.

9. Release emotional tensions.

We often try to manage stress by stuffing our feelings inside a "box" and clamping the lid down tight. Having everything stashed away feels good at first, but as more and more things get jammed inside the box, the pressure builds. Eventually the lid pops, spilling out the contents with a fury. Perhaps more concerning is that permanently tucking away feelings can lead to something worse than stress—it can lead to feeling nothing. Numbness takes hold when feelings seem too difficult to access or process.

The goal of this strategy is to learn to release emotions from your box in a controlled way so they don't explode, keep you up all night worrying, or distance you from your feelings. Here are some ways to release, or channel, emotions:

- Talking to someone you trust helps you understand you're not alone.
- Writing in a journal helps clarify your thinking.
- Prayer connects you with your inner thoughts and perhaps allows you to connect to a higher force.
- Meditation focuses thoughts.
- Crying has a cleansing effect.
- Laughing hits the reset button and gives you energy to start over.
- Playing allows your mind to run free.
- Writing poetry or prose, working on an art project, performing or composing music, doing photography, dancing, or acting allows you to express your feelings creatively.

All of these emotional releases prevent feelings from being trapped inside. The strategies are useful at night so that you do not take your swirling thoughts to bed.

10. Go outside yourself and contribute to the world.

Doing volunteer work or helping out a friend or family member can be deeply satisfying. If you think back to the Seven Cs of Resilience,

Contribution was on the list. Knowing others need you can help put your problems in perspective. It feels good to have people genuinely appreciate what you're doing, Kids who are surrounded by thank-yous instead of disapproval will live up to high expectations and be less likely to turn to the quick and easy fixes. They know they are role models and are being watched. Perhaps most important, people who experience the rewards of helping others may be more likely to ask for help themselves readily and without shame, something you want your teen to be able to do in times of stress.

～ THE PLAN ISN'T ALWAYS THE ONLY ANSWER

Your teen can draw up a personalized stress-reduction plan by going to my Web site FosteringResilience.com.

The Ten-Point Stress-Management Plan won't solve all of your teen's worries or make stress go away forever. It might also not be enough for your teen. In Chapter 30, we'll talk about how to recognize that your child might need the added support of professional counseling to get through a particularly stressful time.

We chose to talk about coping before we handled the next three topics that drive so much parental anxiety—peer pressure, sex, and drugs—because your child will be much less at risk of getting stuck in destructive behaviors or sidetracked from a positive path when she possesses a repertoire of positive coping strategies.

CHAPTER TWENTY-SEVEN

~

Peers

Relationships, Influence, and Sometimes Pressure

PEER PRESSURE IS often seen as a lurking sinister force just waiting to lead our innocent children astray. As our kids approach adolescence, we gird ourselves to do battle with all those mean girls, tough guys, and delinquents who may stand in our children's way, lead them away from virtue, or just hurt their feelings. Our inability to bubble wrap our kids or send them to school with a bodyguard leaves us feeling powerless. Experts who inform parents that their influence is diminished during adolescence, and that only peers matter, magnify the sense of hopelessness and fear. (FYI, they're wrong.)

Reality check. Peer pressure is nothing new; it has always been a factor in teen life. In fact, some aspects of it contribute to healthy development. Young people who learn to handle the peer world well get good practice for dealing with workplace dynamics and friendships throughout life.

Let's take some pressure out of this discussion. Instead of peer pressure, let's talk about peer relationships. Sure, some of those relationships are uncomfortable and others may be dangerous. Our job is to prepare our children to maneuver the challenging relationships relatively unscathed and with an ability to follow their own compass—to stand on their own two feet in peer-charged situations.

There is so much more to this topic than just teaching your child to resist a bottle of vodka being passed his way. You want your teen to understand the essentials for developing trusting friendships and the importance of seeking relationships that are supportive and secure enough that the other person can challenge your teen when your teen needs guidance or is headed for trouble. Finding a cheerleader is easy; it's harder to find a coach. You want your child to learn that although it is comfortable to hang in a homogeneous crowd, people who are different from us often have the most to teach us.

THE IMPORTANCE OF peer dynamics has had a subtle, though sometimes unspoken, role throughout this book. Each time you considered *When* your child was ready for something, on some level you may have been looking around to see what other parents (your peer group) were allowing and other kids (his peer group) were doing. When adolescents are ready for a given privilege is determined by when they are physically, emotionally, and cognitively ready . . . and when *they* think they're ready. Whether they think they are ready for a new privilege has a lot to do with what they perceive as "normal" in their peer group. In other words, they are likely to want to mimic what others are doing.

Some kids always want to be the trailblazer—they want to be the first kid in the class to have a cell phone or a girlfriend. Other kids' temperaments guide them to observe, hang back, and let their peers work out the kinks first. Some kids simply don't feel ready to drive, for instance, even though state laws say they are old enough. Ditto for dating—they are not there yet, even if the school calendar says in bold print JUNIOR PROM.

Most of the behaviors we fear—sex, drinking, drugs—are tightly intertwined with peer behaviors. Adolescents are forever on the alert for signs of what's normal in their peer group, or in a crowd which they aspire to join. Parents need to counteract the often negative and sometimes misleading portrayal of teens in the media and in communities because those messages can give teens a distorted and dangerous view of how they are "supposed" to act. The fact that teens are so influenced by cues around them isn't a character weakness. Think about the burning questions that all adolescents must answer—"Who am I?" and "Am I normal?" Those questions require that they look inward—while keeping an eye out for everything going on around them.

~ WHY PEERS MATTER: A DEVELOPMENTAL VIEW

To better understand the importance of peers to your teen, let's circle back to a few points about development. During adolescence, your child is developing on multiple fronts—physically, intellectually, morally, sexually, emotionally, socially. It's all part of the journey from dependence to independence. In pre-adolescence, a child sees himself primarily as part of a family unit. This is a wonderful thing, but if he is to become independent, he also has to begin seeing himself in a broader context. Remember, the answer to the question "Who am I?" has to be in part "I am not my parents," which helps explain why your child must look to peers both for support and to try out new identities.

In early adolescence, roughly age eleven to thirteen, kids begin to look outside their family for close relationships and cues on how to interact with the world. Friendships tend to be intense one-on-one relationships with members of the same sex. This is the time of BFFs. Exposure to people of the opposite gender usually occurs in group settings.

In mid-adolescence, around age fourteen to sixteen, conformity to the peer group is critical, and teens are certain everybody is watching them. What peers say takes on paramount importance—they help set the tone for what your child wears, how your child talks, what your child's priorities are, and even whether your child considers herself attractive. This is the time when teens are aggressively independent from their parents—"I'm my own man!" The irony is that these fiercely independent beings dress and act just like their friends. How they fit into the peer landscape means everything and they scramble to find a group. Sadly, this is also the meanest time of adolescence, when groups are defined by rigid roles and who's in and who's out. Many wildly popular teen shows catch on because they address teen anxieties by giving permission to be yourself—more than a brain, jock, or band geek. In mid-adolescence, dating becomes more common, but much of the motivation in picking a romantic interest may focus on social status and what—or who—looks good.

The heavy influence of peers starts to wane in late adolescence, beginning around age seventeen, as teens become more confident in their own identity and values. Friendships remain important, but having friends who are different becomes attractive—especially to kids with a "growth mindset." Romantic relationships become more about emotional intimacy and sharing—more of a private than public thing. It is a step toward living in the adult world, where the primary relationship will likely be with a spouse.

The shift from being primarily family-focused to being largely peer-focused is a normal and exciting part of adolescent development. It will happen even if your teen thinks you are the most amazing parent on the planet. Don't take it personally, but also don't retreat from your teen's life just because her friends or a romantic interest are more in it. Even if you think your child isn't listening, she is, and even if she complains about going to Grandma's house or playing Scrabble on Sunday nights, she takes comfort in the traditions and rituals that have always been part of your family. Even as peers become increasingly influential in adolescents' lives, parents remain critically influential, particularly as role models.

～ PROTECTING OUR TEENS

Despite occasionally high-risk or thoughtless behaviors, teens do not think they are invincible, although they do sometimes behave that way, especially when around friends. Knowing that your teen might act differently in a peer group than on his own provides a rationale for taking some basic steps to protect your teen from worrisome peer influence:

- **Teach your child to avoid large groups and crowds, or at least to stay on the periphery.** Even adults can have groupthink take over when in a large group. It can be exhilarating at a sporting event or concert, but it is also how riots can begin. Even people with a strong safety-minded orientation can get carried away by the fervor of a crowd. You can teach your child to remain vigilant at large events and to follow her instincts that something is about to get out of hand. It's even better if her instincts tell her when to avoid an event altogether.

- **Provide a reasonable level of monitoring and supervision, even for your older teen.** Because teens don't always think well on their feet, it helps them to know someone is watching out for them and that they will be held accountable. Your teen can always blame your backward rules for why he can't let a gang of kids descend on your house while you're out.

- **In situations that require particular focus, don't allow peers as a distraction.** The standout example here is prohibiting inexperienced drivers from taking peer passengers. The rationale for this is much more complex than kids goading drivers to speed. It is also about the fact that early drivers do not yet have well-honed automatic responses; they really need to think things through. Even calm passengers pose a distraction to a rookie driver.

- **Because your child's emotions can be heightened, you need to be the calm force.** It's easy to get swept up in peer drama because it isn't pleasant to see your child feeling slighted or rejected. Since adolescents can sometimes have an exaggerated response to what a peer says to them, don't add fuel to the fire. Be a good listener so that your child can sort through what's really happening and come up with a strategy for how to respond. "Nobody likes me anymore" might very well mean that a friend or two misinterpreted something your child said; perhaps a clarification or simple apology on her part is all that's needed to make things right.

∼ SOME PROBLEMS TO CONSIDER

You hope, of course, that your child never suffers because of peers, but the truth is that most kids experience some uncomfortable interactions. There are three major ways that your child could be harmed by peers. The first is if their peers encourage them to engage in worrisome behaviors. The second is if your child becomes part of a peer group that does not have an achievement orientation. The third is through bullying. We'll talk later in the chapter about ways to prevent those first two possibilities, but we'll begin here with bullying. Although you can prepare your child for the possibility of bullying, it is your vigilance and ability to react that may be the greatest help here. We will discuss three forms of bullying: physical bullying, emotional bullying, and cyber-bullying, even though there is something artificial about dividing bullying into these categories since they can all be emotionally jarring to your child.

Bullying has gotten a great deal of attention recently because of some extreme (rare) cases that resulted in serious injury or suicide. Less extreme cases are an all-too-common occurrence and can significantly affect the victim. The American Academy of Child and Adolescent Psychiatry states that as many as half of schoolchildren are bullied at some time, and at least 10 percent are bullied on a regular basis. The American Psychological Association noted that regardless of whether young people are bullies or victims, there may be associated depression and anxiety. They view bullying as a mental health problem and strongly suggest appropriate evaluation and treatment when necessary.

There are some bullying interventions worthy of attention. Many of these are based at least partly on the work of Dan Olweus, a researcher in Norway who developed an approach that both addresses the behavior of victims and bullies and works to affect the environment in which bullying occurs. The essence of his prevention philosophy is this: The solution to bullying has to involve more people than the bully and the victim.

First, let's look at the bully. Bullies need to be identified, held accountable for their actions, and offered help. It has long been understood that bullies tend to be unhappy and have a low opinion of themselves. They pick on other kids to try to make themselves feel better; they thrive by controlling or dominating others. They may be depressed or angry about their life circumstances. But a major research project on adolescent bullying conducted by researchers at the University of California, Los Angeles, presents a different view of bullies: Many bullies are popular and considered to be cool by their classmates. The research, under the direction of Jaana Juvonen, a professor of psychology, and Sandra Graham, a professor of education, has found, among other things, that bullies enjoy a certain notoriety. Many classmates admire their toughness and may even try to imitate them. The research has also found that not all bullies suffer from low self-esteem. Some have quite high opinions of themselves that they use to rationalize their offensive behavior.

Our expanded understanding that there is not just one psychological profile of the bully explains why there is no one-size-fits-all intervention. If your child exhibits bullying behavior, he deserves immediate evaluation both because he is harming others and because bullies can have serious academic, social, emotional, and even legal problems. Bullies need to be guided to develop strategies that will help them control their misplaced anger.

Next, let's consider the victim. Kids who are vulnerable to bullying can fall into any number of categories, but they often tend to be kids who are seen as "different" by their peers. They are often passive or easily intimidated. But the UCLA research indicates that there are also temporary factors that increase a child's likelihood of being targeted, including being new at a school or shifting alliances.

Do not assume that surviving bullying is a rite of adolescence and builds character; rather, it makes victims more vulnerable. Victims can suffer harm that can interfere with their social and emotional development, as well as their engagement in school. If your child becomes withdrawn or depressed, has a decline in school performance, or is hesitant to return to school, a supportive intervention is urgently needed. Victims will likely need support that helps them maintain or develop positive views of themselves and works to prevent them from blaming themselves for their experiences.

If your child is a victim, it is important that he seeks the involvement of adults. Kids who are vulnerable need to be given the tools that will make it less likely they'll be targets. We advise victims to walk away and ignore the bully, because attention only feeds the aggressor who is searching for a response, but that is sometimes hard advice to follow. We certainly don't want victims fighting back, but sometimes a few assertive words that demand being left alone can be helpful. Traveling in groups is also helpful, since bullies are less likely to try to intimidate kids in groups.

Bullying likely would not exist if the only players were the bully and the victim. Bullies thrive on the fact that other kids see what they do. When kids stand by and do nothing or somehow get caught up in group dynamics that support the bullying, they give the bully the go-ahead to torment even more. Adolescents want to feel "normal" and one of the ways they achieve that is by flagging someone else as "abnormal." Why call a bully on the carpet and draw attention to yourself? It could only be a matter of time before you're targeted, so better to lay low.

This is not a problem parents should handle alone. Central to the Olweus model of bullying prevention is that communities and schools create an environment where bullying is not tolerated. A code of conduct is taught where acceptable behavior is clearly defined and core values of empathy and caring are reinforced. Students and teachers are taught to convey the message that there is no place for bullying. The presence of adults is felt throughout the hallways, classes, and playgrounds. Students are taught that reporting bullying is their ethical responsibility, not an act of cowardice or disloyalty. Everyone in the school setting learns that there is no such thing as an innocent bystander. All of this is done while also attending to the emotional needs of the victim and the bully.

∼ MEAN-GIRLS PHENOMENON

The classic portrait of a bully is that of a big tough guy on the playground pushing around a scrawny kid. But girls can bully just as much as boys can, although the bullying tends to be emotional, not physical. Occasionally girls are physical bullies, but more often they attack with words and relational aggression. These nonphysical tactics can be very damaging.

Movies and TV shows have given rise to the stereotypical image of "mean girls," but female bullies don't always look like alpha girls. Middle schools in particular are breeding grounds for less-than-nice girl behavior because everyone is trying to figure out where they fit in, how to make themselves as attractive as possible to peers, and how to protect their status in the social order.

The truth is that movie-level mean behavior is not so common, but spreading gossip and degrading others are very common, and these behaviors are not limited to girls. In middle school culture, alliances among kids can quickly rearrange. What you wear, how you walk, and whom you're seen with in the hallways might all provide ammo for your "frenemies." If you're at the top of the social order, you might have to do everything you can do to stay there. If you're trying to get to the top, you might want to knock someone down a few notches to earn your spot. Gossiping and cruel put-downs can serve to make you look better at someone else's expense. There's also a sexual undercurrent at play in mean-girl behavior—if you're at the top of the social order, you might appear more attractive to peers. Mean-girl behavior happens in high schools, too, but the phenomenon tends to be most common among younger teens.

Even the sweetest of girls can fall into this behavior, whether directly or by giving the mean girl a pass out of fear of being her next victim. You the parent may find your well-adjusted child can also become a target of the mean girls since the social lineup in adolescence is forever changing. Mean-girl behavior should not be tolerated, and it's also important for you to set high standards on what you consider acceptable talk. All you have to do is watch TV for a few minutes and you'll see that sarcasm is everywhere— teens put each other down and it's supposed to come across as funny, not mean. Your child needs to understand that put-downs such as "You're so gay" or "She dresses like a skank" might be tossed about casually by teens, but such comments can be highly destructive, especially at a time in life when everyone is feeling unsure of their own footing.

～ RELATIONAL AGGRESSION, SHUNNING

We've already talked about the emotional abuse that can develop in romantic relationships (see Chapter 17 on dating, and there's more in Chapter 29 on healthy sexuality), but similarly unhealthy relationships can take hold among peer groups. The emotional abuse is characterized by the use of humiliation, lies, revealing someone's private information, and exclusion—all used to put a peer in her place or hold power over her. A typical scenario: One peer shames another in front a group of kids or betrays a secret that is painfully personal. When carried to an extreme, a peer group might actually shun someone, creating a dynamic where that person feels isolated and worthless. Being ignored during adolescence can be as painful as being tormented.

~ CYBER-BULLYING

The instant access afforded by computers and cell phones can bring out the worst in peer dynamics. It used to be when a disagreement unfolded at recess, everyone went home and slept on it. Time defuses a lot of things. But now, texting, instant messaging, and Facebook postings keep disagreements alive and fuel gossip exponentially. A couple of clicks and dozens of kids are in the loop. It doesn't feel quite so mean because you're not looking anyone in the face. But reputations really can be ruined, and these messages can haunt the sender, too, because nothing in the cyber world ever truly goes away. It may be hard for an adult to relate to how devastating being cyber-bullied can feel to a teen; it's just words on a computer. But remember that a large portion of a teen's social life today exists in cyberspace.

~ SOME CONVERSATIONS TO PREPARE THEM

As a parent, you have to accept that the peer world is an exciting place and that it's a good thing your child is forming relationships outside of his family circle. Peers are not alien forces that parents should spend their energy fighting. Besides, we know that if you offer your well-intentioned advice on specific friends, you will be crossing that personal boundary beyond which you are not welcome.

The focus instead should be on helping your child gain the skills needed to travel the sometimes bumpy terrain ahead. You want your child to learn to cultivate healthy and fulfilling relationships that will bring out the best in him. All kids want to be liked, but that doesn't have to come at the expense of making choices that will harm their well-being.

Here are some topics to cover with your adolescent, both in heart-to-heart talks (not lectures) and by seizing on teachable moments that allow your child to reach his own wise conclusions.

In relationships, it's quality not quantity that matters. It's nice to be popular, but what you really want your child to have are a few intensely satisfying relationships. Most of us probably have only a few truly deep friendships that have carried us through thick and thin. We have work friends, neighborhood friends, childhood friends, but out of that group only a handful of people would meet the description of someone you trust fully to bear your soul to. Good friends allow you to be comfortable with who you are and sometimes challenge you to stretch to be even better.

Loyalty is key to friendship, but so, too, is encouraging the other person to act with restraint. Loyalty is an admirable quality and one that seems to be lacking too often. People jump ship all the time in politics, business, and marriage. It's important to teach your child the importance of loyalty because it is a very protective quality amid peer fickleness. But being loyal does not mean ignoring behavior that could put a friend in danger. It's the "friends don't let friends drive drunk" attitude. It's important to have friends who support your views but who also are willing to speak up when you need to hear the truth. Sometimes being a loyal friend means telling a friend to knock if off or calling upon an adult to help. Real friends protect each other.

Some of the most successful people in life are those who were "out of the box" in high school. If only we could allow each teen to go into a time capsule and go to their ten-year high school reunion. They would see that the people they might have envied at the top of the pecking order are not always the most successful or happy. Those kids who had the creative edge and innovative spirit and were willing to be different tend to be poised to take on the world

Exposure to diverse thought is great preparation for life. Because of how badly kids want to be normal, they tend to gravitate toward kids who are like them. Sometimes external appearances allow a kid to too easily determine who is like them at the expense of finding like-minded individuals who look different. Sometimes it is people whose backgrounds are so very different from ours who enrich us the most because they allow us to experience things from a new vantage point. The world is becoming increasingly diverse and people who are prepared to embrace diversity and negotiate through differences will be best prepared to lead in the future.

Like it or not, kids will sometimes try to drag you down with them. This is a hard topic because you don't want your child to become cynical or to automatically view people with suspicion. But it's human nature for people who are not feeling good about themselves to pull others into their web. For example, teens who drink or do drugs like to have their friends join them, in part because it lessens the conflict they're feeling. Teens who are trying to change harmful habits serve as a reminder to those still dabbling in the behavior that perhaps they should change, too. Sabotaging a friend's efforts to change in a positive direction, whether intentional or not, helps those feelings of guilt or conflict go away. That explains why sometimes it's just better to avoid certain people, places, and things because you know they will drag you down. That simple but vitally important point is part of the Ten-Point Stress-Management Plan (see Chapter 26).

Listen to your gut. In Chapter 3, we talked about the importance of parents listening to their gut when making decisions. This is a skill we need to teach our kids, too. Even amid the crowd, kids can have a gut instinct that something isn't quite right or that things are going to end badly if they don't move on. Teach your child that he shouldn't ignore nagging feelings, especially when safety is concerned. More often than not, their gut is right on target.

If a situation seems dangerous, don't hesitate to get an adult's help. If you want your teen to always come to you when she either is in hot water or she senses a friend is approaching a crisis, reach an agreement beforehand that she won't ever be punished for seeking your help to get out of an uncomfortable or potentially dangerous situation. In other words, she can always count on you to get her out of trouble without fear of getting into trouble as long as she comes to you first. We have to make it okay for kids to admit they're in over their head. There are some things teens simply aren't equipped to handle—such as a friend threatening to hurt himself or others—and getting an adult to help is the best thing they can do. Reinforce that the greatest act of friendship—the highest form of loyalty—is keeping someone safe.

Being smart in the cyber world will make your life easier. A lot of the messiest situations with peers happen in cyberspace. Be sure to reinforce these points:

- Follow the twenty-four-hour rule. Never respond immediately to a highly charged text or IM because if you say something you regret, you can't take it back. Better to sleep on things to see if your thinking changes.
- Anything you post online, whether comments or photos, can be used against you by peers. In addition, things you might not be proud of could surface years from now when a potential employer is checking your credentials. Just like a tattoo that never goes away, neither do cyber photos and postings. Having the reputation as a wild party guy or gal might be something you find appealing at sixteen, but not when you're twenty-eight and want to be taken seriously in your chosen field of employment.
- Reputations can be ruined in a minute. The passing about of salacious photos or a juicy tidbit of gossip, even if it's true, can damage a person's psyche. Stop and ask yourself: Would you want someone to do this to you?

Be proud to make a stand, but don't always expect a pat on the back. A hero's salute does not always await a person for doing the right thing in the face of adversity. Most of the satisfaction for making the right choice comes from within, and the largest benefit comes from the positive direction life will take you. Taking a stand for others may not be visible to spectators, but the person who is the recipient of your kindness or respect often knows it. One of the key lessons of life is that what goes around comes around. We are usually paid back for doing the right thing in one way or another.

∼ WAYS TO IMMUNIZE YOUR TEEN AGAINST TROUBLING PEER INFLUENCES

Those heartfelt conversations we just discussed certainly will get your teen thinking and will go a long way in having her understand your values and consider which ones she should adopt as her own. But it is also important to put some strategies in place that will create the needed structure to support your child as she navigates through teen relationships.

Reinforce the social skills that can enable your teen to resist peer pressure. Kids want to do right thing, but there is so much stress and frenzy in the peer world that they can't always think on their feet. You can't expect even the brightest, most mature teen to think through options when in a panic, and all teens worry to some degree that they might lose their friends if they don't go along with the crowd. That's why three "survival skills" need to be practiced so they become automatic. (See Chapter 6 for full details.)

1. Say no with conviction, and then suggest something else to do to signal that you want to be friends with the person. ("No, I can't hang out at the park tonight. But do you want to do something tomorrow?") (See Chapter 28 on drug prevention for some examples.)
2. Shift the blame for your decision to your parents. Having a check-in rule allows kids to accuse their parents of ruining their fun. ("My dad looks in my eyes when I get home and he doesn't miss anything.")
3. Use a code word to summon a parent's help in an awkward or potentially dangerous situation. ("I forgot to feed the dog" means "Come get me!")

Encourage a diversity of friendships. You can't choose your teen's friends, but you can encourage her to move in more than one circle of friends. Having multiple bases of friendship helps kids get through those inevitable times when they feel on the outs with a certain friend or feel like they don't quite fit into their crowd. Teens also gain a more accurate picture of themselves if they're not always viewed through the same lens. At school, a kid might be seen as a brainiac who couldn't possibly handle a ball, while at Scouts he's known as a strong kid who's good at pitching tents. Different circles of friends also help adolescents during that transition time when they don't know whether to play like a kid or act like an adult. Your young teen might still like to play flashlight tag with her neighborhood gang, but enjoys shopping with school friends. Also, if one group of friends is into a risky activity your teen wants to avoid, your teen has another outlet to turn to.

Don't fight them; join them. Some parents try to keep their teens away from peer influences by drawing them even more into family activities. While keeping family rituals is important, you're going to breed resentment if you don't recognize that your teen needs to spend more time away from you as he is achieving independence. The peer world is exciting and you can't compete with it. You can, however, bring your adolescent's friends a bit into your world by encouraging your teen to invite a friend along on an outing. Food is guaranteed to attract kids to your home. You can learn a lot about your teen and his friends by just watching them interact with each other. Let me state strongly here, however, that I am not suggesting you become your teen's best friend or make your home the party house.

Be the kind of parent your teen wants to talk to. Parents often think they'll keep their kids out of trouble if they somehow know every little thing going on. That's not a good expectation because part of a teen's becoming independent is carving out an existence that doesn't require reporting in on every little thing. You don't want to turn into a secret agent when your kid becomes a teen, though you certainly want to remain involved in your teen's life. That happens best when you're the sort of parent your teen feels comfortable disclosing things to. That requires that you turn off the parent alarm, can the lectures, and concentrate on being a patient and nonjudgmental listener.

If you think back to the four styles of parenting we discussed in Chapter 4, teens seem to thrive best when their parents use an authoritative style—offering a nice balance of warmth, support, and monitoring. Kids want their parents to care and offer boundaries that will keep them safe and give them a face-saving out with friends. They don't want their parents overly controlling, nor do they want them overly permissive. They sometimes interpret permissiveness as a sign that their parents don't care.

Remember what Judith Smetana, the University of Rochester researcher, has found: Kids consider it okay for their parents to care about their safety and how they conduct themselves in the world, but it's not okay for parents to meddle in friendship issues. You shouldn't say, "I don't want you to go to Abby's house because I think she's out of control and a bad influence on you." But you can say, "I worry for your safety and don't want you to go to a house where parents aren't home." If you judge friendships, your kids will stop telling you about them. If friends come up in conversation, listen, don't react. Store the point you want to make and then teach it later in a way that is disconnected from the friend, and ideally make it about safety.

Some parents erroneously assume that if they adopt a permissive style of parenting—acting more like a friend than a parent—their kids will tell them everything going on with them and their peers. In fact, children raised by permissive parents are often masters at hiding things.

Nancy Darling, a developmental psychologist and researcher at Oberlin College, makes the point that teens raised by permissive parents don't disclose what's on their minds because they are trying to protect their relationship with their parents. They don't want their parents to be disappointed in them, so they occasionally lie and more often keep their mouths shut. They don't see it as lying if they choose not to tell the full story—they are just sparing their parents.

Darling also makes the case that parents should create a home environment where arguing (two-way discussions, not fighting or hostility) is okay. Even if you wish your daughter's tone was a bit sweeter, respect (and appreciate!) that she has something to say. Remember that arguing is verbal wrestling with someone you think is worth engaging; it's much better than your child choosing to lie or remain silent. Reconsider your decision if your kid makes a good point because it sends a signal that reasonable negotiation works and continued engagement is worthwhile. Teens remain more likely to disclose what's bothering them or pushing them to their limits when they view their parents as fair, flexible, and open-minded.

Get to know your kids' friends' parents. The idea isn't to gossip about your kids or compare them, but to put in place a few more layers of protection around them. When you can put faces to names, you'll likely be more comfortable calling other parents to check whether someone will be home and confirm they are in agreement with the plans. Also, if you can create common rules, kids will be much more likely to comply, because they can still do so while being normal.

Role-play. Because so many peer-driven situations are predictable, you can help your adolescent get prepared. Say things like, "What would you do if . . . ?" Or "What if someone says . . .?" As much as certain TV shows might drive you crazy, you can take advantage of the plotlines to trigger conversations on how your teen would handle a similar situation. Again, when your child is facing a crisis or is in the midst of a panic, she will not be good at thinking on her feet, even if she completely understood what you were saying when you calmly and rationally discussed a string of scenarios ahead of time with her. Role-playing affords her the ability to turn to automatic responses.

Sometimes you just have to separate your kid from peer distractions. Kids really do need to sometimes focus on one task at a time. Homework is a good example here. Carving out a turn-all-devices-off time in your home helps not only with studying, but it gives kids a needed break from the frenzy of peers. You may find this particularly difficult to institute because so many kids now do homework together online. This cyber-study space may be helpful at times, but the challenge is how many other distractions are going on simultaneously in the social media world.

Find ways to tell your kid you like him just the way he is. The peer world is forever telling kids that they better change this or be like someone else. You don't want to shower your teen with hyped praise or flattery, but when you notice specific instances of your kid's goodness and talents shining through, you remind him that he's got a lot going for him. You don't have to add the line, "This is true no matter what other people say," but trust that he will recall your unconditional love when he needs a boost.

As always, be a good role model. This is a familiar theme by now, but worth repeating. Your child learns how to treat his peers by seeing how you treat yours.

- Focus on the qualities you like in your friends, not on their credentials or what car they drive.
- Demonstrate how much you rely on your friends for pleasure, for advice, and sometimes for calming wisdom when you are heated up.
- Avoid gossip.
- Avoid being quick to judge or overly critical.
- Show forgiveness.
- Show that you work hard to maintain your friendships.
- Demonstrate that you like to meet new people, including people very different from yourself.

It will help your child to know that your friendships don't always go smoothly but that they sustain you no matter what. Be a good friend and your child will be one, too.

CHAPTER TWENTY-EIGHT

~

DRUG PREVENTION

THERE'S PERHAPS NO bigger tendency for parents to lecture than when it comes to drinking and drugs. The lecture (no way is it a conversation) can hit full-throttle quickly: "If you drink (or do drugs) you're going to get bad grades and not get into college. You'll end up unemployed or in jail or dead."

If you want your child to make the right choices about alcohol and drugs, feverish rants aren't going to be much help. Your teen will probably roll his eyes and tune you out, figuring such an extreme demise could never happen to her. How can a kid reach that cognitive "aha" moment where she figures out on her own how to make the right decision if she's fuming at you for your irrationality and feeling stupid for not even comprehending what you're trying to say?

This chapter is going to teach you how to calmly approach a subject that is hard to stay calm about. Drugs can get kids in trouble with school and the law, and those mistakes can be personally and financially costly. Drug and alcohol use are also associated with other troubling behavior—impaired driving and car crashes, physical violence, unprotected sex, and date rape.

The focus of this chapter will be squarely on prevention. You'll learn why it's important to make this primarily a safety and health issue, not a character one. There are different reasons why adolescents turn to cigarettes, alcohol, or drugs, and it isn't because they're "bad kids" or have a "weak character." Some kids are experimenting or looking for fun. Or maybe they use drugs to cope with the stress of school or family issues. In rare cases they use them to defy their parents or prove to themselves that they can make their own decisions.

Even with the best prevention strategies in mind, there are some realities that can't be denied. Drugs can be enjoyable to use in the moment. They make you feel relaxed, bonded to the friends you're hanging with, maybe even philosophical. Drugs also provide a fairly easy means of rebelling. The thought of doing something your parents or other authority figures don't want you to do is enticing.

It may be impossible for you to completely prevent experimentation or thrill-seeking behavior, but you can have a big influence on whether your adolescent turns to drinking or drugs out of misplaced rebellion or because she hasn't found better ways to deal with stress.

∼ GETTING GROUNDED

For simplicity's sake, I'm going to use the word *drugs* generically in this chapter. There are a few reasons for that. While you may not think of it this way, alcohol is a drug that falls into the classification of depressant. Cigarettes contain the drug nicotine. There are illegal street drugs and any number of prescription drugs that can be misused.

Because drug trends change and different drugs are more or less of a problem in different communities, I won't talk specifically about any one drug. Instead, at the end of this book, I will refer you to some up-to-date online resources from which you can find reliable information regarding your particular concerns. Because this chapter will focus on prevention, not treatment, those same online resources could be invaluable supplements to what is written here if you suspect your child is using drugs or already has been identified as having a problem.

An uncomfortable fact is that study after study has found that parents underestimate their kids' drug use. Most of that may be just because we all tend to idealize our children. As a society we also make wrong assumptions about who uses drugs. Kids who live in poverty are actually less likely to use drugs than middle-class teens. High-powered kids often use drugs to unwind or escape. Permissive parents might assume their kids tell them everything, including what they do when they're hanging out with friends, but their teens may not disclose their behaviors because they don't want to be a disappointment. Finally, kids who use drugs are masters of disguise. They get really, really good at spinning stories and making excuses that allow them to move from a world where they might function quite well into another one that allows them to dull their senses for a while.

Getting ahead of the curve is extremely important. By teaching your child beginning at a young age about the basics of taking care of her health and making good choices that respect the many needs of her growing body and mind, you're laying the groundwork for drug prevention. Modeling healthy habits is also critical—in fact, it should be the first step in drug-prevention education. Remember, your child is observing your habits, and older kids are especially good at zeroing in on behavior they view as hypo-critical. If you have a routine that involves popping open a beer or pouring a glass of wine the minute you come home from work, your child learns that drinking is an antidote to a tough day. So much for your message that drugs won't solve your problems. On the other hand, imagine the powerful message you'd be sending if *you* gave up cigarettes and took up meditation and exercise instead?

We talked earlier about how parents should have their "absolutes": those areas where your kid knows absolutely where you stand—no gray zone whatsoever. Drugs should be an absolute. Your child needs to be clear that you expect *no use* on his part because you want to keep him healthy and safe at this critical time of development. The brain is still developing during adolescence and it needs to be protected from mind-altering and potentially addictive substances. This is not a subject to be wishy-washy about or to adopt an attitude that your teen is mercifully dabbling in a "lesser of two evils." It is vital here that both parents are on the same page. If your spouse responds to a bit of drinking with a wink or an elbow jab, your child is certain to absorb the lesson that substance use is just a rite of passage into adulthood.

Teens go through a lot of emotional and social change in their quest to answer "Who am I?" and "Am a normal?" But when teens numb themselves with drugs, they can't focus as well on forming meaningful relationships or looking inward to reflect on where they want their lives to head. If teens try to escape the hard emotional and social work that adolescence entails, they arrive at adulthood with lots of developmental growth left unfinished.

Research shows that parents who adopt an authoritative or balanced style of parenting—they are warm and loving but set clear expectations and provide appropriate monitoring—are more likely to raise kids who stay away from worrisome behaviors, including drinking and drug use. When teens view their home as a reasonable place where rules and consequences make sense, they might be less likely to rebel and take part in risky pastimes just to show their parents (or themselves) that they are independent and can't be "controlled."

∼ YOU KNOW MORE THAN YOU THINK

While this topic probably seems daunting, you've already learned a lot in this book that will come in handy. Let's review:

Stress. Helping your child learn to manage stress is probably the best drug-prevention strategy you can undertake. When teens develop the habit of turning to positive coping techniques, they are less likely to latch on to easy fixes when they feel the weight of the world.

Each of the ten points in my Stress-Management Plan (Chapter 26) is helpful, but point number 2 is especially key when it comes to drinking and drugs: Try to avoid people, places, or things that pull your child down. Not only could certain situations bring teens in direct contact with the substance they're trying to avoid, but they could trigger feelings of stress or anxiety that make them want to find a quick remedy for their discomfort. Teens who want to break a bad habit sometimes fare better when they steer clear of kids who engage in the behavior. In taking the step to avoid a potentially tempting situation, it always helps to have a proactive plan for something else to do.

Exercise plays several roles in drug prevention. In the moment, it takes the edge off feelings of stress and nervous energy and can calm racing, disquieting thoughts. As kids start to realize the power of their body— through running or weight lifting or organized sports—they might decide to not mess a good thing up with smoking or drugs. Also, having to physically perform provides a face-saving excuse for teens to skip the partying— "Sorry, I got to keep in shape."

Lectures push a kid toward rebellion. One of the greatest challenges for young adolescents is that they aren't good yet at projecting into the future. That there are consequences is something that doesn't necessarily make sense yet, and people's underlying motivations are hard for kids to figure out. We intuitively know this, but in reaction to our instinctual desire to protect our children, we tell them everything we know by dumping it out in a lecture. We started out this chapter talking about not careening into a lecture because it can backfire. Discussions around drugs may be the best place to learn to hold a conversation that helps kids figure things out on their own and therefore own the solution.

Peers. Peer pressure is often subtle and internally driven. No doubt friends will try to get each other to try drugs (and certainly drug dealers will), but teens also get involved in unhealthy activities because of their own sense of what's "normal" in their peer group and a desire to conform. This is why it's so important to reinforce the fact that most kids are not using, rather than solely paying attention to those who do use.

To deal effectively with the externally driven part of peer pressure, it helps for teens to anticipate what they might encounter. Some drug-prevention programs try to teach kids a variety of comeback lines to use when offered drugs, but the three simple social survival skills we've been talking about throughout this book will help out in most situations:

- Reply with a clear and convincing (but not condescending) *no*. Then suggest something else to do another time so that you let the person know you still want to be friends. ("No, not into it. Want to shoot some hoops tomorrow?")
- Shift the blame for your decision to your parents or some other issue that can be presented as if you have no choice. (See box for some ideas.)
- Use a code word to summon a parent's help if things get hairy. No one will be the wiser.

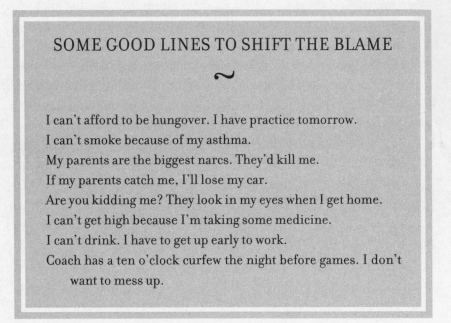

SOME GOOD LINES TO SHIFT THE BLAME

~

I can't afford to be hungover. I have practice tomorrow.
I can't smoke because of my asthma.
My parents are the biggest narcs. They'd kill me.
If my parents catch me, I'll lose my car.
Are you kidding me? They look in my eyes when I get home.
I can't get high because I'm taking some medicine.
I can't drink. I have to get up early to work.
Coach has a ten o'clock curfew the night before games. I don't
    want to mess up.

Knowing your child. While anyone can become involved in drugs, some kids might be more susceptible than others. Research has shown that kids with ADHD are more likely to use drugs, and teens who are stressed, anxious, or depressed are most definitely at risk. Kids who are impressionable might also be more apt to go along with a peer's suggestion to experiment. Peer leaders sometimes feel pressure to "do the adult thing." Kids who are followers or want to break into a new crowd will go out of their way to up their cool factor. If your teen has switched peer groups recently or has radically changed his style, it's a good idea to be alert for signs of potential drug use. Also be alert if your child is going through a stressful time at school or home.

Busy is good—to a point. Kids have a better shot at staying out of trouble when they are involved in sports, clubs, volunteering, or other activities. This generation of kids is so used to constant stimulation—on-demand movies, video games, texting, social networking—that boredom sets in quickly. It's cliché, but boredom can be the enemy. The trick is to help your teen strike a healthy balance between organized activity and downtime in his schedule, so that doing too much doesn't become a source of stress that requires an easy fix and boredom isn't an issue, either.

∼ GETTING THE TONE RIGHT

It might seem as if you're trying to swim against the tide because drug use is everywhere in our society. Entertainment stars become idolized, only to be caught in unsavory off-camera behavior. Drug abuse and addiction haven't spared some of our friends and relatives, either. There are so many examples of drug use all around us that it would be easy to point to a different person every day and tell your teen, "Here's who you don't want to become like."

You want to be careful not to label drugs users as good or bad personally and instead to focus on the behavior that has interfered with their success. Personally knocking your kid's favorite rapper is guaranteed to be a turnoff—kids hate any hint of "See, I knew you had bad taste"—but your teen might gladly engage in a conversation about what might cause celebrities to feel the pressure to get caught up in unhealthy behavior.

You should also avoid labeling family members as bad or derelict—rather than calling someone a drunk or addict, refer to his drinking or drug use problem. The very uncle who struggles to stay sober might be especially loved by your child because he teaches him card tricks and knows a lot of sports trivia. Show compassion, though not resignation or hopeless-ness. Drug abuse shouldn't be one of those dark family secrets that no one dares talk about even though everyone is well aware of what's going on.

Keeping the focus on the behavior, not the person, is especially impor-tant if your concern is about one of your child's friends because teens tend to shut down when their parents tread on friendship issues. Don't cast aspersions. If you're concerned about what is going on in your child's circle, look for an opportunity to bring up something more general, like "I hear your school is worried about kids hanging out after school to smoke pot," and see where it takes you.

~ CONVERSATIONS YOU NEED TO HAVE, STARTING NOW

Early education is key to when it comes to drug prevention because elementary-age students and young adolescents usually are more open than older teens to what their parents have to say.

No matter what your child's age, however, it's important to deal in facts, not hyperbole. One cigarette will not give you lung cancer and one beer at age fifteen does not an alcoholic make. You want to get in the habit of presenting information without exaggeration or drama so that your child comes to expect that what you say is reliable, even if he doesn't neces-sarily want to hear it.

While TV provides endless teachable moments for drug education, real-life examples on the downsides of drug use as well as the benefits of avoidance and recovery are everywhere, too: a frustrated-looking teen or office worker standing on the sidewalk smoking; a panhandler working a crowd for change; a neighbor running his first road race after making a commitment to stay sober.

The goal, remember, is to allow your child to arrive at his own wise conclusion rather than thrusting a one-sided lecture on him in the hope he'll see the light. "What do you think about . . . ?" is a good way to get a conversation going.

Here are some points you want to cover:

Anyone can become addicted, although some people are more at risk than others because of their genetic makeup. If alcohol or drug addiction runs in your family, your child deserves to know that your family's genetics make it more likely that she, too, could become addicted. Avoidance altogether is a smart consideration if family members struggle with addiction.

Health is at stake. There is no need to turn drug use into a moral or character issue. In fact, it could work against you. Teens all know kids who do drugs and they probably like them. Keep focused on the health implications that can happen in the short term and over the long haul. (The Web sites listed at the end of this book will give you excellent specifics.) The brain is still developing right on through early adulthood and this work in progress must be nurtured and protected—by good nutrition, intellectual stimulation, and avoidance of harmful substances.

Success is at stake. You should also stress that habits that can hurt academic and job performance can set in early and quickly. Habits can be extremely hard to break, so better not to start at all. The same substances that help you chill for a while also diminish your drive over the long term. (Marijuana is a classic example.)

This is about safety, not control. As teens march toward independence, they often look for evidence that their parents are out to control them. If you stay consistent to your overall parenting message—that you will do everything you can to keep your child safe and healthy—then drugs won't fall into a special category that seems to beg for your teen to rebel against. You want your child to be safe in all her choices, and teens want to be safe, too. Again, the notion that teens feel invulnerable is false; do not write off their desire to make wise decisions. When they have reasonable rules and proper monitoring, they feel secure.

Don't forget that alcohol is a drug. Some parents apply a different standard to alcohol because it is a legal and socially acceptable substance and seems less harmful than other substances their children could be using. Teens need to hear straight facts about alcohol, too. Kids think of the upsides of alcohol—it makes you relaxed, silly, more talkative, more comfortable in a crowd—but it also makes you dumb and brave, leaving you regretting the actions that were so easy to take. Alcohol is a depressant that can leave a person feeling down after the initial buzz. For kids prone to depression, the effect can be particularly marked, leading to a dangerous cycle. You drink because you are feeling stressed or down. Life is still there when you get sober but you are further behind. You drink again in the hopes of feeling better. Your problems grow and your health deteriorates.

There are indications that more young people are engaging in binge drinking—downing multiple drinks quickly with the sole intent of getting drunk. Binge drinking is especially scary because it can be a factor in sexual assault, gun injuries, and physical fights. It can also land someone in the emergency room for alcohol poisoning, and numerous fatal injuries, including car crashes and falls from ledges and windows, have been linked to binge drinking. You don't want your teen to drink at all, but as part of prevention education your child should understand the numerical side of alcohol consumption. The National Institute on Alcohol Abuse and Alcoholism defines binge drinking as five or more drinks in two hours for a man and four or more drinks in two hours for a woman. It doesn't take a lot of drinking to lose control of your senses.

Drug dealers might be your friends. There's the classic image of the drug dealer: He hangs out on the street corner, cap pulled low, making deals, and then running when he gets the word that the cops are near. The truth is that drugs dealers are everywhere—they're down the block, in your math class, on your team, bunking with you at camp. It's important that you dispel the stereotypical image of the drug dealer (though some do meet that description) so that your child becomes savvy on how dealers operate. They start out friendly and may offer drugs for free in the hopes of enticing kids to try them. The hope is that a few trial runs will lead to a steady-paying customer.

Here's an example of a cognitive "aha" conversation that might be particularly useful for an adolescent. Notice that the parent is not lecturing, but rather facilitating a thought process by asking directed questions to get to the point we just described. A kid will own the solution because he figured it out himself.

PARENT: Did you know that sometimes drug dealers give out drugs for free?

KID: No. That's doesn't make any sense.

PARENT: Well, why do you think they'd do that?

KID: I guess because they'd think I'm cool.

PARENT: Well, let me ask you a question. Why do store owners give out coupons for cereals?

KID: To save people money.

PARENT: So if I buy the cereal because it's cheap, what's going to happen next?

KID: Dumb question. I'm going to eat it.

PARENT: But if you like the cereal and I don't have a coupon next time I go to the store, are you still going to ask me to get it?

KID: I guess so.

PARENT: So why would a drug dealer give you drugs for free?

KID: Got it, Dad.

The manipulation factor is not limited to friends. Companies that market cigarettes and alcohol also have an interest in getting young people to use, even if they claim otherwise. Kids need to understand that companies stand to make a lot of money off them. The antitobacco "truth campaign," which dates back to the late 1990s, was built on the idea that teens would become indignant and turn against smoking if they understood that Big Tobacco companies were attempting to manipulate them for huge profits. The campaign is widely cited for reducing smoking among teens.

Even the best of friends don't always have your best interests in mind. One of the core values of adolescence is to stick by your friends. That means doing what they want to do and never being a buzzkill. It may mean going against your own values or decisions if it prevents your friend from being alone. Kids who use drugs as a habit feel conflicted and guilty. It isn't easy to sustain a lifestyle that is built on lying to parents, making excuses when commitments fall by the wayside, and worrying about getting caught by the police for underage drinking or drug possession. Teens will encourage other kids to join in, partly because it makes them feel less conflicted about their behavior and more like they're doing what's acceptable for their peer group. "Well, I could change, but everyone else is doing it." Your teen needs to understand that it's not an act of friendship to help someone "drown his sorrows" or "toast a victory." Good friends protect each other and sometimes that comes about by saying, "No, I don't want to party. But do you want to do something else?" Kids also need to understand that even close friends may be thinking more of themselves than their good buddies. "Come on, I want to party with you" may feel like a flattering invitation but may not be about your child at all. This is another point that can be made using a cognitive "aha" conversation.

PARENT: Suppose one of your friends was doing drugs. Would you do it with him?

KID: Of course not.

PARENT: But what if your friend says he really wants to hang out and get high with you. Why do you think he'd want to do that?

KID: We're friends and he likes to hang with me.

PARENTS: How do you think he would feel about the fact he's doing drugs?

KIDS: I guess he'd be high and chillin'.

PARENT: I don't mean how does he feel when he's high. I mean how does he feel about being high?

KID: I guess he's feeling guilty because he knows it's bad for him.

PARENT: Well, how does he feel about the fact that you're not also doing drugs?

KID: Lonely.

PARENT: Do you think maybe your not doing drugs reminds him he has a choice, too?

KID: I guess so.

PARENT: So why would he ask you to join him if he feels guilty?

KID: I guess so he can feel like he's not alone, like everybody's doing it.

PARENT: Exactly. Your doing drugs makes him feel better, like it's not a big deal and like he doesn't have a choice about it. So what is the best way to be a good friend?

KID: Saying no, I don't want to do it.

PARENT: Right. Now your friend has a reason to make a good choice, too.

Teens need to know that the most loyal thing they can do is model good behaviors. This is particularly true for kids in recovery who have a real opportunity to be role models for peers who are struggling.

The "Friends Don't Let Friends Drive Drunk" public health campaign, first rolled out in the 1980s, tapped into the sense of loyalty teens feel toward one another. The advertising campaign has been credited with significantly increasing awareness among teens of the dangers of drinking and driving. It transformed the prevailing thought that friends partied together and never ever judged each other into one that made kids understand that there is nothing more loyal than keeping your friends alive.

~ YOUR WATCHFUL EYE

Some of your best drug-prevention tools might already be in your parenting repertoire—stating expectations and potential consequences ahead of time and then following through; the check-in rule each time your teen comes home; calling other parents to check on arrangements; making sure parents are home when teens gather at a house; having an absolutely clear no-drinking-or-drugs policy when teens gather at your home. Simple things such as telling kids to not bring in water bottles and casually suggesting they stash their backpacks and purses in a common corner of the house until they leave help prevent the smuggling in of alcohol and drugs. Asking kids not to come and go from the house is also wise.

You always need to operate from the positive standpoint that teens want to do the right thing. When you provide an appropriate level of monitoring, you show you care and help your child make the right choice. Your teen is more likely to disclose the challenges he's facing around drugs if you listen without judgment and switch your parent alarm to the off position.

EVEN WITH ATTENTIVE monitoring, your teen might come home drunk or high. You need to look at the bigger picture in deciding how best to respond. The first important question to ask yourself is whether the behavior is a one-time event or part of a pattern. The second is whether the behavior has the potential of putting your child in serious danger if it is repeated. Let's consider a few scenarios:

- If the behavior is part of a pattern, you shouldn't be focusing on punishment. Your child needs professional help to sort through why she's fallen into harmful habits.
- If the behavior is a onetime event, or a rare occurrence, and your child called you to get out of trouble, whatever you do, don't punish him. If you lay on a punishment, next time he probably won't call and that could jeopardize his safety. Tell him that while you don't approve of whatever he did, you're glad he's safe and thought enough to call you.
- If the behavior is a onetime event and your child didn't reach out for help, roll back privileges for a while to the point where your child was making good choices. For instance, if your teen comes home with alcohol on her breath after staying out until midnight, return her curfew to eleven and see how she does. Let your teen know that you're eager for her to regain your trust by acting responsibly once again. The worst thing that can happen is for your child to lose your trust and decide, "What the heck? There's no point in trying to regain it." I urge you to stay away from grounding—all it does is breed resentment and the punishment always feels worse than the crime. If you fear your child's safety is at risk, grounding with the intent of breaking a cycle of exposure to certain people or places does make sense.

- If you find that your child has been driving impaired, serious action is warranted, because this falls into the serious danger category if it is repeated even once. Roll back or rescind car privileges until your teen can prove he's to be trusted. You need to be clear that there is no room for error when you're behind the wheel. Likewise, you should have no tolerance for your teen driving with a friend who has demonstrated irresponsible behavior with substances while driving.
- If your child gets in trouble with the law, you want him to realize that there is a price to pay. Of course you don't want him to go to jail, but he should face the judge and pay the fine. You aren't protecting him if you keep him from important life lessons.

～ THE QUESTION PARENTS FEAR: DID YOU DO DRUGS?

A lot of parents struggle with whether they should reveal their past when kids ask the question "Did you do drugs?" I wish I could answer this with scientific certainty, but you can imagine how hard this research would be to conduct. There are experts who come down on both sides: Honesty is always best versus kids don't really want to know.

I come down along the middle. I think being honest up to a point is the best approach.

You don't need to reveal every detail of what you did in your youth. Answer only what you're asked with an emphasis on what you learned from the choices you made. Try something like, "I made some bad choices and I'm not proud of them. My own experiences on what drinking (or drugs) can do to a person make me want to do everything I can to help keep you safe and healthy." Or, "I wasted a lot of valuable time in college. I'm glad I could get myself turned around and back on track."

You can also stress that not as much information about the potential harm of mind-altering substances was known back then. That's not an excuse, but it gives some perspective as to why you expect your child to make smarter choices than you did.

Some parents inadvertently condone the indiscretions of their youth when they get together with friends and swap stories about the good old days. Kids hear their parents talk with great glee about getting high to their favorite albums or chugging contests at fraternity parties and they absorb the message that such behavior is part of being a teenager. Make sure you don't glorify your days of drinking and doing drugs because it will add to the strong allure that's already calling to your teen.

∼ IF YOU SUSPECT DRUG USE IN YOUR CHILD

Unfortunately, many kids who use drugs are excellent liars. It's not that their parents are stupid or even lax—kids can be quite good at keeping a good face on when they need to.

Some of the signs suggestive of drug use—fatigue, edginess, anger, a sloppy appearance, falling grades, changes in social routines, tension with you—can also be indicative of something else, such as depression, so parents shouldn't necessarily assume substance abuse is at play when something changes with their teen.

You need to approach your child not with accusations, but with concern. State that you're worried about her. You sense something has changed. Tell her you love her and want to help.

Try to avoid confronting your teen when he's drunk or high. A person who is not thinking straight cannot process what you're saying. You will be met with belligerence. Better to wait for a calm moment after you've done a bit of preliminary thinking on how you might go about getting help for your teen (see Chapter 30).

You can expect to be met with outright denial ("I'd never do drugs), indignation ("I can't believe you think I'd do that"), or a partial admission ("Yes, I've tried some pot, but it wasn't a big deal—I won't do it anymore"). But if you're worried here, trust your gut and get someone involved who's got the expertise and can do an objective assessment that few parents can do on their own child. Tell your child that you want to trust her, but this is too important to leave to chance. Tell her your monitoring will be even closer and that to regain your trust fully, you need someone else to be involved.

Understand that the most important question is not *what* your teen is doing, but *why* he is doing it. I don't approve if a kid is partying to fit in or to have fun, but I really worry more about kids who use drugs because they say they need to chill. That is a young person who uses substances to deal with stress and who is at risk of using habitually to manage life's challenges.

Always remember to focus on the behavior and not attack your child personally. Shaming will only increase your child's guilt, stress, and sense of worthlessness. Don't try to shift the focus to you—"I can't believe a child of mine would do such a thing" or "How could you do this to me after everything I've done for you?" This isn't about your reputation and it isn't a referendum on your parenting skills. It's about your child getting help to move on from unsafe and unhealthy habits. Focus on safety, focus on health, and remind your child that you love her no matter what and that you will settle for nothing less than her getting better.

I repeatedly find in my work as a doctor that teens who abuse drugs are very loveable and acutely sensitive kids who just take the world very seriously and sometimes prefer that their senses are dimmed. Kids will tell me their "heads are spinning" and they want it to stop. They also might have a lot of pride invested in making people think they are too cool to care—and drugs definitely polish that image for them.

I urge you to focus on the positive attributes of your child and remind yourself of all the ways you take delight in him. Yes, it's a hard time. But let him know that you believe in his goodness and strength and that together you *will* get through this. His sensitivity might be causing pain for you and for him now, but as he gets past this phase it will serve him well far into the future.

CHAPTER TWENTY-NINE

~

HEALTHY SEXUALITY

SEX. This is likely the topic that you either turned to first or wish we could skip altogether. It clearly is an adolescent issue—timed to when they need it, not a moment before. Actually, if I could have one topic in this book addressed as early as possible, it would be this one. The more we put this topic off for THE BIG TALK on the eve of puberty, the more we dread it as something to be gotten past, the more the talk becomes about an event— sex—rather than a healthy part of our nature—sexuality. Most critically, the more this topic remains a mystery, the more kids will make every effort to figure it out on their own.

Your child has already had an enormous exposure to sex "education." Entertainment media is filled with titillation and implied intercourse, but portrays little of the emotional complexity and consequences that accompany sex, and nearly nothing about sexuality in the broader sense. Peers teach freely about sex; they know it all or pretend they do. But their messages are sometimes steeped in spoken or unspoken pressures and often filled with misinformation. The Internet offers sex education only a click away, but just a small portion is professionally written, factual, and developmentally appropriate. Pornography gives its own explicit education—distorted by exploitation and rarely delivered in the context of relationships. My point is you really don't have a choice about shielding your child from education about sex. The choice you make with your personal involvement is to be certain that your child will receive accurate information infused with your values.

~ SEXUALITY IS ABOUT A LOT MORE THAN SEX

What parent didn't dread the Big Question—that moment when your son or daughter asked how babies are made? You sat down, cleared your throat, stared at the floor, and told your kid the "facts of life" or some abbreviated version of them. The parallel now is the eve of puberty ... or the dreaded first date (way, way too late, incidentally). Sex won't be an uncomfortable subject if you stop thinking of it as a biology lesson and instead replace sex with sexuality. It's not just about anatomy; it's about love, relationships, respect, making you and another person you care about happy and fulfilled. We hope our children view sexuality as a cherished part of the human experience and see sex itself as such a valuable part of sexuality that it's worth being certain that the time, place, and person are right. The goal of developing healthy sexuality is not just to get children safely through adolescence, but to up the chances that they'll have meaningful, lasting relationships as adults.

When we teach our children that relationships rarely look like movie fantasies and instead take commitment and effort because they require compromise, self-advocacy skills, and mutual respect, we prepare them for a healthy partnership. Teaching children from a young age that they have the tools to keep their body safe and healthy lays the groundwork for them to feel empowered later on to reject unhealthy relationships and put a stop to unwanted sexual advances.

The earlier you talk about relationships, the more natural it will be to delve deeper into the topic of sexuality, including physical expressions of affection. As in most subjects, children of varying ages and temperaments will receive the message differently. There likely will be a phase when you are the last person they want to hear from about relationships or sexuality. Be assured, however, that they are hearing what you say even when they do not seem to be listening.

∼ DISCUSSING SEX DOES NOT GIVE A MIXED MESSAGE

Just thinking about broaching the topic of sex paralyzes many parents. Some parents worry that discussing sexuality openly will signal to their children that they think the time is right to have sex or that teaching young people about protection implies permission to have intercourse. Also, throughout this book I've talked about the importance of holding your child to high expectations. You may wonder whether this is the ideal place to draw a line in the sand and say, "I expect you to wait." For these reasons, you might be troubled about whether you are sending your teen a mixed message.

Our children are already showered with mixed messages. Essentially, our society teaches kids that sex is evil and dirty, carries deadly diseases, and can ruin their life through an unplanned pregnancy . . . then tells them to save it for the person in their life they love the most! Our message should be clear and honest. "Sexuality is a wonderful part of being human, and sex is a physical way of sharing intimacy with another person. It also brings the greatest imaginable gift, the joy of parenthood. But sex also can have serious consequences, including sexually transmitted infections and a baby before your life is on track and you are ready to give parenthood your all. Because sex is a way of deeply sharing yourself with another person, it also sets you up to be emotionally hurt because you weren't yet ready to be close to that person. For these reasons, I don't believe you are ready to have sex while you are a teenager. But one day you will be ready, so I think it's important you learn how to protect yourself from diseases and unplanned pregnancy. Most important, I want to be able to discuss with you my thoughts on building healthy relationships."

This message does hold teens to the highest of expectations. It tells them that we expect them to be informed, think critically, and use good judgment. It tells them that we want them to think of sex as an act of intimacy in the context of a caring relationship, rather than only a physical act of pleasure. Most important, it tells them there is no subject that you can't discuss with them.

Taking the position that your teen won't have sex may be comforting to you but will do nothing to promote healthy sexuality. Research demonstrates that adolescents who have talked with their parents about sex are more likely to postpone sex, to talk to their parents about sex when they do have it, and to use birth control. Authoritative parenting (a good balance of warmth, emotional support, and setting boundaries) has the greatest influence on healthy sexuality. Authoritarian parents (rules only) raise children who postpone sex, but then tend to keep the information as a closely held secret from parents and are less likely to protect themselves.

Betty had good reason to give careful thought to how she would handle the topic of sex with her kids. She got pregnant when she was seventeen and had a miscarriage three months later. Now, nearing forty, she can still feel the sting of having her private life exposed for her family and classmates to see.

"I was naive. I had sex, unprotected sex. I couldn't be open with my mom. I couldn't talk to her about any of it," she said. At it turned out, Betty regrouped after the miscarriage and went on to college. She eventually married the boy who had gotten her pregnant in high school and together they have three children.

"I can't keep my own kids free from sex, but I can tell them, 'Talk to me. Talk to me!'" Betty said. "I want to be open about things because I should have been able to talk to my mom. I don't want my kids to only be able to ask outside people about something so important. If they come home with a slang word for something, I say, 'Let me tell you about that.'"

Betty has a good motivation for wanting her kids to know about sex—she doesn't want them to repeat her mistakes. But rather than using scare tactics, she made a deliberate decision to do two things. If a question arises, she answers it in an informed, matter-of-fact way. But then she seizes on

every opportunity she can to talk about sex in the context of healthy relationships and the bigger picture of what her children hope to achieve in life.

"I want my kids to know they have choices and that if they have goals
for life, they can make them happen," Betty said. "I pray every day my kids
won't have sex, but I also want to do everything I can to keep them safe."

Francine, another mom, was put to the test when her daughter came
to her at age seventeen and said she wanted to be intimate with her boyfriend. Francine had always stressed the fact that sex should be in a context
of a loving, caring relationship between two committed, mature people,
but she had also talked about the importance of making safe choices
around sex.

"This was an opportunity where I could either go nuts or for me to
keep my word," Francine said. "I had always told my daughter, 'Come to
me, I'll help keep you safe. I may not agree with your choice, but I'll do
whatever I have to do to keep you safe.'"

～ TAKE THAT BREATH

All right, so I've just beaten you into the ground about the fact that I think
you should be the one to teach your child about sex. Deep breath. Let me
soften that directive: You *may* be the best one to teach about sex, and it is
ideal if you can cover all aspects of sex and sexuality with your child. But
either your own discomfort or your child's deeply rooted sense that it is
creepy to learn about the physical act of sex from someone she's sure did it
only once (or more if there are siblings) may have earned you a pass on
discussing sex. If your best judgment tells you that you are not the one to
give explicit information, make sure your child receives factual information from a reliable source. You might choose to make books readily available; if so, leave them in view without checking whether they are being
used. You might make certain that accurate information is available in the
school. I recommend that your child have regular checkups with a health
professional who addresses sexual health as a part of routine adolescent
care. You might also request a relative or friend to have discussions with

your teen. Aunt Teresa might be considered the most asexual person on the planet by her own children, but she might be precisely the right person for your daughter to connect with about a new boyfriend. Just make sure that your trusted adult approaches your teen in a comfortable, natural way. The "assignment" might backfire if your stamp of approval is too evident. "Your mother said I should talk to you about sex" may not go over well.

Although you may have dodged THE BIG TALK, there is no better way for your child to learn about sexuality than from you. You can have a big influence on whether your teen makes safe and healthy choices around relationships and sexual activity. Ideally, you will have begun early to foster healthy attitudes about sexuality, using suitable vocabulary and detail at various stages of development. By presenting sexuality as a way of thinking, acting, and being, instead of merely the physical act of intercourse, you open up avenues to talk about love, relationships, respect, and the joy that comes with bringing pleasure to someone you care deeply about. See, didn't that just get easier?

∾ HOW TO FRAME THE DISCUSSION

You'll use your best parenting skills here as in every other topic. Let's recap and put some of the general points we've discussed into the context of sexuality:

- Parents need to address issues directly. Children need factual information, guidance, and a listening ear. When we don't teach our children, others do and we are not in control of the message.
- Listen more than you talk. Sexuality is far too complex for you to be giving answers. You want your child clarifying for herself how she feels. This means you should use open-ended questions like "How do you feel about that?" rather than questions like "Does that make you uncomfortable?" which can be answered with a yes, no, or grunt.
- Be authoritative, loving, and responsive. Set limits and offer appropriate freedoms.

- Try not to focus on what not to do. Instead, focus on what they can do. Rather than decrying the dangers of sex, talk about the emotional advantages of delaying sex. Rather than banning intercourse, talk about the pleasure of sharing great conversations while hugging.

- Avoid the lecture! You want your teen to own the solution here, not to feel that you are condescending or judgmental.

- Frame the conversations about safety whenever possible. Avoid the personal areas whenever you can. You can do this by discussing generalities about "people" and less about specific friends. When you talk about safety, make sure you're not just focusing on dire circumstances like HIV or pregnancy, but also on the real and frequent challenges to emotional safety.

- Teach navigational skills whenever possible. Teens who know the right thing to do, but who don't know how to do it without embarrassment or isolation, often choose to do things against their better judgment.

- Help your child understand that ambivalent messages like "well, maybe, but I'd rather not" lead to a loss of control. There is nothing wrong with a clear *yes* or clear *no*.

- Make sure your child has a wide repertoire of healthy coping strategies. The last thing you want is your teen seeking sexual relationships for solace.

In addition to those general parenting points, there are specific approaches to discussing sexuality you may want to consider:

- **First, acknowledge how much changing bodies can worry adolescents.** Most teens have many unspoken fears about being physically abnormal. Adolescent boys may worry about developing nipples, which are a product of surging hormones, or they may worry that all the other guys are sprouting a beard, but not *them*. Girls, who suddenly see hips and bottoms where there were none, may complain of "getting fat." Acne can be devastating when looking attractive becomes a priority. A little reassurance from you or a health professional can go a long way.

- **Consider avoiding the word *abstinence.*** It is too tightly tied to culture wars. Besides, abstinence can be equated with sacrifice. How about postponement? That acknowledges that one day they will have sex. It also gives you room to talk about safe, less intimate sexual behaviors.
- **Talk about the fact that sexuality involves a range of feelings and intimacy involves a range of behaviors.** You may have to battle the fact that the entertainment media usually inserts a blank space between kissing and intercourse (more later). People don't like blank spaces, and I worry that this pushes kids toward what they do know about—intercourse. Let them know either through your own words or from appropriate literature that there are lots of intimate activities in between. It can take years to round the bases. Everyone knows a home run is the greatest success, but playing the game is pretty fun anyway.
- **Do not belittle butterflies, holding hands, or kissing as puppy love.** Those are real entries into sexuality. And they should be acknowledged as a big deal. You want your child feeling sexual for just having his breath taken away. You don't want him to feel as though he needs to do something more advanced to have his sexuality taken seriously. Simple observations such as "It's sweet how Grandma and Grandpa hold hands" convey the message that romance is part of being sexual and that holding hands *is* sexual.
- **Similarly, do not belittle any emotions your teen is having by implying they are naive or "young love."** The feelings are real and very intense. She will stop talking if she feels her emotions are invalidated.
- **Don't criticize her choice of partner.** Remember that you are not the one who has to date the person. If you believe there is a safety issue, that is another matter altogether.
- **Help your child think about tomorrow.** Today the new boy in her life seems like the man of her dreams, and she'll do anything to be closer. Help her understand how many people have felt that way, only to be disappointed or burned. Again, don't be against the relationship; only suggest that it move slowly to withstand the test of time.

- **Address double standards between males and females.** Both men and women should be appreciated for their brains, integrity, and character. Men should be able to be sensitive and no less manly for choosing to postpone sexual involvement.
- **Talk about levels of intimacy.** Help your teen consider how different levels of touching and sexual behaviors need to be reserved for people who have really earned trust. Here's a good way to think of it. You don't share the same level of information with everyone you meet—you share some basic information with people who ask, you have personal information you share with trusted friends, and then you have have even more private information that is only shared in the closest and time-tested relationships. In the same way, you allow different levels of access to your body depending on your degree of closeness with the other person. Anybody can pat you on the back or offer a warm handshake. A tighter group of people can offer a hug. You might be comfortable kissing or holding hands with someone who you want to display affections with. But the more private touching, and certainly intercourse, is reserved for someone who has demonstrated their trustworthiness over time. Your body should never be used to buy love or earn closeness; rather, the physical part of a relationship follows the closeness. In this way, the conversation focuses on how close you want to be rather than on how far you want to go sexually.

∼ MEDIA IS YOUR FRENEMY

The bad news is that the entertainment media consumed by our kids rarely portray a well-rounded view of sexuality. Women often get what they want by offering or withholding sex. Beauty and seductiveness are the sources of their power. Men get what they want through coercion or the use of power, money, or sex. Manipulative lines abound.

There is a great deal of attention on the pursuit of sexual behaviors (hoping for that first kiss) and then on intercourse, but very little on the sexual behaviors in between. On TV, people meet each other and fall into bed before the first commercial. For those of us raised on the bases, it is a new world. We know that there were multiple steps in between that made us sexual without having intercourse, but the range of sexual behavior not involving intercourse is rarely shown.

The media shows the excitement of the sexual chase, and even the throes of passion. It less frequently shows the challenges of rejection and rarely has story lines about consequences of sexual behaviors. It is easy to find seduction and the strategies we use to find a sexual partner, but it very rarely shows the negotiations to make sure the relationship is mutual, safe, and responsible. In a similar vein, our society allows abundant exposure on TV to sexual enhancement medications—we all know the jingles—but considers contraceptives and STD (sexually transmitted disease) prevention strategies far too explicit.

On shows and in movies specifically designed to appeal to young people, sex is portrayed as a rite of passage; successful, popular teens are the ones who do it. Many teen-oriented shows have characters made up to be particularly unattractive who are always in pursuit of sex but who will never get it. Implicit message: They don't deserve to be sexual. Prove you're not a loser, too.

The good news is that entertainment media can be part of the solution because they bring up every subject you would ever want to discuss with your adolescent. TV shows and movies are full of opportunities for you to jump-start the conversations we've just described and even to launch into impromptu role plays.

∼ TEACHING NAVIGATIONAL SKILLS

No matter how open and respectful your discussions, regardless of how clear your teen is about his own values, he still has to deal with the real world. He has to navigate the sexual forces that suggest that sex itself is the goal. He might want to keep his own time line and control his actions, but it is hard to think everything through in the moment. That is why sexuality education must also include practiced skills. Here are a few strategies for you to use to prepare your teen.

ROLE PLAYS

Role plays are rehearsal for real life. They allow adolescents to explore hypothetical situations and learn how their decisions or choice of words will influence outcomes. It is through role plays that your adolescent will learn the words to use in the other techniques. When you think about role-playing with your kid, keep the following pointers in mind:

Set up a role play casually. Don't announce, "Let's role-play." I promise that if you do, your kid will refuse.

You can spontaneously (and subtly) start role-playing almost anywhere. A car ride is ideal because you are passing situations that you can just ask about and you can avoid that dreaded eye-to-eye contact. "Did you see that guy coming on to that girl? What kind of great line do you think he's using? Yeah, what should she say back?" Or create hypothetical situations that might involve strangers. These are often "safer" teaching opportunities because the focus isn't on your teen.

You won't have to wait long to use TV to your advantage. For example, you walk into the living room and notice an over-the-top scene on the screen. You sit down beside your daughter and watch silently for a while. At the commercial, you ask, "Why do you think that girl fell for that guy's line?"

"What line?"

"When he said, 'I love you so much it hurts. I really want to prove it to you.'"

"I guess he was trying to sleep with her."

"Yeah, and he got his way. What if she didn't want to do it? What could she have said?"

Sexual story lines are usually predictable, so it's pretty easy to see patterns. I caution against using too critical a tone ("How could he be so stupid?") because your teen will note your reaction and be afraid you could be as equally judgmental toward her. This is the kind of thing that makes teens "spare" you by withholding information. Instead, talk about how all people make mistakes and that is why it is so important to be prepared for someone trying to pull one over on you.

Some reminders:

- Avoid confrontational dialogue. Regardless of where it leads, stay calm so your child thinks instead of reacts.
- Use short phrases and let your teen do most of the talking.
- Use neutral situations that don't involve your teen or her friends directly; otherwise your teen will feel defensive or think you are intruding on personal territory.
- Don't try to sound cool yourself. That is a guaranteed turnoff.

REINFORCE THE POWER OF *No* . . . AND IMPORTANCE OF *Yes*

Young men and women receive very different messages in our culture about their role in the sexual dance. Men are to be the aggressors. Women are to be pursued. Men who do it are studs. Women who do it are less than virtuous. Although these standards are changing, they set teens up for some very serious problems. Men feel forced to pursue sex before they may be ready. Women do not have real control over their actions—if they want to engage in a sexual behavior, they have to act as if they were seduced. They can't say yes; they need to say no with just enough ambivalence that the boy is prodded to become more aggressive. They can't protect themselves in the moment because that took planning and foresight that is not permitted. Add to this that girls are taught from a young age that "no" is not a feminine word . . . it's not nice. Ambivalent *nos* are a setup for date rape. We need to have frank discussions about the importance of a clear no. And, we have to be brave enough to suggest that a yes when you mean yes allows you to remain in control.

The best way to handle this is through a heart-to-heart conversation, but it can also be taught through a role play. For example, pick a sexual come-on scene you both see on TV and ask your daughter how she would have handled it. She will be embarrassed by the line of questioning and will likely respond with a sheepish or demure "I would have said no." That is your opportunity to teach how *no*s have to be stated with conviction. Similarly, you might ask your son, "Did she look like a willing partner? I mean she said no." "Yeah, Dad, but it was obvious she wanted it because she was smiling the whole time." That is the opportunity to talk about how he is morally and legally responsible to understand that the word *no* means no, regardless of how it is said. He also needs to learn that a yes mixed with alcohol or drugs is a legal no.

Don't Forget the Code Word to Shift the Blame

There are myriad opportunities in the world of teen sexuality where the judicious and quick use of a code word could get your child out of trouble. She could use it in a call to you when she wants to leave a party where alcohol is pouring and sexual pressure abounds. Or she might use it to find a polite way to get out of a date: statement with code word inserted, followed by "Mom, we're all going to the movies. Okay?" You'll know she wants you to take the blame because she doesn't want to go. Tell her that it is not okay to go to the movies.

∼ SPECIAL TOPICS

There Is a Range of Sexuality

Not all people are heterosexual. All kids are curious about this and your adolescent's questions do not imply that she or he has a homosexual orientation. Kids want to know what it means to be gay and why it seems to be such a big deal that everybody—or nobody—talks about it.

Younger adolescents grasp that to call someone "gay" is an insult, but what it really means likely remains a mystery. People fear what they do not understand and are more likely to repeat the insults as long as they remain uninformed. Tell them simply that a heterosexual person may be attracted to someone of the opposite gender, a homosexual person may be attracted to someone of the same gender, and a bisexual person may be attracted to people of both genders. Inform them that various organizations of mental health professionals do not consider this a choice, rather that it is just about who someone is. Explain that other than sexual attractions, there is no difference between heterosexual and homosexual people. They are driven by the same hopes and dreams and hold the same capacity to love people, serve the community and country, and be good neighbors.

Sexuality is a difficult topic for all teens trying to figure out who they are, but is an all-consuming one for sexual minority teens. There is no evidence that talking about this subject will steer a young person toward being homosexual. There is enormous evidence that gay kids who grew up in homes where homosexuality was never discussed, or was condemned, have tormented adolescent years and engage in self-harming behavior to cope with the stress and isolation.

Most sexual minority kids do not disclose to their parents, so it is unlikely you will know if your child is struggling with this issue. For that reason, and because you want to raise your children with good character, it is important to create a home where hate language and judgment toward any minority group (including sexual minority groups) is considered unacceptable.

If your child asks you if he may be gay, tell him that all people have strong sexual feelings as teenagers and that some of them are confusing. Many people have strong emotions and sometimes attractions toward people of the same and different sex. Reassure him that over time he will figure out who he is and who he is attracted to. Tell him that no matter whom he chooses to love, one thing is certain and that is that your love for him will never change. If your teen tells you that he is gay, recognize him for his self-awareness, thank him for choosing to share with you, ask him how you can be most supportive, and reassure him of the constancy of your love.

Even the most well-intentioned parents sometimes struggle as to how best to support their sexual minority children. Further guidance is available from Parents, Families and Friends of Lesbians and Gays (www.pflag.org).

NOT ALL RELATIONSHIPS ARE HEALTHY

Your teen must know warning signs that suggest a relationship is unhealthy. Abusive people rarely start out nasty. They often enter relationships with flattery and display early signs of jealousy that adolescents find cute. When jealousy triggers isolation from others, kids need to heed this as a major warning sign. Controlling people start by asking you to cut off contact with former relationships, then with opposite-gender friends, then with all friends, and then finally with family. Kids need to know that a relationship is not healthy if you have to change to satisfy your partner. They also need to know that words themselves can be abusive. They also need to view unpredictable mood swings and explosive anger as a danger sign because it is likely only a matter of time before the wrath will be directed toward them.

~ YOU'RE THE ULTIMATE ROLE MODEL

I'll bet you're not a bit surprised that we're going to end this chapter by telling you to take care of your own relationship first. Especially during the teen years, kids are watching what you do much more than they are listening to what you say. If you model a healthy view of sexuality, your adolescent will learn to embrace that view, too.

Your child is picking up cues on how to treat a romantic interest when he sees you kiss your spouse or surprise her with a night out.

Whether you are with your spouse or single and navigating the dating world again, you should demonstrate integrity and commitment. Your children should learn through your actions that listening, occasional compromise, and unwavering respect can get you through almost anything when it comes to relationships.

As in all topics with adolescents, what you say matters less than what you do.

CHAPTER THIRTY

~

REACHING FOR PROFESSIONAL HELP

WHILE YOU MAY not think twice about hiring a math tutor for your adolescent, you might view reaching out to a mental health professional as a sign that you've fallen short on the most important role of your life. To the contrary, turning for outside support could end up being one of the wisest acts of parenting you ever take.

You tackle parenting with passion and purpose, and there's an understandable frustration and even sadness in realizing that what you're doing isn't enough to meet the needs of an adolescent who is not adjusting as smoothly as you'd like. Parents can't be truly objective when assessing their own child, but you do have a strong instinct about when your child is struggling. Learn to trust that gut feeling.

It would be so easy to know what to do if adolescents shared every frustration and emotion they felt and told us of every obstacle they face. That's not reality for most parents, not because we're doing something wrong but because the struggle with independence makes adolescents feel they need to conquer some challenges alone. Remember the chasm they need to cross? We wish we could build them a bridge to get across, but they need instead to step a few paces back before taking a flying leap with covered eyes. Remember also that occasionally they need to convince themselves that they hate us—precisely because of how deeply they love us. We are also sometimes left in the dark because they withhold information for fear of disappointing us or as a misguided effort to protect us. To frame it positively, sometimes kids don't want their parents to know how much they're hurting because they don't want to hurt their parents. For all of these reasons, be glad that you have such a well-honed instinct for sensing that something's not quite right rather than bemoan the fact that you can't fix everything on your own.

⁓ WHY PARENTS SOMETIMES MISS WARNING SIGNS

Parents sometimes miss that their kids are in trouble because they have begun to take their teen's withdrawn behavior or irritability as a matter of course. It's normal for teens to act out at home and express frustration as part of their pursuit of independence. Some teens withdraw into their rooms to avoid confrontation, or even interaction. Although generalizations are always too simplistic, girls tend to engage in conflict and argue every point, whereas boys tend to withdraw.

As uncomfortable as these changes are, they grow to feel like normal behavior. Parents can lose their objectivity in determining when excessive irritability and anger or withdrawal might be signs of more serious problems. It's important to know, however, that teen depression may look quite different from adult depression. Depressed teens might become lethargic, sleep a lot, and stop taking care of themselves, much as depressed adults do, but teen depression just as often shows up as extreme irritability and anger. Part of this is likely a biological difference between teens and adults, but part is just a matter of teen pride. It's hard for a teen to admit "I'm sad or nervous" or "I'm afraid." It's a lot more comfortable to act like the whole world pisses you off and that you don't care about anything, especially your family.

Parents also can mistakenly assume their teen is okay because he earns all As and has assembled an impressive list of colleges to apply to. Driven teens, especially those perfectionists we talked about, can be good at making it appear to the outside world that everything is going great while inside they're being consumed by stress and anxiety. They are more likely to see small setbacks as catastrophes and worry incessantly that they will be exposed as imposters. It's not normal for a teen to worry all the time, obsess about the future, or lose sleep night after night doing schoolwork.

Parents also need to be careful not to write off a child's indifference as laziness. Too often parents determine that their child just can't be reached because nothing seems to matter to him. As we discussed earlier, stressed kids sometimes create a facade of carelessness or a lackadaisical attitude to mask how deeply they do care. Teens who believe they will never live up to people's expectations exit the playing field because of how much easier it is to say "I don't care" than it is to say "I care too much, but don't believe I can do anything about it." Always consider the possibility of perfectionism or a learning disability, including ADHD, before believing your child genuinely has lost interest.

～ TROUBLING SIGNS YOU WANT TO NOTICE

There are many good checklists available on the Web or from your health care provider on warning signs that your adolescent may be having a problem with depression or substance abuse, or that your relationship could be strained. I will include the red flags here, but also want to focus on the troubling patterns that can set in with teens and their families that can lead to a deterioration of everyone's quality of life now or predict a dysfunction later. Not all of these have to do with what your teen is or isn't doing behavior-wise, because how you're functioning is an equally important consideration. If you find yourself stuck in a vicious cycle with your teen or derailed in other aspects of your life, you need to get yourself back on track.

Here are some questions to think about:

- Has your teen's behavior changed? Has she lost interest in activities, has she taken up with a new group of friends, or is she spending much more time alone? Have her eating or sleeping habits recently changed? Is she much more irritable or withdrawn? Does she seem hopeless?
- Is she worried or nervous much of the time?
- Is she suddenly doing poorly in school? School is her job and a substantial change in school performance is often the first clue of emotional distress.
- Is your teen ever saying that life is not worth living, or threatening to hurt himself? Never ignore these statements or assume that they are only attention-getting remarks. You need a professional assessment immediately. Even if these statements are being made "to get attention," then respond by giving your full attention. Your teen is reaching out for help.
- Does your teen complain of physical symptoms that can't be readily explained, such as extreme tiredness, headaches, stomachaches, body pain, or insomnia?
- Is your teen in trouble at school or with the law? One infraction for skipping class or underage drinking is not reason to panic, but you should be concerned by a pattern of taking risks or defying rules and authority figures.
- Has your relationship with your teen become distant, angry, or even hostile? Have the mutual respect and trust you once enjoyed eroded? Do most of your exchanges revolve around what you think your teen is doing wrong?
- Is the son in your house disrespectful or dismissive of his mother? If so, it's imperative that you find a way to make this relationship healthier now so that your son can grow up to have positive relationships with other women in his life. Is your daughter's relationship with her father distant or is he overbearing? If so, you need to make this relationship healthier now so that your daughter will seek out a life partner who is warm and supportive of her views.

- Does your home no longer feel like the safe, happy oasis it once was? Is it filled with tension and conflict even if there is no outright arguing going on?
- Do you spend so much time and negative energy on your adolescent that you shortchange relationships with other family members? Are you underperforming at work, experiencing insomnia, or fighting with your spouse because of issues with your adolescent? Do you spend all of your precious time with your spouse talking about your teen?
- Are you feeling anxious or depressed? Are you disillusioned or hopeless about what lies ahead for your teen? Even if these feelings have nothing to do with your teen, you still deserve help—because you deserve to feel better and that, in turn, will help your family.

Some of these questions might have surprised you because you are used to a list of warning signs that may suggest dire danger. Don't worry, they were included, but so were items designed to get you thinking about mental *health* (in the best sense of the word) and healthy relationships. We tend to think of going to a doctor mostly when we're sick or a mental health professional when we just can't take it anymore. But if you assume a prevention mode of thinking, your goal should be to prevent a downward spiral with your adolescent rather than to wait until you're in the midst of an undeniable crisis. I want the teen in your house to thrive and your relationship to flourish. Not being broken isn't good enough. If your instinct says that things are not as good as they could be, then you deserve outside help. You don't want to put off repairing alienation or disrespect in your relationship with your teen if you hope to enjoy a close relationship twenty years from now.

Isabelle and her husband decided to seek out family therapy, not because there was any particular crisis looming but because their once peaceful home had deteriorated into bickering as one person played off another depending on the situation of the day. Their third child in particular was the focus of attention because she had a learning issue and needed guidance with her schoolwork. They noticed that as they focused their energies on that adolescent, their other kids would act out and fight with each other, as if to say, "Notice me, too. I am equally as deserving of your time and attention."

"Our family was just not getting along," Isabelle said, though they looked like the perfect family on their annual vacation photos. Her older children rolled their eyes at the suggestion of counseling, but Isabelle said they all learned a few things about how to function better as a couple and as a family unit.

~ HOW PROFESSIONALS CAN HELP

A first step to seeking guidance might be found at school. Your teen's school has teachers, each of whom are child professionals, as well as guidance counselors. Some families are hesitant to turn to their child's school for help, fearing a breach of confidentiality. I urge you to rethink that attitude—if your child had a physical sickness that was affecting school performance, you would do everything you could to make sure the school was aware of his needs. But mental health issues unfortunately make us nervous. When Cheryl's youngest daughter developed depression in high school, she and her husband realized they could either go it alone or make the school community a part of the team helping to get their daughter better. An art teacher turned out to be particularly helpful, making a point to invite their daughter to spend time in the art room. It became a place for her to creatively express her feelings and get away for a bit from the demands of a competitive school.

"We could have hidden what was going on with our daughter, but that wasn't fair to her," Cheryl said. "We wanted to make sure there were connections among school, home, and therapy. We took the attitude, 'We're really struggling with our child as parents and we need your help.'"

Your child's health professional is another important resource. Health professionals who serve children and adolescents view health as much more than physical well-being. Much of what we do involves promoting and supporting emotional, behavioral, and social health. The health professional, educator, or counselor will provide support for your teen and for you, hooking you up with reliable mental health resources and, if you like, parent support groups in your community that can provide a source for ideas from families who are dealing with similar challenges. With an expanded team on hand to help your teen, you can concentrate once again on the most important job of parenting—loving and caring for your child—instead of being in the position of constantly assessing him.

I can tell you from my work with families that parents almost always end up feeling tremendous relief when they get a professional on board, preferably before a crisis hits. It's reassuring and empowering to receive an objective assessment from someone who is looking at your child with a fresh set of eyes and ears, but also with the experience of having seen plenty of other kids just like him.

There are many different approaches a counselor or therapist may use to help your child deal with challenges or to help your family better function. A first step is to determine whether the efforts should focus on your teen or on the entire family. Sometimes family therapy that concentrates on helping all of you communicate more effectively can be the best approach to helping both you and your teen.

Parents are often surprised at how teens ultimately embrace the very treatment they at first balked at. It goes back to that idea of feeling good. Teens want to feel physically well and emotionally strong and they want to get along with people they care about. Sneaking around, making excuses, lying, fretting over missed assignments and bad grades, or being in a state of constant turmoil at school or home is exhausting. My experience is that even those teens who get practically dragged into my office by their parents end up taking comfort in having a safe, face-saving place where they can be honest about what they're feeling and experiencing.

A skilled professional really can get your teen to talk about things he would hesitate to tell you—that perhaps he's scared about failing, not lazy; that he's sad, not mad; that he so doesn't want to disappoint you that he does everything he can to create distance between the two of you. Once teens admit the truth to themselves about what they're feeling, they start to be honest with their parents, and that honesty becomes a launching point for change.

Even if your communication with your teen is good, he will likely find that the weight on his shoulders gets lighter by having an added outlet of talking about what's going on in his life. With the right strategies put in place and you as his best ally no matter what, your teen will begin to see the many opportunities in front of him.

∿ HELPING ADOLESCENTS SEEK HELP WITHOUT SHAME

I can't tell you that your teen will jump at the suggestion that you think she would benefit from added professional help, but how you approach the topic will make a difference in her reaction. The first step is being fully comfortable yourself with reaching for outside guidance. Your teen will sense if you have mixed feelings.

I appreciate how hard it can be for parents to feel comfortable getting professional advice. We've already tackled the biggest point: Seeking help is not a sign of your own failure; it is an active demonstration of your love. Some parents see going to a therapist or psychiatrist as embarrassing, something "normal" people don't do. They might worry that their teen will get labeled or teased if friends find out. Although reaching out for help might surely feel like a big deal while you're contemplating it, be assured that it is extremely common.

Another barrier is that many parents were raised to tough it out, so why shouldn't their kids? If this is the way you were raised, I want you to reflect for a moment on how you felt then. Sure, you may have turned out okay, but how did it feel then to know that your feelings were either disregarded or devalued as something you just needed to get over? Your children deserve to know that their emotions matter and that they will be heard.

Remember that your goal is to raise a resilient teen who will bounce back from adversity. Teens become resilient when they know they will receive unconditional love through good times and bad and will be held to high expectations. Sometimes the best way of receiving unconditional love is to understand that the people who care about you aren't going anywhere no matter how hard you try to push them away, and in fact they will fight to get you what you need. In this context, "high expectations" means that you expect them to be emotionally healthy.

Other parents may take the attitude that "all things will pass," and so, too, will the contentious, dysfunctional relationship they have with their teens. They might be right. It might be that with no action things will still turn out okay. But is that a chance worth taking? The resilience mind-set says that with every challenge comes an opportunity for growth. If you and your child work on improving your relationship now, including learning more effective approaches to communication, it will pay dividends far into the future. It will prepare your teen to have richer, more meaningful adult relationships in years to come. It may also contribute to building that long-term healthy *inter*dependent relationship you hope to have with your adult child.

Even if you have the most positive feelings about mental health care, your teen may at first reject seeking help. The middle of a highly charged situation is not the time to tell your teen that you want her to see a therapist, an addictions counselor, or some other specialist. If you blurt out that you believe your child needs help while you are angry, it may mistakenly communicate that you are judging or that counseling is a punishment. If possible, wait for a calm moment and don't expect to necessarily reach an agreement as a result of your first talk. Try using open-ended questions such as "How do you think things are going for you?" and "What do you think about how our family is getting along?" to begin a productive dialogue.

You might suggest that as a first step your teen sees his regular health care professional or school guidance counselor, who will then refer him to someone else or to a suitable program as needed. You want to stress that he'll have a say in what's a good fit and that reaching for help doesn't mean he's signing up for lifelong counseling. It might only take a few sessions to get clarity on what's amiss.

A key message you want to convey to your teen is that seeking added help is not punishment or an indication that you're giving up on her. Make it clear that you're in parenting for the long haul, but that you humbly recognize that you need assistance for your child and you need to get through this rough patch or crisis. You need to state your unwavering love for your teen and the idea that accepting professional help is an act of strength because it says, "I want to feel better, and I know that with some guidance I can." A therapist or other professional isn't going to "solve" or "fix" your teen's problems, but rather help him find his own solutions to what's caused him to get sidetracked. In fact, the best therapists build upon each person's existing strengths. Seeking help is not about being broken; it is about becoming even stronger. Weakness is about not believing you can grow or feeling undeserving of feeling okay; strength is taking the action steps to reach your potential.

~ DON'T IGNORE YOUR OWN NEEDS

We've talked a lot in this book about how *Letting Go* of your adolescent is a lot about you. In that same spirit, getting help for your teen sometimes has to begin with you.

So many parents say they spend all of their waking moments taking care of others—their children, their partner, their aged parents—that they end up neglecting their own physical and mental health and borrowing from the energy that is required for sustaining good relationships. While your teen might very well need help, so might you to figure out how best to deal with your own emotional struggles and all that's on your plate.

Think back to the list of questions I posed earlier in this chapter because a number of them had to do with how you're functioning in light of your child. When you have a troubled teen or even an adolescent going through a rough period, the whole family can be turned upside down. If you spend every moment with your spouse talking or fighting about your teen or you have no time left for your partner, your marriage will suffer. That's unfortunate on multiple levels because growing up in a happy, stable family will help your teen turn out to be a well-adjusted adult. Likewise, giving all your attention, even if it's negative, to your teen can breed resentment in your other children, which in turn could generate problems in them. It's not uncommon for siblings to learn that to get their share of attention they have to do whatever it takes to get you worried enough to notice them, too.

If your marriage feels strained or joyless, getting help for the two of you will help your kids, too. No matter how hard parents work to put on a good face, children can sense when their parents are struggling. Parents shouldn't reveal all their personal issues to their children, but there's something very honest in sharing that you know what it's like to be overwhelmed and that you have or are benefiting from reaching out to someone—whether a mental health professional, a workplace counselor, or a wise aunt. It's reassuring for your teen to know that the one or two people they count on most aren't going to fold under pressure. Your example also reinforces the message that there's no shame in getting help and that, in fact, mental and emotional health should be valued as much as physical well-being.

It took Joshua a long time to come to the realization that his top priority needed to be him if he was going to preserve his relationships with his kids. He was growing increasingly anxious, his marriage was blowing up, and things were falling apart at work. His middle school son was beginning to act "like the man" and assumed an air that he didn't care much about school. Joshua responded to all the pressure he was feeling by clamping down on his kids even more, becoming hyperfocused on everything from homework, to cooking dinner, to his daughter's dance lessons. He became inflexible in dealing with even routine issues.

"When I couldn't control my work, I tried to control my kids," said Joshua, a lawyer. "Back then I would do anything for my kids, but ended up doing nothing for myself."

Joshua emerged from the rubble of a divorce and a lost job as a result of professional help. He said he is a different dad now than he was five years ago, finally able to truly enjoy his kids for who there are, not what he wanted them to be. He's remarried and happy at work, and he and his ex-wife have come together to work in their children's best interests.

"What's caused the change is that I've changed," Joshua said. "What I've learned is that I can step back and let my kids figure things out for themselves. I try to start now with compassion, rather than judgment."

Many parents are resistant to demonstrating self-care, but Joshua's story underscores just how much how your child's well-being rests on your emotional health and resilience. I have enough experience with parents to know that if I approach you solely focused on *your* well-being, you might appreciate it for the moment but will likely forgo caring for yourself if you perceive it will divert energy from focusing on your teen. I therefore need to emphatically state to parents that caring for yourself is a selfless and strategic act of good parenting. Your burning out is not an option. Attending to your own needs is precisely what maintains your energy to give to others.

Never forget that you are a role model. You display a resilient mind-set when you view challenges as opportunities for growth. Your teen is watching you as you demonstrate healthy coping strategies at home and at work. You can make it safe to admit vulnerability and recognize personal limitations without shame. When you address problems, you actively reject stigma. When you reach your limits, you model that strong people take active steps to find guidance. You model that connections with others is what gets you through hard times.

The bottom line is that the first step in a teen's healing can come from the security she feels when she sees you healthy and happy.

∼ HAVING A CHALLENGING KID . . .
CAN BE A CHALLENGE

We have so far ignored an uncomfortable reality. Sometimes having a teen going through troubling or challenging times can make us more than worried, it can make us angry. It might even make us resentful of what our teen is doing to our lives, and there may be moments when, even though you continue to love your child, you don't like him very much. These feelings may make you feel ashamed or disappointed in yourself, but they are very normal, and quite temporary. Nevertheless, your feelings will be known by your teen because teenagers really do have Geiger counters that read our emotions. Your understandable disappointment or anger may make your teen feel the need to put up an even tougher facade.

All parents reach the breaking point at times. What can you do at these moments? A first step is to reassure yourself that adolescence is full of its ups and downs. On the other side of a crisis may be a stronger person and a deeper relationship after you have proven how valuable your connection remains.

The key is to never lower your expectations. The worst thing that could happen would be for your teen to feel that there is nothing more to lose because she has already lost your trust. I've seen that attitude lead to even more use of alcohol and drugs, and depression. I have seen other teens worsen their behavior to maximize the only kind of attention they believe they can get from their parents.

It is time to give yourself that gift of falling back in love with your teen. Your child might be a challenging teen now, but inside is the infant you held, the toddler you protected, and the child whose hand you held walking into the first day of kindergarten. Your teen may not be quite as "cute," but hasn't it been wonderful to witness his growth and the complexity through which he now views the world?

Reconnecting with this love may be what you need to break the dysfunctional cycle of shame and anger that invades your home during challenging times. Take a vacation from the present conflict and remember those moments that made you swell with pride when you realized how special your child was. Was it his love of animals? The patience he showed with smaller children or the respect he paid to elders? The time he took care of you when you had the flu? Seeing the little boy inside of the young man causing you anguish or the pint-sized girl inside of the teen scorning you may be just what you need to hit the reset button that will once again allow you to hold your teen to the very highest expectations.

∾ A FINAL THOUGHT

Most kids really turn out very well, even those teens who worry their parents during adolescence. Please understand that sometimes it's the very "best kids" or the most sensitive kids who run into trouble. Adolescence is a challenging time for everybody, but teens who are born pleasers or are especially emotionally sensitive can feel the ups and downs most intensely. The very same traits of empathy and sensitivity that cause them pain now may serve them very well later in life. Bear that in mind because it will give you strength as you guide your teen through present struggles.

EPILOGUE

~

Letting Go with Love and Confidence

So much has happened since we started writing this book. My daughters turned fifteen and are freshmen in high school. They are wonderful kids. Warm, compassionate, and committed to fairness. Hardworking but fun loving. I don't think I could have been given children more perfect for me. Not perfect. Perfect for me. That doesn't mean there aren't *moments* where I look at them and think, "Do I know you?" I also sometimes stop in my tracks and wonder whom I am looking at? They are young women. Where are my little girls?

I still get nostalgic a lot, and imagine that the drive to college will be filled with deep, mixed emotions. But I really am more ready, perhaps because it's less overwhelming to imagine my fifteen-year-olds being independent than it was to visualize my thirteen-year-olds on their own. Writing this book helped me process my feelings and reaffirm that *Letting Go* is indeed a loving act. It is far easier now for me to celebrate my girls' emerging independence.

This book was written so you also will be well prepared to guide your child along the road toward self-sufficiency. The philosophy driving both the *When* decisions and *How* discussions is that independence is a good thing. Your job as a parent is to serve as guide and monitor, always with safety in mind and an eye toward ensuring that your child will become a responsible, contributing adult.

The truth is that your child's independence is destined to be, and teens are wired to prove (for better or worse) that they can handle life on their own. Once your older teen or young adult gains confidence in his ability to stand alone, he'll look around and realize he'd rather be standing alongside you. He'll come back for the interdependent relationship you long for if he trusts that you value and respect his ability to manage himself.

Let's recap of some of what you've learned. Let's hope that when your adult child looks back at adolescence, he or she will be able to describe your relationship and your approach to parenting in these ways:

- You knew it was more important to listen than to talk. Active listening communicated that you trusted in your teen's ability to develop solutions.
- You recognized that the answer to *When* she was ready for something had little to do with age and everything to do with whether the baby steps had been mastered.
- You always believed in the essential goodness of your teen. Even during the most trying moments, you communicated that you never gave up, were not going anywhere, and still held her to the highest of expectations.
- You weren't best friends; you were a parent. You knew your teen had lots of friends and that you needed to fill a different role.
- You sometimes grew weary of the arguments, but on some level you appreciated the "fight" because you understood he was figuring out where he stood.
- You had the attitude that the best way to prevent rebellion was not with an iron fist, but rather with a disciplinary style that made it clear you would happily grant increasing privileges as long as they were earned with demonstrated responsibility.

- You didn't get into cycles of nagging and hostility. Instead, you disciplined clearly enough that there were plenty of opportunities for the quality time that holds families together.
- You prioritized family. That meant that even if the world was always wired or rushing, your family took time to cherish each other. Cell phones off. TVs off. Family time on.
- When your child came to you with a dilemma, you trusted his ability to grow. You guided him rather than judged him.
- You appreciated that as she grew there was more of her to love.
- You were more interested in what she was learning than her grades or what she was scoring.
- You monitored enough that she knew she could spread her wings within safely defined limits.
- You let him go out in the world, but always with an understanding that you were the one he could turn to. You worked out strategies with him so he could blame you, allowing him to save face with his friends even while doing the right thing.
- You were his role model. You never pretended to have smooth sailing all of the time, but you consistently demonstrated how to navigate the waters in a healthy way.

～ SOME FINAL STORIES

When I thought about how best to wrap up this book, I decided that we wanted to end with a gift—the gift of reassurance. I won't offer you a false pat on the back that everything at every moment will be just fine with your teen, but I can share with you a few final stories from parents of young adult children who serve as proof that after the struggles of your adolescent achieving independence will come an even more satisfying interdependence for both of you.

It's not possible, nor fair to them, to tell you the details of their travails or the depths of some of the challenges they sometimes faced. Some of the people interviewed believed they were at their rope's end, perhaps more

than once, but all kept an abiding faith in their children that paid off. Some
had a relatively smooth ride through their children's adolescence, and their
challenge was more a sentimental one that we all feel as our babies grow to
teens. All of us, though, no matter how wonderful our children or how
perfect (there's no such thing!) our approach to parenting, feel occasionally
rejected by our growing teens. Remember that they, too, are getting ready to
let go. They have to reject us to know who they are, and they have to convince themselves they don't need us precisely because of how much they do.

Before we leave you with these parents' thoughts and experiences,
please understand they have something that you do not yet have: They
have hindsight. They hold the long view after having dealt with challenges. Now you are planting the seeds, nurturing the roots, and fighting
the occasional storm. You do this with trust that your efforts will bear fruit,
and they will.

Dana comes to mind first. She has six children, ages sixteen to thirty-
two, and doesn't hesitate to say she feels "younger now at fifty-eight than I
did at thirty-six." Part of that good feeling has to stem from the wisdom
she's gained from raising a big family and living with them all around the
globe—the Philippines, Japan, and Italy, as well as multiple cities in the
United States. When they all get together, stories fly.

"They'll reminisce about the good old days and point out things I may
not have noticed," Dana said. "When you're in charge of your children,
you think you're the director of the play and you think you know everything going on. But then you find out there was plenty of unscripted stuff
going on."

All of the moving may seem exotic, but for Dana it was never without
some worry. Would her children do okay without the roots and continued
presence of extended family? Would they grow to understand the importance of family and community, her very core values, if they were frequently uprooted?

Dana takes pride in seeing that her grown children are so much more
than repackaged versions of herself or her husband. "Your children are not
just an extension of you," she explained. "They're individuals who have
their own feelings and desires and gifts. You're responsible for who they

are on some level, but you see that they have friends who have no connection to you and they work hard and achieve things separate from you."

Still, the key values she taught them—including commitment to family and giving back through service—are very evident. When Dana's father lay dying in the hospital, her one son, unprompted, took over her bedside vigil so she could get some sleep.

"You come to realize that your children are capable people who *you* can depend on," Dana said. "They know how to step up."

With two adult children out of the house and one starting her first job, Cheryl said she realizes she'll never totally stop worrying about her kids—moms and dads are wired that way for life. Her youngest daughter's adolescence was especially tumultuous because she struggled with depression that required her to take time off from school for a while. It is difficult to describe the anguish and even self-doubt Cheryl felt at times. Could she have done more to prevent it? What kind of a mother can't cheer up her kid? Professionals helped her understand that not only was it not her fault, but that she was part of the solution.

Her daughter's depression is being managed well now and Cheryl can see ahead to the day when her daughter will be independent and happy. She is beginning to understand that the life lessons her daughter will draw from in picking herself up from a low point may have ingrained a lifelong sensitivity and empathy that will serve her and others well.

"Our goal was to help them develop their 'tool kit'—faith, ritual, family, education—and then to step back and let them go," Cheryl said. "Sure, they make mistakes. But there is comfort in knowing that our children know how to stumble and get back up again."

Cheryl and her husband thought they'd feel lonely when the sports games and school events were history, but they've discovered that their adult children are still very much in their lives, though in different ways.

"It's fun to watch them as *they* make the next decision on their careers, their love lives. They share with us what's in their hearts and souls," Cheryl said. "They *want* to have dinner with us!"

Cheryl and her husband also are discovering a new relationship with each other. Up next: a winter sports vacation, just the two of them!

"We have to build our next life and go for it," she said. "The greatest gift we give our kids is to show them how to live. They see from us that we're not afraid to try new things."

Rich is another parent whose experience is testimony to the good things to come. He and his wife went through some rough stuff with their kids— fender benders, uneven school performance, mismanaged finances, frustrating job searches. Each of those problems sounds so casual when simply listed, but each felt like a crisis in the moment. There were times when Rich worried quite a bit about his kids' futures, but now he's reveling in seeing them finding their strides. He makes a point to book lunch with each of them on a regular basis because he so thoroughly enjoys their company.

We caught up with Elaine just as she was retiring from a longtime job with the military, so she was understandably feeling nostalgic. Elaine was a highly successful career woman who tried to model for her daughters a commitment to service, professionalism, and balance. But the truth is, she worked very hard and had generations of other "children" because she was a leading teacher in her field. Her career also required frequent travel. Although her daughters had a happy childhood and a relatively smooth adolescence, Elaine always felt conflicted. Was she stretched too thin? Was she paying enough attention to her own children? Was she serving others at the expense of caring for her own family? Was she modeling for her daughters how to be a strong but balanced woman?

She talked about a recent experience when she accompanied her twenty-two-year-old daughter to a doctor's appointment. As Elaine stood at one end of the hall talking to someone she knew, she got a glimpse of her daughter in a doorway at the other end.

"I wanted to yell, 'Hey, Mom is here,' but I caught myself. I saw her framed in this doorway, walking away from me, and it just hit me that my baby is a lovely young woman who is standing on her own two feet and articulating for herself her health care concerns," Elaine recalled. "It was one of those moments when I suddenly saw my child as this independent adult young woman."

Elaine is a lucky woman. On the occasion of her fifty-fifth birthday, her college-age daughter sent her this e-mail: "Mom, thank you for supporting me, for caring about me, and for being there for me, for encouraging and inspiring me, for setting a good example of what a strong and spiritual woman is, for making me smile and comforting me, but most of all for being understanding, patient, and loving me even when I make mistakes. I love you."

I guess she did successfully strike that balancing act between being a professional, a caring role model, and loving, attentive mother.

～ GO FOR IT

So in the end, *How* do you know *when* it's finally right to let go? Our job isn't to finish our kids or produce perfect kids, but to start our kids. While I'm not there yet with my two girls, parents far more seasoned than I am say that I'll recognize—perhaps gradually, perhaps in a moment's insight— that the child before me is started indeed. They say you will know it's okay to let go when you recognize that your child doesn't have all the answers but is asking good questions. The time is right when you say good-bye to your child not with worry or one more round of advice, but with complete joy in the time you've spent together. You know you're ready to let go when you no longer yearn for sharing everything with your child, but look forward to telling each other what you've experienced.

In the end, *Letting Go* won't be full of regret because you've taken an incredible journey with your adolescent and arrived at a new destination filled with even more possibility. You're confident and ready to let go—and then to take hold again of the adult child that you got started in a wonderful way. This new hold will not be as obvious as the hand that guided your child through these first years, but it will be every bit as loving, and always there.

RESOURCES

~

You may find the following resources helpful if you want to further explore areas of interest or concern. The list is by no means exhaustive; nor can I endorse every point in every book or Web page. But you will find plenty of valuable information that will supplement what you read in this book.

A good starting point is my previous book *Building Resilience in Children and Teens: Giving Kids Roots and Wings*, written with Martha M. Jablow (Elk Grove Village, IL: The American Academy of Pediatrics, 2011). The book will take you deeper into the topic of resilience, including a comprehensive plan on how to build the Seven Cs of Resilience (Competence, Confidence, Connection, Character, Coping, Control, and Contribution) in children and adolescents. It also focuses intently on how to strengthen parent-child ties.

You may also find my Web site, FosteringResilience.com, useful. It explains how to apply resilience-based strategies in home, school, and community settings, and includes handouts and information sheets for you to download.

OTHER RESILIENCE-BASED PARENTING BOOKS

Benson, Peter. *Sparks: How Parents Can Help Ignite the Hidden Strengths of Teenagers*. San Francisco, CA: Jossey-Bass, 2008.

Lerner, Richard M. *The Good Teen: Rescuing Adolescence from the Myths of the Storm and Stress Years*. New York: Three Rivers Press, 2008.

Mogel, Wendy. *The Blessing of a B Minus: Using Jewish Teachings to Raise Resilient Teenagers*. New York: Scribner, 2010.

Reivich, Karen, and Andrew Shatté. *The Resilience Factor: 7 Essential Skills for Overcoming Life's Inevitable Obstacles.* New York: Broadway, 2002.

Seligman, Martin E. P. (with Karen Reivich, Lisa Jaycox, and Jane Gillham). *The Optimistic Child: A Proven Program to Safeguard Children from Depression and Build Lifelong Resilience.* New York: Mariner Books, 2007.

OTHER RESOURCES ON BUILDING RESILIENCE IN CHILDREN AND COMMUNITIES

The Search Institute. The Search Institute framework includes forty developmental assets that young people need to achieve their potential. To see a list of assets modified for each developmental level, go to www.search-institute.org/assets.

Communities That Care. The CTC Prevention Strategies Guide lists fifty-six tested and effective prevention programs and policies that communities can use to protect teens and reduce the risk of problem behaviors. www.communitiesthatcare.net

Kids at Hope. This organization is committed to helping families and communities create an environment where all kids will thrive. www.kidsathope.org

BOOKS ABOUT SUCCESS

Dweck, Carol. *Mindset: The New Psychology of Success.* New York: Ballantine Books, 2007.

Elkind, David. *The Hurried Child: Growing Up Too Fast Too Soon.* Cambridge, MA: Da Capo Press, 2006.

Hallowell, Edward M. *The Childhood Roots of Adult Happiness: Five Steps to Help Kids Create and Sustain Lifelong Joy.* New York: Ballantine Books, 2003.

Hirsh-Pasek, Kathy, and Roberta M. Golinkoff (with Diane Eyer). *Einstein Never Used Flash Cards: How Our Children Really Learn—and Why They Need to Play More and Memorize Less.* Emmaus, PA: Rodale Books, 2004.

Jones, Marilee, and Kenneth R. Ginsburg (with Martha M. Jablow). *Less Stress, More Success: A New Approach to Your Teen Through College Admissions and Beyond.* Elk Grove Village, IL: American Academy of Pediatrics, 2006.

Levine, Madeline. *The Price of Privilege: How Parental Pressure and Material Advantage Are Creating a Generation of Disconnected and Unhappy Kids.* New York: Harper Paperbacks, 2008.

Pope, Denise Clark. *Doing School: How We Are Creating a Generation of Stressed-Out, Materialistic, and Miseducated Students.* New Haven, CT: Yale University Press, 2003.

Rosenfeld, Alvin, and Nicole Wise. *The Over-Scheduled Child: Avoiding the Hyper-Parenting Trap.* New York: St. Martin's Griffin, 2001.

STRESS AND THE MIND-BODY CONNECTION

Benson, Herbert (with Miriam Z. Klipper). *The Relaxation Response.* New York: Harper Paperbacks, 2000.

Ratey, John J. (with Eric Hagerman). *Spark: The Revolutionary New Science of Exercise and the Brain.* New York: Little, Brown and Company, 2008.

Sapolsky, Robert M. *Why Zebras Don't Get Ulcers.* New York: Holt Paperbacks, 2004. This classic book helps the reader understand the connections between the mind and body.

Stricker, Paul R. *Sports Success RX! Your Child's Prescription for the Best Experience: How to Maximize Potential and Minimize Pressure.* Elk Grove, IL: American Academy of Pediatrics, 2006.

OTHER RESOURCES ON SUCCESS

Challenge Success. This organization is committed to championing a broader vision of success for youth. Its mission statement: "We believe that real success results from attention to the basic developmental needs of children and a valuing of different types of skills and abilities. Challenge Success endorses a vision of success that emphasizes character, health, independence, connection, creativity, enthusiasm, and achievement." www.challengesuccess.org

OVERCOMING PERFECTIONISM

Adderholdt, Miriam, and Jan Goldberg. *Perfectionism: What's Bad About Being Too Good?* Minneapolis, MN: Free Spirit Publishing, 1992.

Greenspon, Thomas S. *Freeing Our Families from Perfectionism.* Minneapolis, MN: Free Spirit Publishing, 2001.

———. *What to Do When Good Enough Isn't Good Enough: The Real Deal on Perfectionism: A Guide for Kids.* Minneapolis, MN: Free Spirit Publishing, 2007.

EMOTIONAL INTELLIGENCE

Goleman, Daniel. *Emotional Intelligence: Why It Can Matter More Than IQ.* New York: Bantam Books, 2005.

Gottman, John (with Joan DeClaire). *The Heart of Parenting: Raising an Emotionally Intelligent Child.* New York: Simon and Schuster, 1998.

ADOLESCENT HEALTH INFORMATION

The American Academy of Pediatrics' site, healthychildren.org, offers a wide variety of health and development information in its "ages and stages" section on teens and young adults.

Children's Hospital Boston offers health information for girls and young women at www .youngwomenshealth.org, and information for boys and young men at youngmens healthsite.org.

Nemours, a pediatric health system, has an online teen and parent health web site at: www .teenshealth.org.

The American Medical Association has published two paperback books especially for teens: *AMA's Girl's Guide to Becoming a Teen* (Kate Gruenwald, author; Amy B. Middleman, editor [2006]); and *AMA's Boy's Guide to Becoming a Teen* (Kate Gruenwald Pfeifer, author; Amy B. Middleman, editor; [2006]). Hoboken, NJ: Jossey-Bass.

CHILD AND ADOLESCENT DEVELOPMENT

The American Academy of Pediatrics publishes authoritative books to help parents understand and support healthy development. These books can be previewed at www .healthychildren.org/bookstore.

PARENTING YOUR ADOLESCENT

Steinberg, Laurence. *You and Your Adolescent: The Essential Guide for Ages 10–25.* New York: Simon and Schuster, 2011.

TEMPERAMENT

Carey, William B. (with Martha M. Jablow). *Understanding Your Child's Temperament.* Blomington, IN: Xlibris Corp., 2004.

STRESS MANAGEMENT: THE IMPORTANCE OF NUTRITION

The United States Department of Agriculture interactive site allows users to individualize a nutrition plan. www.mypyramid.gov
The National Institutes of Health offers information on nutrition for parents (WIN: Weight-control Information Network) at www.win.niddk.nih.gov/publications/child.htm.
The Canadian Public Health Agency offers a guide for nutrition and activity for children and adolescents at www.phac-aspc.gc.ca/hp-ps/hl-mvs/pag-gap/index-eng.php.

CHILD SAFETY

de Becker, Gavin. *Protecting the Gift: Keeping Children and Teenagers Safe (and Parents Sane).* New York: Dell, 2000.
The National Center for Missing and Exploited Children offers a wide range of outstanding materials that prepares children, teenagers, and parents to navigate a world that can be exploitative to children. www.missingkids.org

TEEN DRIVING

The Web site www.teendriversource.org is produced by The Center for Injury Research and Prevention at The Children's Hospital of Philadelphia. It has separate sections for teens and parents. It includes the site (http://parentingmyteendriver.org) that teaches parents how to apply authoritative parenting practices to teen driving.

PREVENTION AND CRISIS MANAGEMENT

Students Against Destructive Decisions (SADD) is dedicated to preventing destructive decisions, particularly underage drinking, other drug use, risky and impaired driving, teen violence, and teen suicide. www.sadd.org

The Covenant House Nineline is a national, 24-hour, toll-free hotline for kids and parents across the United States that addresses adolescent crises and homelessness. Counselors offer guidance and support can link callers to community services. Visit www.nineline.org or call 800-999-9999.

The National Campaign to Prevent Teen Pregnancy. www.teenpregnancy.org

DRUGS AND OTHER SUBSTANCES

The National Youth Anti-Drug Media Campaign offers a site that features strategies to counter drug use. www.theantidrug.com

National Institute on Alcohol Abuse and Alcoholism (NIAAA) offers easy-to-read material covering a wide range of alcohol-related topics. www.niaaa.nih.gov.

National Institute on Drug Abuse (NIDA) has materials developed specifically for students and young adults at http://nida.nih.gov.

More information about specific drugs is available at http://nida.nih.gov/drugpages.

U.S. Department of Education (this source has tips on drug prevention starting in the pre-school years): http://www2.ed.gov/parents/academic/involve/drugfree/index.html

U.S. Department of Health and Human Services, Substance Abuse and Mental Health Services Administration. www.samhsa.gov

National Anti-Drug Strategy, Government of Canada. http://www.nationalantidrugstrategy.gc.ca/parents/parents.html

The Partnership at Drugfree.org. www.drugfree.org

Students Against Destructive Decisions. www.sadd.org

RESOURCES FOR SEXUAL MINORITY YOUTH AND THEIR FAMILIES

Parents, Families and Friends of Lesbians and Gays (PFLAG) offers you guidance and support if a young person you care for may be struggling with his or her sexual identity; or if he or she shares a homosexual or bisexual orientation with you, and you wish to learn how best to be supportive. Visit www.pflag.org or call 202-467-8180.

The GLBT National Health Center offers the GLBT National Youth Talkline at 800-246-7743, and online support and information at www.glnh.org.

The Trevor Lifeline, a 24-hour crisis hotline for sexual minority youth, is available at 866-488-7386.

REACHING FOR PROFESSIONAL HELP

It is ideal to ask your child's pediatrician or other health care professional, school counselor, or clergyperson to help guide you to find a mental health professional that is the right match for your child and family. However, many mental health professional organizations offer online referral resources.

United States

National Institute of Mental Health (NIMH) offers free, easy to read brochures and fact sheets on mental health issues at http://nimh.nih.gov/health/publications/index.shtml.

American Academy of Child and Adolescent Psychiatry offers information for psychiatrists
and families about developmental, behavioral, emotional, and mental disorders affect-
ing children and adolescents at www.aacap.org.
American Mental Health Counselors Association. www.amhca.org
American Psychiatric Nurses Association. www.apna.org
American Psychological Association. www.apa.org
American Association for Marriage and Family Therapy www.aamft.org
National Association of Social Workers. www.socialworkers.org

Canada

Canadian Academy of Child and Adolescent Psychiatry. www.cacap-acpea.org
Canadian Association of Social Workers. www.casw-acts.ca
Canadian Psychiatric Association. www.cpa-apc.org
Canadian Psychological Association. www.cpa.ca

ADDITIONAL REFERENCES THAT INFORMED THIS BOOK

Advocates for Youth. www.advocatesforyouth.org
Darling, N., P. Cumsille, L.L. Caldwell, and B. Dowdy, "Predictors of adolescents' disclosure strategies and perceptions of parental knowledge." *Journal of Youth and Adolescence*
35(4) (2006): 667–78.
Darling, N., P. Cumsille, and M.L. Martínez. "Adolescents as active agents in the socialization process: Legitimacy of parental authority and obligation to obey as predictors of
obedience." *Journal of Adolescence* 30 (2007): 297–311.
————. "Individual differences in adolescents' beliefs about the legitimacy of parental
authority and their own obligation to obey: A longitudinal investigation." *Child Development* 79 (2008): 1103–118.
Darling, N., P. Cumsille, I. Pena-Alampay, and J. D. Coatsworth. "Individual and
Issue-Specific Differences in Parental Knowledge and Adolescent Disclosure in Chile,
the Philippines, and the United States." *Journal of Research on Adolescence* 19(4) (2009):
715–40.
Darling, N., and B. Dowdy. "Monitoring, Disclosure, and Trust: Mothers' and Adolescents'
Reports. In K. J. Rotenberg, ed., *Trust and Trustworthiness During Childhood and Adoles-
cence,* 203–22. Cambridge, England: Cambridge University Press, 2010.
Fact Sheets: Binge Drinking, Centers for Disease Control and Prevention. www.cdc.gov/
alcohol/quickstats/binge_drinking.htm
FastStats: Obesity and Overweight, Centers for Disease Control and Prevention. www.cdc
.gov/nchs/fastats/overwt.htm
Families and Work Institute. familiesandwork.org
Galinsky, Ellen. *Ask the Children: What America's Children Really Think About Working Parents.* New York: William Morrow, 1999.
García-España, J. F., K. R. Ginsburg, D. R. Durbin, M. R. Elliott, and F. K. Winston. "Primary access to vehicles increases risky teen driving behaviors and crashes: National perspective." *Pediatrics* 124(4) (2009): 1069–75.

Ginsburg K. R., D. R. Durbin, J. F. García-España, E. A. Kalicka, and F. K. Winston. "Associations between parenting style and teen driving safety-related behaviors and attitudes." *Pediatrics* 124(4) (2009): 1040–51.

Juvonen, Jaana, Sandra Graham, and Mark A. Schuster. "Bullying Among Young Adolescents: The Strong, the Weak and the Troubled." *Pediatrics* 112 (2003): 1231–237.

Juvonen, Jaana, and Alice Y. Ho. "Social Motives Underlying Antisocial Behavior Across Middle School Grades." *Journal of Youth and Adolescence* 37 (2008): 747–56.

Kaiser Family Foundation. "Generation M2: Media in the Lives of 8- to 18-Year-Olds." January 2010. www.kff.org/entmedia/mh012010pkg.cfm

Love Is Not Abuse. www.loveisnotabuse.org

Monahan, Kathryn C., Joanna M. Lee, and Laurence Steinberg. "Revisiting the Negative Impact of Part-Time Work on Adolescent Adjustment: Distinguishing Between Selection and Socialization Using Propensity Score Matching." *Child Development* 82 (2011): 96–112.

Mortality Among Teenagers Age 12–19 years: U.S. 1999–2006, NCHS Data Brief, No. 37, May 2010.

Olweus Bullying Prevention Program. www.olweus.org

Pew Internet & American Life Project. "Mean Teens Online: Forget Sticks and Stones, They've Got Mail." June 2007. pewresearch.org/pubs/527/cyber-bullying

Ramey, Garey, and Valerie A. Ramey, "The Rug Rat Race." *Brookings Papers on Economic Activity* (Spring 2010), 129–76.

Smetana, J. G. *Adolescents, Families, and Social Development. How Teens Construct Their Worlds*. Hoboken, NJ: John Wiley and Sons, 2010.

Smetana, J. G., M. Villalobos, M. Tasopoulou-Chan, D. C. Gettman, and N. Campolone-Barr. "Early and middle adolescents disclosure to parents about activities in different domains." *Journal of Adolescence* 32(3) (2009): 639–713.

Smetana J. G., A. Metzger, D. C. Gettman, and N. Campione-Barr. "Disclosure and secrecy in adolescent-parent relationships." *Child Development* 77(1) (Jan–Feb. 2006): 201–17.

Supportive Listening. supportivelistening.org

Teen Drivers: Fact Sheet, Centers for Disease Control and Prevention. www.cdc.gov/Teen_Drivers/teendrivers_factsheet.html

TRU (formerly Teen Research Unlimited). www.tru-insight.org

INDEX

~